GREAT QUESTIONS IN

Governing by Campaigning

The Politics
of the Bush Presidency

GEORGE C. EDWARDS III
TEXAS A&M UNIVERSITY

PEARSON
Longman

New York   San Francisco   Boston
London   Toronto   Sydney   Tokyo   Singapore   Madrid
Mexico City   Munich   Paris   Cape Town   Hong Kong   Montreal

Editor-in-Chief:	Eric Stano
Senior Marketing Manager:	Elizabeth Fogarty
Production Manager:	Denise Phillip
Project Coordination, Text Design, and Electronic Page Makeup:	WestWords, Inc.
Senior Cover Design Manager:	Nancy Danahy
Cover Designer:	Base Art Co.
Cover Illustration/Photo:	© Corbis
Senior Manufacturing Buyer:	Dennis J. Para
Printer and Binder:	R.R. Donnelley and Sons
Cover Printer:	Phoenix Color Corporation

Library of Congress Cataloging-in-Publication Data

Edwards, George C.

Governing by campaigning : the politics of the Bush presidency/George C. Edwards III.

    p. cm.

Includes index.

ISBN 0-321-43767-5

1. United States—Politics and government—2001– 2. Bush, George W. (George Walker), 1946– I. Title.

E902.E29 2006

973.931—dc22

2006003679

Please visit us at www.ablongman.com

ISBN 0-321-43767-5

1 2 3 4 5 6 7 8 9 10—DOH—09 08 07 06

To Ira Sharkansky—
Mentor and Friend

Brief Contents

Detailed Contents

Preface

Elected in 2000 on what seemed to be a moderate platform in domestic policy and a cautious approach to international relations, George W. Bush has sought to revolutionize policy in both areas. The administration's response to the 9/11 terrorist attacks, its desire to reorient fundamental aspects of domestic policy, and its efforts to build a lasting Republican majority are some of the most important political developments in the past generation.

Yet the president was first elected without even a plurality of the vote, the country is closely divided politically, and partisan polarization is at its highest level in modern times. Thus the president's base is firm, but it is also narrow. There is certainly not widespread popular demand for transforming public policy. Revolutions are usually not built on such modest foundations.

In this book I explore the politics of the Bush presidency, focusing especially on how the administration has attempted to make sweeping changes in public policy without broad support for doing so. At the core of this effort is the strategy of governing by campaigning. To increase his political capital, the president has taken his case directly to the people more than any of his predecessors. The White House has based this strategy on the premises that

(1) Congress would respond to public opinion regarding the president and his policies; (2) the president must actively take his case to the people; and (3) through the permanent campaign the White House *can* successfully persuade or even mobilize the public.

In recent years there has been a great deal of attention on the permanent campaign and its implications for governing. Critics argue that politicians who attempt to govern by campaigning breed incivility in politics, undermine coalition building, mislead the public, discourage serious deliberation about public policy, increase the role of special interest money in politics, feed partisan polarization, and produce legislative gridlock and public cynicism. Yet it is the core of George W. Bush's strategy for governing. We need to understand better the causes and consequences of governing by campaigning.

To set the context for the president's efforts to govern—and his emphasis on governing by campaigning—I examine the nature of the president's policy proposals and the opposition's response to them in Chapter 1. Chapter 2 focuses on the Bush White House's efforts at going public while Chapter 3 examines the extent to which this effort succeeded in moving public opinion in the president's directions. Chapter 4 investigates the public's evaluation of the president personally. In Chapter 5, I explore the president's relations with Congress and ask, among other things, how much leverage the president's public approval gave him in dealing with the legislature. Chapters 6 and 7 are a case study of the most intensive effort to govern by campaigning in American history: the administration's effort to reform Social Security. In Chapter 8, I take a broader view of the impact of governing by campaigning on the political system.

Although writing is a solitary activity, no author functions alone. I am grateful to the continued support of Texas A&M University for my research and to the Department of Politics and International Relations and Nuffield College at the University of Oxford, where I served as Olin Professor of American Government while finishing this volume. A number of graduate students, including Matthew Eshbaugh-Soha, Todd Kent, Justin Vaughn, Jose Villalobos, and Adam Warber, provided essential assistance. I thank the reviewers who provided helpful feedback on the first draft of this manuscript: Gretchen Brandt, Bucknell University; Richard Conley, University of Florida; Dennis Simon, Southern Methodist University; and Phil Warf, University of Arizona. Eric Stano has been an outstanding editor as well as a close friend, and I highly value both relationships. My wife, Carmella, continues to provide the invaluable gift of a supportive environment conducive to my work. Finally, I am delighted to dedicate this book to Ira Sharkansky, with whom I began my professional journey nearly two generations ago and who taught me how to think about politics.

George C. Edwards III
Oxford

CHAPTER I

Policy and Polarization: The Context of Governing

The presidency of George W. Bush has been turbulent. Beginning with the protracted denouement of his election in 2000 and punctuated by the 9/11 terrorist attacks, wars in Afghanistan and Iraq, the devastation of Hurricane Katrina, and major shifts in domestic policy, the Bush presidency has polarized American politics and left durable impressions on public policy. As befits a president who has sought to reconfigure public policy and build a lasting governing coalition, there are two widely held and highly divergent views of his performance.

To his detractors, Bush is a parochial, intellectually shallow, close-minded, hard-right cultural warrior who combines smug ideological certitude with a stunning indifference to facts and evidence. Opponents dismiss the president as unequal to the demands of the office, incapable of thoughtful reflection, an intellectually passive ignoramus robotically repeating rhetorical platitudes. They see him as impervious to lessons of experience, unwilling to admit or correct mistakes, and unable to adapt his preconceptions to inconvenient realities. They also complain that he suppresses dissent among his advisors and uses them as an ideological echo chamber rather than a source of competing views. Critics regard the president as an irresponsible free spender obsessed with shifting the tax burden from the wealthiest Americans to future generations, as disdaining due process and claiming virtually unlimited power to suspend constitutional liberties, and as alienating millions of America's onetime admirers abroad.

There is a much more positive view, however. In this perspective, Bush is a mature and confident leader who is comfortable with himself and in wielding power. A president who is willing to tackle the big—and difficult—issues like Social Security, his decisiveness and serene resolution more than compensate for any thinness of his knowledge. Moreover, a theoretical orientation drives this administration, which pursues its goals in a highly effective strategic manner. In the final analysis, his supporters argue, Bush is a president in tune with the mainstream of the American public and one who has brought about revolutionary and much-needed changes in public policy.

This is a book about how George W. Bush has tried to govern to achieve his goals. The next six chapters examine the politics of Bush's presidency and his core governing strategy—governing by campaigning. In these chapters I examine his efforts to lead and his successes and failures in obtaining the public's support and by means of it, moving Congress to support his policies.

Before focusing on how President Bush has tried to govern, and the consequences of his doing so, however, it is important that we first understand the president's policy proposals and the opposition's response to them. A president with an ambitious agenda and vigorous opponents is likely to adopt a more aggressive governing style than a president seeking incremental change in a more consensual environment. Thus, before we analyze a president's efforts at governing, we need to know why he has tried to govern that way. What has been George W. Bush's agenda, and what response has it evoked?

LEADING A REVOLUTION IN PUBLIC POLICY

George W. Bush has tried to lead a revolution in public policy. He has broken from the incremental, fiscally prudent, and moderate approaches that characterized the presidencies of both his father and Bill Clinton. Instead, he has boldly reexamined and challenged the basic tenets of decades of foreign, economic, and domestic policy. Let us briefly examine some of the highpoints of the president's policies.

Taxes

The centerpiece of Bush's domestic policy is his belief in the efficacy of tax cuts under any and all circumstances. It was hardly novel for a Republican president to push for lower tax rates early in his term, as Bush did in 2001. Moreover, the budget surpluses then accumulating encouraged opposition Democrats to agree that revenue reductions, slightly smaller in scope, were appropriate. What is different is Bush's insistence that tax cutting should continue, even with the return of budget deficits and even with the prospect of substantial, long-term additional spending on the military, homeland defense, and the war on terrorism. Facing deficits in his second year, Ronald Reagan acquiesced in Congress's rollback of some 1981 tax cuts. In a similar situation in 1990, the president's father made the same concession to a Democratic Congress. Bush, however, pursued tax policy based on the supply side theory that tax cuts would produce such robust economic growth that deficits would substantially decrease.

Bush has not just cut taxes; he has pushed tax cuts with a supply-side bias, aimed at stimulating investment rather than consumer demand. The tax cuts of 2001 left the tax system largely intact, except for abolishing the estate tax. However, the president's 2003 tax proposal sharply cut taxes on investment income and wealth for Americans by eliminating taxes on stock dividends and capital gains. In the end, the president obtained reductions in, but not elimination of, both taxes. The president also wants to allow Americans to shelter larger amounts of income from taxation, as discussed below.

The rationale for these proposed changes is to raise the amount of investment capital available to businesses by allowing investors to keep more of their money. Supporters of the cuts argue that the changes will lead to a permanent expansion in available capital, decreasing its cost to corporations, which would in turn spend more on new initiatives, creating new jobs and stimulating the economy. Advocates of Bush's policies also maintain that lower taxes empower people to spend their income as they wish.

Reducing or eliminating taxes on capital gains and dividends essentially replaces the pre-Bush income tax system with a tax on paychecks. If bigger investment portfolios no longer come with larger tax bills, the tax burden shifts toward those whose income comes from wages. Because wages constitute a larger share of the income of people of modest means than of the income of the wealthy, a wage tax substantially erodes the progressivity of the tax system. A variety of tax-preferred savings accounts, an option the wealthy are most likely to exploit, would have the same consequence of reducing progressivity. It is no exaggeration to call these changes revolutionary.

In a convergence of conservative tax doctrine and social policies, Bush also wants to use the tax code for broader social purposes. The president has articulated a vision of an "ownership society" in which individuals are encouraged to act as investors in their own destiny by saving in tax-preferred personal accounts tied to stocks, bonds, and other securities. The president has even proposed "lifetime savings accounts" without restrictions on withdrawals. These savings could be used, tax free, for any purpose.

Education

Traditionally, the hallmark of conservative thinking about elementary and secondary education has been the insistence on local control of schools. It was conservatives who sought to eliminate the Department of Education. Central to George W. Bush's domestic policy has been the drive to raise the standards and improve the performance of America's schools through a major piece of social legislation, the No Child Left Behind Act.

At the core of this bill are standards of performance, measures of achievement based on systematic testing, and real sanctions for failure. This policy represents the largest expansion of the federal role in education since Lyndon Johnson's Great Society. In response to the new law, many state and local education officials complain that such a regimen stifles teachers' creativity, infringes on local control of schools, and threatens to label so many public schools as failures that public support for private school vouchers would increase. Many states have complained loudly about the problems, and especially the cost, of implementing the legislation.

The president has also called for increased parental choice in the education of their children. Thus, Bush wants choice among public schools for parents of children in underperforming and unsafe public schools and the creation of more charter schools. More significantly, he supports vouchers that parents could use to send their children to private schools, many of which would have religious affiliations. Congress, at the administration's urging, has adopted a voucher program for the Washington, D.C., school system. If adopted more widely, this policy would be another radical change in federal education policy.

Church-State Relations

Bush has backed a continuing effort to shift the line on church-state relations, bringing civil and religious authority much closer together. He proposed direct public funding of parochial schools and applauded when the Supreme Court approved the Cleveland voucher plan, which allows parents to use public funds for religiously affiliated schools. He has lobbied hard for legislation that would route much more federal money aimed at meeting the needs of troubled individuals and families through churches, synagogues, and mosques. When Congress failed to respond to his pleas, he issued an executive order authorizing agencies to award grants to faith-based organizations.

Retirement Security

Bush's proposals for reforming Social Security would also break sharply with the past. First, he wants to allow workers to divert nearly a third of their payroll taxes to individual accounts, which they would invest in stocks and bonds. He views these accounts as a way to obtain significantly higher returns for retirement savings, softening the blow from reducing traditional Social Security benefits and thus reducing the need for substantial new long-term borrowing to pay retiree benefits. The president also proposed progressive indexation of Social Security benefits, which would cut the guaranteed benefits to middle and upper-income workers and thus diminish the role of Social Security in their retirement income.

Despite cautions from members of his own party, strong criticism from the Democrats, and the decline in the stock market, Bush remained committed to his proposals. They are additional examples of his commitment to theoretical notions, often cultivated in think tanks and ideological magazines. Libertarian and conservative research organizations such as the Cato Institute, the National Center for Policy Analysis, and the Heritage Foundation provided the primary nurturing for the concept of private accounts.

Health Care

In 2003, the White House made a full court press to convince Congress to provide a prescription drug benefit for seniors, creating the largest new federal entitlement program since the creation of Medicare in 1965. Once again, the president built on the foundations of one of Lyndon Johnson's Great Society programs, and once again he did so in a nonincremental fashion.

The Medicare revisions of 2003 also created "health savings accounts" that would allow anyone who pays high deductibles for health insurance to save and withdraw money tax-free to pay for medical expenses. This is a radical departure from current policy because the funds in these accounts are not subject to tax at any point, unlike tax-preferred investment vehicles like Keoghs, IRAs, and Roth IRAs, in which owners pay taxes when they deposit or withdraw funds. The ultimate goal of such accounts is to give people a choice about their investment in health care and also slacken the demand for health care services. These accounts separate individuals from employer-provided health care plans.

In addition, as part of the Medicare overhaul in 2003, Congress passed at Bush's urging a pilot privatization test program that will require private health plans to compete directly with Medicare—and with each other. Such plans would be a major departure in health care policy because they would substantially increase the role for private plans in Medicare.

Homeland Security

The president's USA Patriot Act, passed just six weeks after the September 11, 2001, terrorist attacks, gave the government broad new powers for the wiretapping, surveillance, and investigation of terrorism suspects. Attorney General John Ashcroft also eased restrictions on domestic spying in counterterrorism operations, allowing agents to monitor political or religious groups without any connection to a criminal investigation. The Patriot Act gave the federal government the power to examine a terrorist suspect's records held by third parties such as doctors, libraries, bookstores, universities, and Internet service providers. It also allowed searches of private property without probable cause and without prior notice to the owner, limiting a person's opportunities to challenge a search. In 2005, press reports revealed that Bush had ordered the National Security Agency, without the court-approved warrants ordinarily required for domestic spying, to monitor the international telephone calls and e-mail messages of people inside the United States.

In the aftermath of 9/11, the FBI detained more than 1,200 persons as possible dangers to national security. Of these persons, 762 were illegal aliens (mostly Arabs and Muslims), and many of them languished in jail for months until cleared by the FBI. For the first time in U.S. history, the federal government withheld the names of detainees, reducing their access to the courts and to counsel. The government argued that releasing the names and details of those arrested would give terrorists a window on the terror investigation.

In the summer of 2002, President Bush concluded that the only way to overcome the fragmentation of agencies involved in providing homeland security was to create a new department. Congress passed the legislation necessary to create the new department at the end of 2002, the largest reorganization of the federal government in a half-century.

Federal Workforce

Most of the federal government is composed of bureaucracy, and the president has sought to transform it. First, Bush announced plans to outsource up to 850,000 federal jobs—about half the government's civilian work force—to private contractors. Whether his goal is ideological or managerial, requiring government workers to compete for their jobs against private contractors through "competitive sourcing" would be an extraordinary transformation of the federal government. In addition, Bush's appointees at the National Labor Relations Board have helped to make it harder for unions to represent temporary workers.

The president also wishes to give political appointees in the federal agencies greater authority to reward or discipline senior career managers and to give managers more flexibility to promote, punish, or fire hundreds of thousands of civil servants. He proposed eliminating annual raises for the highest ranking civil servants, those who compose the Senior Executive Service, and replacing them with a system of merit ratings. Bush also insisted on a major revision of civil service rules at the Department of Homeland Security, weakening job protections, and wants to expand this change to the entire government.

National Security Policy

Nowhere is the president's tendency toward bold change more clear than in national security policy. In the 2000 presidential campaign, George W. Bush spoke of "humility" in foreign affairs and warned against "nation-building" and overextending America's military. The 9/11 terrorist attacks caused the president to rethink these views, and the administration now talks about meeting America's "unparalleled responsibilities."

The president sees the threat posed by terrorism as presenting new challenges to U.S. national security and the strategies and institutions that kept the peace during the Cold War as unsuited to a twenty-first-century campaign against terrorism. He has concluded that multilateral alliances like NATO and bilateral partnerships like that with South Korea have proven ineffective in dealing with terrorism. Thus, the United States is moving away from a system of formal, structured alliances and into a more fluid system of ad hoc alignments of nations in which the mission determines the alliance.

It is not surprising, then, that national security strategy doctrine issued by the Bush administration in September 2002 is the most dramatic and far-reaching change in national security policy in a half-century.[1] It substitutes preemption of potential threats for deterrence and containment of aggression. In more recent formulations, preemption has expanded from precluding immediate threats to prevention of the development of threats. U.S. national security doctrine also explicitly advocates U.S. preeminence in military capabilities and, if necessary, unilateral action in national security policy, contrary to decades of emphasis on grounding defense policy in alliances.

---

[1] *The National Security Strategy of the United States of America,* September 2002 (Washington, D.C.: Government Printing Office, 2002).

The U.S. invasion of Iraq followed directly from these premises. It was a policy designed to preempt future strikes against the United States and its allies. The absence of support from core members of NATO and the potential damage to our most enduring alliances did not deter the president. Nor did the lack of support from the United Nations, which the president feels has failed miserably—in Rwanda, in Kosovo and now in its confrontation with Iraq—and needs to be made anew. Similarly, the president renounced the 1972 Anti-Ballistic Missile Treaty over the objections of Russia and China, refused to participate in the International Criminal Court, and rejected several environmental treaties.

In his 2005 inaugural address following his reelection, the president spoke to the world, proclaiming that America would stand with those who challenge authoritarian governments and warned those governments to begin liberalizing. These exhortations appeared to represent another major element of Bush's foreign policy, but the administration—including a rare press conference held by the president's father—downplayed the significance of the statements. It remains to be seen how the White House makes the inevitable trade-offs between principle and pragmatism in dealing with repressive regimes. So far, however, it appears as though the unexpected difficulties endured in Iraq since the fall of Saddam Hussein have colored the broader efforts against the "axis of evil" states of Iran and North Korea. Tehran and Pyongyang have felt freer to flout American pressure, secure in the knowledge that the U.S. military is tied down in Iraq. The White House has favored diplomacy with Tehran and Pyongyang, adopting a decidedly pragmatic turn.

Defense Reform

Directly related to rethinking national security policy is reforming the nation's military. Reevaluating weapons systems and potentially skipping a generation to produce more technologically advanced systems is part of the effort. So is changing the force structure to make the armed forces lighter, faster, and more flexible. The administration believes the army is more likely to be fighting "conflicts" than "wars" in the future and therefore needs to be a force organized around smaller, more "modular" combat teams that would fight more efficiently and maneuver themselves on the battlefield with less reliance on divisional headquarters. More effectively coupling intelligence with an increasingly agile military and a greater use of Special Forces are also part of the restructuring—and significant breaks from the past. The president wants the infantry to increase as a percentage of the army, and he wants to reduce spending on the air force and navy to help pay for these changes. He also supports moving specialists from the reserves into active duty. These changes in the force structure are the largest since the 1930s. New approaches to military conflict inevitably follow from such transformations.

POLICIES AND POLARIZATION

To understand how revolutionary Bush's proposals are, it is instructive to examine an apparent paradox in American politics. In one narrow but important sense, Bush has moved the Republican party to the left, espousing compassionate conservatism. Central to his electoral strategy has been preempting traditional

Democratic issues such as education and health care. Both the size of the federal budget and the national debt have grown substantially during his tenure. The very large deficits run up by the administration have certainly angered a number of traditional conservatives. Only a decade ago, Republicans moved into ascendancy in Congress by promoting traditional conservatism, including smaller government, lower budgets, and reduced public services. They vowed to abolish four cabinet-level departments, including the Department of Education. Bush, however, supported adding a prescription drug entitlement to Medicare and substantially increasing federal aid to education. In this sense, then, the president has tried to capture the center for Republicans by advocating more liberal policies than did his Republican predecessors.

On the other hand, Bush is the most polarizing president in polling history. The first Gallup poll of Bush's tenure found that he had the highest level of *disapproval* of any new president since polling began.[2] Similarly, Gary C. Jacobson reported that the public's initial reception of Bush reflected the widest partisan differences for any newly elected president in polling history. In the 28 Gallup and CBS/*New York Times* polls taken before September 11, 2001, Bush's approval ratings averaged 88 percent among self-identified Republicans but only 31 percent among Democrats (Independents averaged 50 percent). This 57-point difference indicates an extraordinary degree of polarization.[3] Yet this gap

---

[2] Gallup Poll, News Release, January 5, 2001.
[3] Gary C. Jacobson, "The Bush Presidency and the American Electorate," *Presidential Studies Quarterly* 33 (December 2003): 701–729.

between the assessments of Democrats and Republicans was just the beginning. In the May 21–23, 2004, Gallup poll, the difference between his approval among Republicans (89 percent) and Democrats (12 percent), was an astounding 77 percentage points! That gap of 70 points or higher has been common since Bush's fourth year in office.[4]

These are extreme and unprecedented levels of polarization.[5] No president, dating back to Harry Truman, has had a partisan gap above 70 points in any Gallup poll in a reelection year. Moreover, Gallup had never before found such a high proportion of partisans with such strongly opposing views of a president. In the May 21–23, 2004, poll, 64 percent of Republicans said they strongly approved of the job Bush was doing as president, while 66 percent of Democrats strongly disapproved. As Gallup put it, "Bush is the only president who has had more than 6 in 10 of his party's identifiers strongly approving of him at the same time that more than 6 in 10 of the other party's identifiers strongly disapprove of him." The only other president to have more than 60 percent of a partisan group disapproving of him was Richard Nixon in the year of his resignation, when 61 percent of Democrats strongly disapproved of him. At that time, Nixon had overall job approval ratings below 30 percent.[6]

Gallup found that 95 percent of Republicans voted for Bush in 2004—but only 7 percent of Democrats did so.[7] Jacobson's

---

[4] See, for example, Jeffrey M. Jones, "Bush Ratings Show Historical Levels of Polarization," *Gallup News Service,* June 4, 2004.
[5] This point is nicely illustrated in Gary C. Jacobson, *A Divider, Not a Uniter: George W. Bush and the American Public* (New York: Longman, 2006), chap. 1.
[6] Jones, "Bush Ratings Show Historical Levels of Polarization."
[7] Jeffrey M. Jones, "How Americans Voted," *Gallup News Service,* November 5, 2004.

analysis of the National Election Studies found the highest level of party line voting in the 52-year history of the National Election Studies. With partisan leaners (those who say they "lean" toward identifying with one party or the other) included, 89 percent of Democrats and 91 percent of Republicans voted for their party's candidates. If we exclude the leaners, 92 percent of Democrats voted for Kerry while 94 percent of Republicans voted for Bush.[8]

Although Bush received a modest five-point bounce in his approval rating after his election in 2004, his 53 percent rating was actually the lowest of any of the last seven presidents who won election while serving as president in the first poll conducted after their elections (see Table 1.1).

The war in Iraq has been the most important policy of the Bush administration. Although the president enjoyed majority support for going to war in the spring of 2003, by 2005 the public's evaluations of both the war, the postwar U.S. occupation of Iraq, and the president's management of it split along party lines. This division was much greater than it had been for any other U.S. military engagement since World War II, widening the partisan gap in overall evaluations of the president in the process.[9]

Strong Government and Conservative Values

How can we reconcile the antipathy to Bush among Democrats with his support of education and healthcare programs? It is true that Bush is not antigovernment in the tradition of Goldwater,

---

[8] Jacobson, *A Divider, Not a Uniter,* p. 190.
[9] Gary C. Jacobson, "The Public, the President, and the War in Iraq" (paper delivered at the annual meeting of the American Political Science Association, September 2005).

TABLE 1.1
Presidential Approval Following Election of Serving Presidents

PRESIDENT	YEAR	APPROVAL (%)
George W. Bush	2004	53
Bill Clinton	1996	58
Ronald Reagan	1984	61
Richard Nixon	1972	62
Lyndon Johnson	1964	75
Dwight Eisenhower	1956	69
Harry Truman	1949*	69

SOURCE: Gallup Poll.
*First poll after 1948 election not taken until January 1949.

Reagan, and Gingrich. He recognizes that Americans do not want to reduce government radically. Instead, they expect it to assuage two of life's greatest fears—illness and old age. Thus, we spend nearly 40 percent of the federal budget on Social Security and health care. People also want help at the other end of the life cycle with improved education—and thus a better life—for their children.

However, the president's basic strategy is to put strong government in the service of conservative values. The central value for Bush is freedom. He is much less concerned with equality, especially equality of condition, which is at the heart of traditional liberalism. Bush aims to expand individual choice and empower individuals—and increase their responsibility for themselves. Thus, the president aims his reforms at offering opportunities and incentives for individuals to become more self-sufficient.

Conservative columnist George Will puts it this way:

> *Standards that measure schools' performances enable parents, exercising the right to choose, to differentiate education products. Medical savings accounts would empower individuals to pursue preferences and, by making individuals into price-sensitive shoppers, the accounts would serve medical cost-containment. Private investment of Social Security taxes would democratize access to wealth creation, reducing dependence on government-provided retirement security. Low taxes expand each earner's freedom by enlarging discretionary income and focus society's attention on improving well-being through individual creation of wealth rather than government redistribution of it.*[10]

Similarly, his prescription drug benefit proposal provides for alternatives to the one-size-fits-all single payer Medicare program. Even competitive sourcing of public services buys alternatives to government bureaucrats, albeit typically for collective rather than individual benefits.

Bush believes that government curtails freedom not by being large or active but by making choices that should be left to people, undermining their individual responsibility in the process. Thus, he is flexible, willing to support expanding, reforming, or shrinking government, as long as it increases people's choices. He wants to change the structure of government, not its size. He is less concerned with how much government spends than with how it spends it. He wants to reduce the demand for government rather

---

[10] George F. Will, "Freedom vs. Equality," *Washington Post*, February 1, 2004, p. B7.

than, as traditional conservatives do, the supply of it. And he wants to accomplish this by, in his words, empowering people.

The nation's safety net developed following the movement from farm to factory and from extended to nuclear families. The Great Depression underscored the vulnerability of the new economy and social structure. To alleviate suffering and spread risk, Franklin D. Roosevelt's New Deal created programs such as Social Security, which protected the working class against the risk of outliving their assets, and unemployment insurance, which protected workers against the vagaries of the economic cycle. In World War II, businesses offered workers broad-based health and pension programs to circumvent wartime controls on wages, buy peace with unions, and help attract workers in an environment of labor shortages. In the 1960s, Lyndon Johnson's Great Society created Medicare to limit the impact of burdensome health costs for the elderly, who were poor candidates for private health insurance because of their high health costs.

The current system broadly spreads the financial risks of the vicissitudes of life over most of the population. It also forces people to save through taxation for Social Security and Medicare and through the incentives provided by employer matching of pension contributions. Bush wants to rewrite the social contract that has defined the past four generations of Americans. He wants Americans to use personal savings to replace some of the nation's social insurance system, including government- and employer-sponsored health and pension plans. Bush wants Americans to self-insure against such risks and give up the national security blanket to determine their own destinies. Liberals have supported tax policies that encouraged savings, especially for lower-income individuals.

Bush's proposals are tilted toward the well-to-do, however, because they pay most of the income taxes. Equally important, liberals prefer savings that supplement government or employer-based programs, while Bush wants at least to partially supplant these programs.

Democrats favor expanding government controls (and thus limiting freedom of choice), to promote equality, such as common dependence on government-provided education, health, and pension entitlements. It seems reasonable to argue that Democratic resistance to Bush's domestic policies such as school standards and choice, medical savings accounts, partial privatization of Social Security, and cuts in individual income taxes reflects a basic fight over the classic goals of equality and freedom. Lowering income taxes, which fall mainly on the wealthy, increases inequality. Tax savings cannot help the poorest Americans, who pay no income tax now. Creating options in public schools, Medicare, and Social Security threatens their comprehensive coverage of the population—and also everyone with a stake in maintaining the *status quo*.

Bush has emphasized shifting decision-making responsibilities from government to the private sector through partially privatizing retirement (through individual investment accounts), education (through vouchers), health care for the elderly (through health savings accounts and partially privatizing Medicare), and welfare (through faith-based charities). Government would still provide or safeguard resources devoted to these programs, but much of the decision making about them would center on individual choice.

Democrats fear that the true intention of the president's proposals is to relieve government of its responsibilities and replace public programs with a free market that values efficiency more than the equality of a social safety net. For example, at the time of the president's second inauguration, 75 percent of Democrats and 54 percent of Independents thought that Bush's plan to reform Social Security was motivated by a desire to benefit Wall Street investment companies more than to help average Americans.[11] Similarly, in May 2005, 76 percent of Democrats and 54 percent of Independents thought the president's real agenda regarding Social Security was to dismantle it rather than to save and strengthen it.[12]

Expanding freedom also increases risk for the less well off. Their lack of slack resources puts them at greater risk from downturns in the stock market (affecting personal accounts in Social Security) or mistakes in evaluating their health care needs or an unexpected inability to save for them. Health accounts could also leave the sick in more traditional plans with higher costs as healthier people opt out of sharing the risk of illness. In addition, individual retirement accounts and health savings accounts make it more difficult for the wealthy to subsidize the poor under Social Security, Medicare, and Medicaid (which covers much of nursing home care). In the end, many Democrats share Senator John Edwards's fear of creating "two Americas" in which there are great disparities in wealth.

---

[11] CBS News/*New York Times* poll, January 14–18, 2005.
[12] Harris poll, May 4–10, 2005.

Conservatives argue that inequalities of outcomes are manifestations of freedom and prerequisites for progress. They believe that Democratic policies produce a culture of dependency by diminishing individual competence and dignity and thwart the benefits that result from competing alternatives. Liberals, in contrast, argue that only by emphasizing equality can society protect its weakest members and guarantee every American a basic dignity of lifestyle. Moreover, they say the evidence is clear that America has prospered in the post-New Deal era and see no reason to change what they view as successful policies. We cannot resolve these differences in outlook here, but we can understand that the stakes are high for the outcome of battles over Bush's policies.

Freedom is not the president's only value, of course. The president also supports big government—a big federal government—where it will help him achieve his goals, preempting states on policy issues in the process. Thus, he supported limiting personal injury lawsuits or removing class action lawsuits from state courts, limiting the discretion of school administrators and teachers, limiting states issuing drivers' licenses to illegal immigrants, and allowing off-duty and retired police officers to carry concealed firearms wherever they travel.

Interestingly, the president had a policy outcome in mind when he proposed shifting class action lawsuits from state to federal courts and away from sympathetic judges and juries. He presumed that federal judges and juries would be less generous to plaintiffs. Similarly, he anticipated that federal judges would order reinserting Terri Schiavo's feeding tube, in contrast to state judges. In essence, he is asking federal judges to make decisions based on political predilections—exactly what he has denounced in other settings.

Equally important, Bush has supported some strong governmental constraints on individual freedom. The president is willing to use federal power aggressively to achieve moral and cultural goals, including limiting abortion and stem cell research and prohibiting gay marriage. Some feel his proposals to use tax revenues to support faith-based schools and social programs violates their protections under the Establishment Clause of the First Amendment. As differences in economic policy decreased during the Clinton years, conflict over differences in moral and cultural issues increased. There is an increasingly strong relationship between religiosity and party identification in the United States. As white, southern evangelicals have moved to the Republican party, the Christian Right has become more central to its success. The Democratic party, on the other hand, has become more assertively secular. It is not surprising, then, that Democrats have disdain for Bush.

Similarly, the president's exercise of the broad investigatory powers authorized under the USA Patriot Act and his claims to executive power to detain suspects without due process of law have concerned those at both ends of the political spectrum. Although the administration argues that the president's actions are aimed at protecting Americans' freedom, many critics view his highly unusual policies as fundamental threats to civil liberties.

Finally, there is foreign policy. At the core of this policy is the fight against terrorism, and the most significant aspect of this fight has been the war in Iraq. We will see in Chapter 4 that for a substantial period following 9/11, the president was at historic highs in the polls, and there was a wide public consensus supporting his efforts to combat terrorism. Yet by the time of the Iraq war, the country was divided and this division deepened as first chaos and then prolonged violence characterized the aftermath of the war. The expenditure of lives and treasure without signs of visible progress certainly contributed to the nation's polarization. More broadly, however, the Bush administration's projection of a muscular foreign policy and its willingness to act without traditional allies raised concerns among a substantial segment of the public. At the core of this group were those who initially responded so enthusiastically to Howard Dean's antiwar candidacy for the Democratic nomination in 2004. In addition, as we will see, the White House's arguments on behalf of the war and its claims of progress soon rang hollow to all but Republicans ears in the public.

Weakening Democrats

Adding to the partisan polarization of the country has been the Bush White House's political strategy of constraining the Democrats' ability to legislate. The first step was to limit the resources available to them. The president chose a large income tax cut as his highest legislative priority. This made good strategic sense for a conservative administration. The president and his advisors felt that the notable victory of enacting a major tax cut early in the administration would signal the administration's competence in governing while unifying the Republican party for the more difficult issues ahead. Equally important, by severely limiting the government's resources, cutting taxes would set the terms of debate for nearly all the policy debates that would follow and restrain the Democrats' ability to use the budget surplus for expansion of social welfare policies.

A related component in this strategy has been to weaken principal components of the Democratic coalition. Tort litigation reform would reduce the incomes of trial lawyers, who represent a main source of Democratic funding. Former Clinton White House chief of staff John Podesta articulated the Democrats' view: "Why would you make this the cause célèbre?" he asked. "The notion that this is a key element of their economic program is laughable. It's important to them ... both in organizing core elements of their business and doctor communities, and at least undermining a financial base of the Democratic Party."[13] Similarly, Bush's education reform plan weakens teachers unions, another group at the Democratic core, because it decentralizes education decisionmaking while increasing accountability.

Trade unions are a key element in the Democratic coalition. Outsourcing of federal jobs weakens public employee unions, which are a mainstay of the Democratic party. The administration's transformation of civil service rules at federal agencies would also limit the power and membership of public employee unions. Trade liberalization weakens them to the extent that their members lose jobs to workers in other countries who cost less to employ. Although the White House's desire to undermine the

---

[13] Quoted in Thomas B. Edsall and John F. Harris, "Bush Aims To Forge A GOP Legacy," *Washington Post,* January 30, 2005.

opposition was not the primary motivation for these policies, the consequence of doing so has added an additional impetus to the president's initiatives—and an additional source of polarization.

A third aspect of the strategy for weakening Democrats, of course, is co-opting their issues. By directly addressing education, health care, and retirement security, for example, the president has been able to improve the Republicans' image as a party concerned with social welfare issues.

The presidency of George W. Bush is an important one. The president wants to transform the face of American policy and politics, and he has generated an unprecedented level of polarization in the process. In the remainder of this book, I focus on the politics of the Bush administration. Given the president's ambitious goals and the intense opposition he faces, how has the White House attempted to engender change? Of course, we cannot presume that efforts—even those of a president—succeed. So I also explore how successful he has been in these efforts. At the end of the book, we will revisit the issue of polarization and ask whether the president's approach to governing contributed to the partisan divisions in the country.

CHAPTER 2

Going Public: A Strategy for Governing

Every president must choose a strategy for governing within the context in which he finds himself. One approach is to seek to pass legislation through relatively quiet negotiations with congressional leaders. The president's father, George H. W. Bush, provided an example with his administration's efforts regarding environmental, education, and budget policy. We have seen in Chapter 1 that George W. Bush came to office with an ambitious agenda that inevitably divided the country. The White House concluded that the president's program was unlikely to pass without increasing its political capital. To achieve his goals, Bush has relied on an alternative strategy to that of his father: taking his case to the people, counting on public opinion to move Congress to support his policies.

Bush's approach is not unique, of course. The president's relations with the public sit at the core of the modern presidency.

Both politics and policy revolve around presidents' attempts to garner public support, for both themselves and their policies. Three fundamental and widely shared premises about the relationship between public opinion and presidential leadership underlay this mode of governance. The first is that public support is a crucial political resource for the president (i.e., it is difficult for others who hold power to deny the legitimate demands of a president with popular support). A president who lacks the public's support is likely to face frustration and perhaps humiliation at the hands of his opponents. As Bill Clinton exclaimed after the Senate acquitted him in his impeachment trial, "Thank God for public opinion."[1]

The second premise supporting the White House's intense focus on public opinion is the view that the president must not only earn public support with his performance in office, but also must actively take his case to the people. Moreover, he must not only do it at reelection time but all the time. As Clinton advisor Dick Morris put it:

> *Once upon a time, elections settled things for the term of office. Now, they are mere punctuation marks in an ongoing search for public support and a functioning majority. Each day is election day in modern America.... A politician needs a permanent campaign to keep a permanent majority.*[2]

The third (and least analyzed) premise sustaining the public presidency is that through the permanent campaign the White House *can* successfully persuade or even mobilize the public.

---

[1] Quoted in Bob Woodward, *Shadow* (New York: Simon and Schuster, 1999), 513.
[2] Dick Morris, *The New Prince* (Los Angeles, CA: Renaissance Books, 1999), 75, 72.

Commentators on the presidency in both the press and academia often assume that the White House can move public opinion if the president has the skill and will to effectively exploit the "bully pulpit." As a result, modern presidents choose to engage in a permanent campaign for the public's support as their core strategy for governing.

The next three chapters explore various aspects of the president's relations with the public. This chapter focuses on the Bush White House's efforts at going public. Chapter 3 examines the extent to which this effort succeeded in moving public opinion in the president's directions. Chapter 4 investigates the public's evaluation of the president personally. In Chapter 5, I ask, among other things, how much leverage the president's public approval gave him in dealing with Congress.

GOING PUBLIC
IN THE BUSH WHITE HOUSE

Much to the surprise of many observers, George W. Bush has chosen to govern by campaigning. Soon after taking office, he launched a massive public relations campaign on behalf of his priority initiatives. At the core of this effort was the most extensive domestic travel schedule of any new president in American history. Bush spoke in 29 states by the end of May, often more than once. The president also used his Saturday radio addresses to exhort the public to communicate their support for his tax cut and education plans to Congress.

The president not only spoke extensively about each initiative, but also went to considerable lengths to focus attention on each proposal in the early weeks of the administration. The faith-based initiative received attention in the week after the inauguration, followed in successive weeks by education, tax cuts, and defense.

The Bush administration has never looked back—and never slowed down—in its efforts to win public support for its policies. To achieve its public relations goals, the White House has typically adopted a highly disciplined and strategic perspective.

Think Strategically

In her extensive study of the Bush White House communications operation, presidential scholar Martha Kumar found that the operation is dedicated to making news on the president's terms and is organized to plan and get ahead of events. As White House advisor Karen Hughes put it about the president, "He'll want to know the plan. What's the plan? How are we rolling this out?" Similarly, Mary Matalin observed, "He's very engaged in the strategic thinking. He has a feel for when is the right time to give the speech. What is our objective? Are we talking to the Congress, are we talking to America, are we talking to the world? . . . He knows when is the time when the iron's hot, if you will, or carpe diem. He gets those moments in ways that we often don't."[3]

President Bush's interest goes down to the operational level as well. For example, he pushed the staff in terms of making certain

---

[3] This discussion draws extensively on Martha Joynt Kumar, "Communications Operations in the White House of President George W. Bush: Making News on His Terms," *Presidential Studies Quarterly* 33 (June 2003): 366–393.

that events related to the administration's response to the attacks of September 11 rose to his level. He was furious when his staff sent him documents to sign at Camp David regarding freezing financial assets. He demanded to know, "Why am I just signing this document and Secretary [Paul] O'Neill is announcing this tomorrow. This is the first strike in this new war against terror." The president wanted more publicity for his action, and the White House communications operation put together a Rose Garden signing event for the following morning.

The president also placed two strategic thinkers, Karl Rove and Karen Hughes, in top positions in the White House. He gave Hughes a broad mandate to think about the White House's message, whether the public understood the president's policies, whether it supported the president's policies, and how to build more support for them. She was also to supervise the elements that might be used in an issue campaign, including speechwriting, media affairs, television, press secretary, and communications.

Top administration officials meet daily with the president and vice president to discuss strategic direction and issues and approaches. Once or twice a month Karl Rove convenes a strategy session to plan several months ahead, focusing on the president's travels, messages, and daily themes. The strategy meetings provide them with a direction for the months ahead even if events outside of their control blow them off course.

In general, the emphasis on strategic planning has aided the president in defining himself and his programs rather than allowing his critics to do so. For example, since early 2001, Democrats have raised the issue of the fairness of the president's proposals for cutting taxes, arguing that most of the immediate benefits of the tax reductions go to the affluent. However, from the beginning, the administration aggressively framed the president's proposals as efforts to benefit much larger segments of the population. Although the public did not necessarily adopt the president's view, the White House's efforts seemed to have blunted the edge of the Democrats' charge and undermined their ability to engage in class warfare.[4]

In the summer of 2002, there was substantial criticism that the administration was losing control of the agenda and not speaking with one voice, especially on the possibility of war with Iraq. However, White House officials argued that the administration was following a meticulously planned strategy to persuade the public, the Congress, and the allies of the need to confront the threat of Saddam Hussein. The White House decided that even with the appearance of disarray it was still more advantageous to wait until after Labor Day to kick off their plan. "From a marketing point of view," said Andrew H. Card Jr., the White House chief of staff who coordinated the effort, "you don't introduce new products in August."[5]

The White House communications operation was especially impressive during the war in Iraq. The White House plotted appearances by officials in a daily communications grid, ensuring that in the first half of the day there was a news briefing by an administration official every two hours, and that everyone was

---

[4] See, Jonathan Weisman, "Bush Blunts 'Fairness Question' on Taxes," *Washington Post,* May 13, 2003, p. A6.

[5] Elisabeth Bumiller, "Bush Aides Set Strategy to Sell Policy on Iraq," *New York Times,* September 7, 2002.

taking a similar line. The White House, Pentagon, and State Department had a 9:30 A.M. conference call about the theme of day and who was delivering it. Starting at 7 A.M., the command center in Qatar held a briefing so that it could run live on the morning news shows to put the administration's spin on overnight battlefield developments. A former deputy in the White House communications office prepped General Vincent Brooks, the chief military briefer. Ari Fleischer, the president's press secretary, held three press conferences per day, and there were additional briefings at the Pentagon and State Department, and sometimes special sessions for foreign reporters.[6]

In January 2006, the White House opened a media blitz in defense of the National Security Agency's eavesdropping program, which had become a high-profile issue. Critics charged the president with exceeding his authority and invading the privacy of innocent Americans through a "domestic spying program." To counter this criticism, the White House went to great lengths to recast the language surrounding the debate and frame the program as a crucial element in the war against terrorism. Bush termed his decision to authorize the interceptions as part of a "terrorist surveillance program," a phrase meant to convey that only members of al Qaeda and their associates were falling into the net of the security agency.

The administration recognized that it was critical that the White House seek to define an issue such as the electronic surveillance program on its own terms. Because public opinion about

---

[6] Elisabeth Bumiller, "Even Critics of War Say the White House Spun It with Skill," *New York Times,* April 20, 2003, p. B14.

the trade-offs between national security and individual rights was nuanced and unresolved, there was more opportunity for the president to influence public opinion than on issues about which people have firm predispositions. Of course, there was also more opportunity for the opposition to define the issue if the White House did not act aggressively.

Despite its efforts to think strategically and plan ahead, the White House has frequently found itself in a reactive mode. One example is the administration's reaction to the issue of corporate fraud, an issue the White House did not anticipate and to which it was slow to react. Months of articles in newspapers and stories on television news detailed the depth of the issues and the connections some of the corporate players had with the White House. By the time the president delivered a speech on the issue on July 9, 2002, the bar representing success had been raised. Although the first day's stories focused on the president's rhetoric, the day two and day three stories focused on the speech's lack of effective enforcement mechanisms. One of the byproducts of a communications operation geared towards action is the difficulty inherent in listening while selling.

Exercise Message Discipline

An innovation of the George W. Bush administration is the control it exercises over the publicity officers in the departments. The White House screens the persons named to these positions and the release of information by departments. Controlling departmental public affairs offices allows the president and his staff to avoid the problem many administrations have faced with such units focusing their attention on the departmental secretary and his goals rather than those of the president.

Coordination with the departments has the advantage of making certain everyone has the same version of events and also that each knows what the other is doing. In addition, coordination with the departments has the advantage of making it easier for the White House to leverage the resources of the departments. Not only can the department secretaries serve as effective surrogates for the president on issues important to the administration, but agencies also have at their disposal resources to send out their message.

The administration also exercised message discipline in its characterizations of people and developments in terms favorable to its policy. U.S. and British troops were "coalition forces." Regime change was "liberation," not "occupation." The paramilitary fedayeen were "death squads." Iraqi troops and fighters were "thugs." The Hussein government was a "regime." These terms became part of the accepted language of describing the war.[7] Later, those fighting the United States in Iraq were not "insurgents" but "terrorists."

Poll the Public

George W. Bush campaigned against governing by poll, presenting himself as a strong leader who did not bend in the political wind. Despite its claims of disdain for polls and focus groups, the Bush

---

[7] Bumiller, "Even Critics of War Say the White House Spun It with Skill."

White House has had extensive involvement in polling. The White House Office of Strategic Initiatives monitors and analyzes the results of numerous national polls, and it has commissioned millions of dollars of its own polls and focus groups. Polls conducted by Republican pollsters at the state level also inform its analyses.[8]

As in all modern presidencies, the White House's goal in much of its effort to poll the public is to determine how to frame the president's message most effectively in order to win public support for his policies. The White House tried to frame the debate over the nomination of John Bolton to be ambassador to the United Nations as one of reforming the UN rather than over Bolton's personality or his handling of sensitive intelligence. When the administration announced its plan to open national forests for more extensive logging, it named the plan the "Healthy Forests Initiative." Similarly, the Environmental Protection Agency's plan to reduce the pollution standards for power plants was labeled the "Clear Skies Initiative." At other times, the White House may be trying to identify possible pitfalls in its path or to clarify the administration's policies. When polls reveal that the public is not responsive to the president's appeals, explanations, or accomplishments, the White House makes great efforts to adjust its language or highlight its successes.

As support for the war in Iraq (and the president) dropped below 50 percent in 2005, the White House hired an academic expert on public opinion during wartime, whose studies helped Bush craft his message. There were a number of ways the president could have sought the public's support, and he was certainly

---

[8] Kathryn Dunn Tenpas, "Words vs. Deeds: President George W. Bush and Polling," *Brookings Review* (Summer 2003): 33–35.

inclined toward perseverance and confidence. In addition, however, the president's rhetoric of resolution and optimism reflected a strategy based on extensive study of public opinion on how to maintain support for a war. These studies concluded that the more resolute the commander in chief and the more the Americans could interpret events in Iraq as making progress toward the United States leaving, the more likely the public would see the difficult conflict through to the end.[9]

PUBLIC RELATIONS TECHNIQUES

There are less direct ways of going public than the president giving a speech. The White House employs some public relations techniques in ways that it hopes will affect broad perceptions of the Bush presidency or structure thinking about issues. These are some of the characteristic patterns in the Bush White House's public relations efforts.

Use the Rolling Announcement

The White House employs a "rolling" announcement format in which it alerts the press that it will be making an announcement about a legislative initiative in coming days, sparking stories on the upcoming news. Then it makes the announcement, generating yet additional stories. Finally, the president travels around the country repeating the announcement he just made, obtaining both

---

[9] Peter Baker and Dan Balz, "Bush Words Reflect Public Opinion Strategy, *Washington Post,* June 30, 2005; Scott Shane, "Bush's Speech on Iraq War Echoes Voice of an Analyst," *New York Times,* December 4, 2005.

local and network coverage of his media events. When journalists asked the president on June 1, 2005, why he kept plugging away on his meticulously staged and unusually repetitive national tour on Social Security (discussed in Chapter 6), he responded that he did so because "most people get their news from the local news. And if you're trying to influence opinion, the best way to do it is to travel hard around the country."[10]

Choose the Venue

Although the president has gone public actively, he has done so in controlled venues. As the *Washington Post* reported in September 2002, Bush had devoted far more time to golf (15 rounds) than to solo news conferences (six).[11] After holding three news conferences in his first four months, he held only five more in his next 24 months—not counting the question and answer sessions he has had with foreign leaders during this period.[12] Indeed, keeping the press at bay characterized his entire first term as he held only 17 solo news conferences. The pace of press conferences picked up for a while in his second term, as he held five in his first five months. But then he skipped five months before holding one in October.

Another controlled venue is the town meeting. Throughout the president's two campaigns for the White House and in his efforts to drum up support for his policies while in office, Bush has utilized "town hall" meetings. These gatherings are ostensibly an opportunity for the president to explain his policies to average

---

[10] Quoted in Dan Froomkin, "Bush, Deep Throat and the Press," *Washington Post,* June 3, 2005.

[11] Dana Milbank, "Bush by the Numbers, as Told by a Diligent Scorekeeper," *Washington Post,* September 3, 2002, p. A15.

[12] Martha Joynt Kumar, "'Does This Constitute a Press Conference?' Defining and Tabulating Modern Presidential Press Conferences," *Presidential Studies Quarterly* 33 (March 2003): 221–237.

citizens and answer their questions. In reality, the audiences at these events have been carefully screened supporters. The meeting organizers deny entry to anyone who seems likely to ask a critical question, so the president always speaks to sympathetic listeners. Leaving nothing to chance in the fight for the president's 2005 proposal for private accounts under Social Security, the advance team rehearsed the questioners the night before the event, with a White House official playing the president.

Emphasize the Bright Side

Another pattern of White House public relations efforts is what one journalist described as "compromise quietly, claim victory loudly." Bush is a pragmatist who makes the best deal he can with Congress and then declares victory. The White House knows that few Americans will notice or care that he did not get all, or even most, of what he wanted. Regarding education policy, for example, the Heritage Foundation complained on July 5, 2001: "Key elements of the president's plan—accountability, choice, flexibility and structural change—have been eliminated or weakened to the point that his design for educational reform is barely recognizable." Two weeks earlier, however, the president projected a more optimistic view: "I'm pleased to say that we're nearing historic reforms in public education," he said. "This is a victory for every child and for every family in America." The administration would rather public commentary focus on the size of the president's victory than on whether there *was* a victory.[13]

---

[13] Dana Milbank, "No Lemons; It's All Lemonade in Bush's White House," *Washington Post*, July 22, 2001, p. B1.

Naturally, the White House hopes that its claims of victory will be self-fulfilling, improving its reputation and thus the chances for future successes.

The Iraqi election in the winter of 2005 provided a critical moment for the administration. Held amid violence and attempts at intimidation by insurgents, the election presented a substantial risk to the president's Middle East policy and his justification for the war in Iraq and served as a critical test of his assertion that the country was on the path to stability. Thus, the White House adopted an aggressive communications strategy to frame the election in the best possible light. The president insisted that the key to success was simply holding the elections at all—not the percentage turnout of Iraqi voters or the nature of the election outcomes. The administration's goal was not only to lower expectations but also to avoid any definition of success to which critics could compare the results of the election.[14]

The White House serves up its upbeat diagnosis each day and again at week's end. Bush's aides send the talking points throughout the White House, to allies on Capitol Hill, and to Republican opinion leaders around town. Interest groups receive customized talking points, such as a list of Bush victories for Hispanics. In an era of 24-hour cable and Internet news, the administration hopes that outlets too pressed for time to put the claims in context will report its talking points, repeated by administration officials or allies.

The White House also tries to avoid associating the president with bad news. When China shot down a U.S. plane in April

---

[14] Elisabeth Bumiller, "Communicator in Chief Keeps the Focus on Iraq Positive," *New York Times,* January 27, 2005.

2001, the White House was determined to keep George W. Bush away from the issue, so he would not appear to be emotionally involved or the negotiator with the Chinese. Secretary of State Colin Powell took the lead—but the White House did not want Powell on television to take the credit when he succeeded in winning the crew's release. The general rule of thumb is that the president delivers good news, but bad news comes from his staff or other administration officials.[15]

If the White House wants to decrease the coverage of an event, it can wait until after the evening news programs or weekends to announce it. Then the story might be buried among the next day's occurrences. (In the age of 24-hour news channels, however, a cable channel is likely to pick it up.) The White House can also pass the word to administration officials to avoid appearing on interview programs or holding press conferences. Finally, the White House can make an announcement right before a deadline, decreasing the opportunity for reporters to obtain unfavorable reactions. Alternately, the president might take another newsworthy action at the same time. In a nationally televised address on June 6, 2002, President Bush announced his proposal for a Department of Homeland Security—just as the Senate Judiciary Committee began hearings on failures of the FBI regarding preventing terrorist attacks.

Another way to emphasize the bright side is to determine who will have access to the public. In August 2002, the White House held an "economic forum" in which various experts and interests offered advice about economic policy. In reality, this was a

---

[15] Bob Woodward, *Bush at War* (New York: Simon and Schuster, 2002), 13.

heavily stage-managed event with carefully screened attendees who lauded the president.

Manage the Image

The Bush White House is also skilled at using the powers of television and technology to promote the president. "We pay particular attention to not only what the president says but what the American people see," said Office of Communications Director Dan Bartlett. He added:

> *Americans are leading busy lives, and sometimes they don't have the opportunity to read a story or listen to an entire broadcast. But if they can have an instant understanding of what the president is talking about by seeing 60 seconds of television, you can accomplish your goals as communicators.*[16]

Thus, the White House has hired experts in lighting, camera angles, and backdrops from network television to showcase the president in dramatic and perfectly lighted settings. In May 2003, at a speech promoting his economic plan in Indianapolis, White House aides went so far as to ask people in the crowd behind Bush to take off their ties so they would look more like the ordinary people the president said would benefit from his tax cut. For a speech that the president delivered in the summer of 2002 at Mount Rushmore, the White House positioned the platform for television crews off to one side so that the cameras caught Bush in profile, his face perfectly aligned with the four presidents chiseled

---

[16] Elisabeth Bumiller, "Keepers of Bush Image Lift Stagecraft to New Heights," *New York Times*, May 16, 2003, pp. A1, A8.

in stone.[17] When the president delivered a speech at a Missouri trucking company, volunteers used stickers to cover up the labels on boxes around him that read "Made in China." Behind him, the White House constructed a backdrop of images of boxes that said "Made in the U.S.A."[18]

To trumpet his first-year legislative agenda, George W. Bush visited inner city schools to talk about education, senior citizens' centers to discuss his proposal to provide prescription drug coverage for the elderly, military bases to explain his plan for increased pay and benefits for uniformed personnel, and groups of citizens to promote his tax cuts. On May 24, 2005, the House passed a bill to expand federal financing for embryonic stem cell research, defying Republican leaders and a veto threat from President Bush. Just hours before the vote, Bush appeared in the East Room of the White House with babies and toddlers born of test-tube embryos and warned the measure "would take us across a critical ethical line."[19] The children were born from embryos donated from one couple to another.

Perhaps the most elaborate White House event was Bush's speech aboard the *Abraham Lincoln* announcing the end of major combat in Iraq. The Office of Communications choreographed every aspect of the event, including positioning the aircraft carrier so the shoreline could not be seen by the camera when the president landed; arraying members of the crew in coordinated shirt colors over Bush's right shoulder; and placing a banner reading "Mission Accomplished" to perfectly capture the president and

---

[17] Elisabeth Bumiller, "Keepers of Bush Image Lift Stagecraft to New Heights."
[18] Elisabeth Bumiller, "Keepers of Bush Image Lift Stagecraft to New Heights."
[19] *President's Remarks: President Discusses Embryo Adoption and Ethical Stem Cell Research,* White House, May 24, 2005.

the celebratory two words in a single camera shot. It also specifically timed the speech so the sun would cast a golden glow on Bush. One of the president's aides proclaimed, "If you looked at the TV picture, you saw there was flattering light on his left cheek and slight shadowing on his right. It looked great."[20]

A centerpiece of the president's strategy to gain public support for the war with Iraq was the president's nationally televised speech on September 11, 2002, which was to serve as the emotional precursor for a tougher speech about Iraq that the president delivered to the United Nations General Assembly the following day. The White House picked Ellis Island in New York Harbor as the place where President Bush would deliver his address to the nation, because the television camera angles were spectacular with the Statue of Liberty aglow behind the president.[21]

In the world of public relations, image often trumps reality. In 2004, the president went to Rome and visited Pope John Paul II. The public relations could have gone badly as the pope rebuked the president over the war in Iraq, reading a statement reminding Bush that the Vatican had opposed the war in Iraq and declaring that the "deplorable events" at Abu Ghraib were troubling to the conscience of the world. Presidential senior political advisor Karl Rove was delighted, however, because after the pope read his statement Bush praised him as a "hero of our time" and presented him with the Presidential Medal of Freedom. Thus, the image in many people's minds (especially those of American Catholics) was of the pope warmly thanking Bush.[22]

---

[20] Bumiller, "Keepers of Bush Image Lift Stagecraft to New Heights."
[21] Bumiller, "Bush Aides Set Strategy to Sell Policy on Iraq."
[22] Carl M. Cannon, "The Architect," *National Journal*, March 12, 2005, 760–761.

The talking points we mentioned earlier not only put a positive spin on the news; they also give focus to the message of the day. The goal is to give the press one story to cover and, by getting everyone in the administration to say the same thing, they reduce the chances of contradictions or disagreements to stimulate new and less positive stories.

Change Justifications

The Bush administration has been skillful in adapting rationales for its policy proposals to changing circumstances. The president advocated tax cuts as a way to return money to taxpayers when the government ran a budget surplus, as a way to constrain future government growth, as an insurance policy against an economic downturn, and as a means of stimulating a stagnant economy. The White House ignored the facts that the surplus soon disappeared, that government had to grow substantially as a result of the war on terrorism, that an economic downturn occurred, and that most of the tax reductions would not occur for years (and thus could not provide a stimulus).

On the issue of regime change in Iraq, the administration sought first to link Iraqi President Saddam Hussein to al Qaeda and the September 11 attacks. When those links proved tenuous, the administration proclaimed a shift in U.S. strategic defense doctrine from deterrence and containment to preemption of those who would use weapons of mass destruction. When critics at home and abroad complained that the United States was ignoring its allies in pursuit of unilateral action, the president went to New York and declared that Iraq's refusal to comply with United

Nations resolutions *required* multilateral action to preserve the viability of the world organization. Similarly, the president responded to criticism that he had usurped the legislature's war powers by going to Congress and asking for a strong resolution of support for the use of force against Iraq.

After the war, as the United States failed to find weapons of mass destruction in Iraq, the president changed his focus to destroying programs with the *capability* to produce such weapons in the future rather than the weapons themselves. Then he developed yet another rationale for the war against Saddam Hussein: Iraq was to be the "linchpin" to transform the Middle East and thereby reduce the terrorist threat to the United States. When public support for the war continued to wane, Bush again played his trump card of terrorism. It was ironic that before the war Bush argued that Saddam Hussein's control over Iraq could make the nation a haven for terrorists. Yet two years later he was asserting that the tumult that has followed Hussein's removal created the same threat. Thus, Iraq had become such a magnet for foreign terrorists after the war that winning the current battle there was critical to America's security.

Stay Resilient

The Bush administration has continually demonstrated resilience in its relations with the public. The summer of 2002 provides an excellent example of this pattern. By June, only 54 percent of the respondents felt Bush had strong qualities of leadership. Even worse, only 42 percent expressed confidence in his ability to deal wisely with an international crisis and only 45 percent thought he had the skills necessary to negotiate effectively with world leaders. Fifty-seven percent felt the administration favored the rich.[23] The next month, the public split evenly on whether Bush or his aides were running the government. A plurality of 48 percent felt the United States was on the wrong track, 58 percent viewed business as having too much influence on Bush, and 66 percent felt the same way about business influence on the administration. Sixty-one percent of the public felt the administration's proposal for reforming corporate accounting practices showed it was more interested in protecting the interests of large corporations than those of ordinary Americans.[24]

The White House did not allow events to overtake it, however. In the week following its biggest drop in the Gallup poll since the September 11 rally began, it announced ("hurriedly" in the minds of critics) its proposals for a new Department of Homeland Security. This returned it to a proactive stance and also provided a distraction from congressional hearings that were critical of the federal bureaucracy's performance.

In August 2002, the administration again seemed to be adrift. As it stepped up its rhetoric against Saddam Hussein and advocated a unilateral strategy for regime change, the United States found its allies reluctant partners. Indeed, many were openly critical of the president's policy. Even more damaging were highly visible cautionary warnings from Republican establishment figures such as James Baker, Brent Scowcroft, and Lawrence Eagleburger. Moreover, more than two-thirds of the public signaled

---

[23] CBS News/*New York Times* poll, June 14–18, 2002.
[24] CBS News/*New York Times* poll, July 13–16, 2002.

that it was necessary to obtain resolutions authorizing going to war with Iraq from both Congress and the United Nations—authorizations the administration argued it did not require. Fifty-eight percent of the public felt the White House had not done a sufficient job of explaining to the American public why the United States might take military action to remove Saddam Hussein from power.[25] In addition, the public remained quite pessimistic about the economy.

Once again, the administration turned the tide. Putting on a full-court press, the president turned the tables on its critics by asking the UN for multilateral action and Congress for a resolution authorizing force. In short order, a majority of the American public concluded that the administration had made its case for going to war clearly.[26] As the public became convinced that there would likely be a war with Iraq and that the White House was meeting its critics at least halfway, it began moving behind the president and his approval ratings reversed some of the losses sustained over the summer. As public attention turned from the economy, corporate malfeasance, and failures in the intelligence community to responses to the Iraqi threat against the United States, the president's approval ratings stabilized and even increased slightly.

As the UN weapons inspectors searched for illegal weapons of mass destruction in Iraq early in 2003, the administration yet again found itself in danger of losing control of events. As international pressure built to give the inspectors more time, it appeared

---

[25] CNN/*USA Today*/Gallup Poll, September 2–4, 2002.
[26] The switch was from 37 percent agreeing the administration had made a clear case in late-August to 52 percent in mid-September. Pew Research Center poll, September 12–16, 2002.

that opponents of the war in the UN were setting the terms of debate. In response, the administration launched a carefully coordinated series of speeches by leading figures in January and February, culminating in the presentation to the Security Council by Secretary of State Colin Powell.[27] As a result, support for invading Iraq with ground troops rose to its highest point since 2001 (see Table 3.3).

In late-2005, the president's job approval ratings dropped to the lowest point of his tenure. The White House concluded that the core of the problem was Iraq, and it decided to launch a sustained public relations effort to recapture some of the middle of the public. Thus the president made a series of four high-profile speeches to military, diplomatic, and political audiences; gave interviews with key television anchors; provided briefings for congressional centrists; delivered a prime-time Oval Office address on December 18, and held a prime-time East Room press conference. By the end of the year, the direction of the trend in president's approval had reversed and he began to regain some of the public support he had lost (see Figure 4.1).

Focus on Values

The Bush White House copied a page from Bill Clinton's (and Dick Morris's) playbook by frequently focusing on values rather than issues. For example, it has staged events around the country that focused on family-friendly issues such as fitness, homeownership, reading, and adoption—typically providing largely symbolic

---

[27] Elisabeth Bumiller, "War P.R. Machine Is on Full Throttle," *New York Times*, February 9, 2003, p. 13.

support. It designed such efforts to appeal to suburban women, one of the most sought-after groups of votes, and to reach people who do not focus on politics by relating to issues in their personal lives. Local media typically gave substantial coverage to these events.

Such events were natural outgrowths of the 2000 presidential campaign in which Bush emphasized returning dignity and integrity to the presidency, "an era of responsibility," "leave no child behind," and, of course, "compassion." The war on terrorism provided new symbols for the president to exploit, focused around the most basic of public concerns, that of safeguarding people from attack in their homes and workplaces.

An emphasis on values paid off again in the 2004 election. Those for whom values were the determinant of their vote supported the president by large margins. Groups associated with the Republican party, especially those that form the religious right, energized their members by emphasizing issues such as gay marriage, stem cell research, abortion, and general religiosity. Although the president's stances were not congruent with the views of a majority of Americans, they were aligned with an intense minority for whom they were especially salient.

In November 2005, the president found himself under attack from all sides. One element of the criticism was the president's credibility. A *Wall Street Journal*/NBC News poll was typical in finding that a clear majority of the public felt that Bush "deliberately misled people to make the case for war with Iraq."[28] The

---

[28] NBC News/*Wall Street Journal* poll, November 4–7, 2005.

president needed to answer his critics, and he did so by attacking them and appealing to patriotic values. He declared that anyone accusing his administration of having "manipulated the intelligence and misled the American people" was giving aid and comfort to the enemy.

> *These baseless attacks send the wrong signal to our troops and to an enemy that is questioning America's will. As our troops fight a ruthless enemy determined to destroy our way of life, they deserve to know that their elected leaders who voted to send them to war continue to stand behind them. Our troops deserve to know that this support will remain firm when the going gets tough. And our troops deserve to know that whatever our differences in Washington, our will is strong, our nation is united, and we will settle for nothing less than victory.*[29]

In this case, the president's words seemed to do little to restore the public's trust in him or his policy in Iraq.

Control the Message

The Bush administration has aggressively used a well-established tool of public relations: prepackaged news reports that look indistinguishable from authentic newscasts. At least 20 federal agencies, including the Defense Department, have made and distributed hundreds of television news segments. Local stations

---

[29] "President Commemorates Veterans Day, Discusses War on Terror," Tobyhanna Army Depot, Tobyhanna, Pennsylvania, November 11, 2005. See also "President Delivers Remarks at Elmendorf AFB on War on Terror," Elmendorf Air Force Base, Anchorage, Alaska , November 14, 2005.

across the country have broadcast many of them without any acknowledgement of the government's role in their production.

Agencies produced some reports to support the administration's most cherished policy objectives, like regime change in Iraq or Medicare reform. Others focused on less prominent matters, like the administration's efforts to offer free after-school tutoring, its campaign to curb childhood obesity, its initiatives to preserve forests and wetlands, its plans to fight computer viruses, even its attempts to fight holiday drunken driving. They often feature "interviews" with senior administration officials in which questions are scripted and answers rehearsed. The reports exclude critics of the administration, however, as well as any hints of mismanagement, waste, or controversy.

Although federal agencies are usually forthright with broadcasters about the origin of the news segments they distribute, they design the reports to fit seamlessly into the typical local news broadcast. In most cases, the "reporters" are careful not to state in the segment that they work for the government. Their reports generally avoid overt ideological appeals. Instead, the government's news-making apparatus has produced a quiet drumbeat of broadcasts describing a vigilant and compassionate administration.

It is illegal for the government to produce or distribute such publicity material domestically without disclosing its own role. At least twice recently, however, agencies of the federal government have been caught distributing prepackaged television programs that used paid spokesmen acting as newscasters and, in violation of federal law, failed to disclose the administration's role in developing and financing them. The two best-known cases of such video news releases—one concerning the prescription drug

provision under Medicare and the other an antidrug campaign—
drew sharp rebukes from the Government Accounting Office,
which issued a blanket warning that reminded federal agencies
they may not produce newscasts promoting administration policies without clearly stating that the government itself is the
source.

Even if agencies do disclose their role, those efforts can easily
be undone in a broadcaster's editing room. Some news organizations simply identify the government's "reporter" as one of their
own and then edit out any phrase suggesting the segment was not
of their making. In essence, video news releases exploit a growing
vulnerability of television news: Even as news staffs at the major
networks are shrinking, many local stations are expanding their
hours of news coverage without adding reporters.[30]

Reporters discovered even more about message control in
2004 and 2005. They disclosed that the administration hired a
conservative commentator, Armstrong Williams, to promote the
administration's No Child Left Behind education measure—
without revealing that the government was paying him. The
Department of Education also commissioned a newspaper article
praising its role in promoting science education. The article
appeared in numerous small newspapers around the country, but
it did not inform readers that it was the department itself that
wrote the article. Similarly, the department disseminated a prepackaged television story that said that the president's program

---

[30] David Barstow and Robin Stein, "The Message Machine: How the Government Makes News; Under Bush a New Age of Prepackaged News," *New York Times*, March 13, 2005; Anne E. Kornblut, "Administration Is Warned About Its 'News' Videos," *New York Times*, February 19, 2005.

for providing remedial instruction and tutoring to children "gets an A-plus" without mentioning that it was the administration making this claim about its own performance. In 2005, federal auditors found that these actions as well as hiring a public relations company to analyze media perceptions of the Republican party's stance on education violated a statutory ban on the government spreading "covert propaganda" in the United States.[31]

Manipulate Information

Controlling information is another, even less unsavory, public relations technique. The goal is to influence public opinion by controlling the information on which the public bases its evaluations of chief executives and their policies and which it analyzes to determine if there is cause for concern. If the public is unaware of a situation or has a distorted view of it, then presidents may have more flexibility in achieving what they desire—which often is public passivity as much as public support.

DE-EMPHASIS.   In August 2005, the administration fired Lawrence A. Greenfeld, the director of the Bureau of Justice Statistics in the Justice Department. Four months earlier, he complained that senior political officials at the department were seeking to play down newly compiled data on the aggressive police treatment of Hispanics and African Americans. Officials at the White House and the Justice Department denied that they had applied political

---

[31] Robert Pear, "Buying of News by Bush's Aides Is Ruled Illegal," *New York Times*, October 1, 2005.

pressure on the statistics branch. There is no question, however, that as statisticians at the agency were preparing a press release to announce the results of a major study on traffic stops and racial profiling, which found disparities in how racial groups were treated once they were stopped by the police, political appointees within the Office of Justice Programs ordered Greenfeld to delete certain references to the disparities. Greenfeld refused to delete the racial references, arguing to his supervisors that the omissions would make the public announcement incomplete and misleading. As a result, the Justice Department opted not to issue a news release on the findings and posted the report online, all but assuring the report would get lost amid the avalanche of studies issued by the government.[32]

WITHHOLDING. The classification of information under the rubric of "national security" is a frequently used means of withholding information. Most people support secrecy in handling national security affairs, especially in such matters as defense plans and strategy, weapons technology, troop movements, the details of current diplomatic negotiations, the methods and sources of covert intelligence gathering, and similar information about other nations. However, there has been controversy over the amount of information classified and whether the president and other high officials have used classification strategies to influence public opinion. An official might withhold crucial information from the public in order to avoid embarrassment. But this may hinder the

---

[32] Other senior statisticians divulged that the administration had been applying pressure on the Bureau of Justice Statistics. Eric Lichtblau, "Profiling Report Leads to a Demotion," *New York Times*, August 25, 2005.

public's ability to evaluate an official's performance and ask fully informed questions of public policy. In an attempt to increase or maintain support, an official may provide a distorted view of reality.

For example, an FBI agent working at the military prison in Guantanamo Bay, Cuba, concluded that controversial interrogation practices used there by the Defense Department produced intelligence information that was "suspect at best." However, the Justice Department, which reviewed the memo for national security secrets before releasing it, redacted (edited out) the agent's conclusion. The department, acting after the Defense Department expressed its own views on which portions of the letter should be redacted, also blacked out a separate assertion in the memo that military interrogation practices could undermine future military trials for terrorism suspects held at Guantanamo Bay.[33]

There are other means of withholding information. One of the highest priorities of the George W. Bush administration in 2004 was to pass a prescription drug provision under Medicare. Many members of Congress were concerned about the program's cost, especially at a time of record budget deficits. Richard S. Foster, Medicare's nonpartisan chief actuary, concluded that the bill would cost considerably more than the administration projected. Thomas Scully, the presidential appointee who administered the agency overseeing Medicare, ordered him not to provide Congress the most recent estimates of the cost of the bill while Congress considered it. As a result, Foster's cost estimate did not become

---

[33] R. Jeffrey Smith, "Justice Redacted Memo on Detainees; FBI Criticism of Interrogations Was Deleted," *Washington Post,* March 22, 2005, p. A3.

known until after Congress enacted the legislation. Congressional Republicans were furious when they learned of the "real" cost.[34]

Regulating mercury emissions from power plants is one of the most important responsibilities of the Environmental Protection Agency (EPA). In 2004, the *Los Angeles Times* reported that EPA staffers said they were instructed not to undertake "the normal scientific and economic studies" required to regulate mercury. The administration turned instead to industry lobbyists to write much of the new regulation . Bruce C. Buckheit, who served in major federal environmental posts for two decades and who had retired in December 2003 as director of the EPA's Air Enforcement Division, complained that "there is a politicization of the work of the agency that I have not seen before. A political agenda is driving the agency's output, rather than analysis and science."[35]

The administration continued to withhold information, however. When the EPA unveiled a rule in 2005 to limit mercury emissions—a rule less strict than critics felt the Clean Air Act required—officials emphasized that the controls could not be more aggressive because the cost to the industries producing the emissions already far exceeded the public health payoff. What these officials did not reveal is that a Harvard University study paid for by the EPA, co-authored by an EPA scientist, and peer-reviewed by two other EPA scientists had reached the opposite conclusion.[36]

---

[34] Robert Pear, "Inquiry Confirms Top Medicare Official Threatened Actuary over Cost of Drug Benefits, *New York Times,* July 7, 2004.

[35] Tom Hamburger and Alan C. Miller, "Mercury Emissions Rule Geared to Benefit Industry, Staffers Say," *Los Angeles Times,* March 16, 2004, p. A1.

[36] Shankar Vedantam, "New EPA Mercury Rule Omits Conflicting Data; Study Called Stricter Limits Cost-Effective," *Washington Post,* March 22, 2005, p. A1.

In June 2005, the *New York Times* revealed that Philip A. Cooney, chief of staff for the White House Council on Environmental Quality, repeatedly edited government climate reports. A lawyer with a bachelor's degree in economics, Cooney had no scientific training, but he removed or adjusted descriptions of climate research that government scientists and their supervisors, including some senior Bush administration officials, had already approved. In many cases, the changes appeared in the final reports. The dozens of changes, although sometimes as subtle as the insertion of the phrase "significant and fundamental" before the word "uncertainties," cast doubt on the link between building greenhouse-gas emissions and rising temperatures, and tended to produce an air of doubt about findings that most climate experts say are robust. Before going to the White House in 2001, Cooney led the oil industry's fight against limits on greenhouse gases as a lobbyist at the American Petroleum Institute, the largest trade group representing the interests of the oil industry.[37]

White House officials claimed the changes Cooney made were part of the normal interagency review that takes place on all documents related to global environmental change, but critics replied that although all administrations routinely vetted government reports, it should be scientists reviewing the scientific content in such reports. In response to these revelations, the White House said that Cooney would not be available to comment. "We don't put Phil Cooney on the record. He's not a cleared spokesman."[38] Cooney resigned two days later. The White House said Cooney's

---

[37] Andrew C. Revkin, "Bush Aide Softened Greenhouse Gas Links to Global Warming," *New York Times*, June 8, 2005.
[38] Revkin, "Bush Aide Softened Greenhouse Gas Links to Global Warming."

decision was unrelated to revelations about the documents.[39] Within a week, Cooney accepted a job with Exxon.

In a broad indictment of the administration, more than 60 prominent scientists, including 20 Nobel laureates, issued a statement and a report in 2004 asserting that the administration had distorted scientific fact in the service of policy goals on the environment, health, biomedical research, and nuclear weaponry. The scientists accused the administration of repeatedly censoring and suppressing reports by its own scientists, stacking advisory committees with unqualified political appointees, disbanding government panels that provide unwanted advice, and in some cases refusing to seek independent scientific expertise.[40]

President Bush introduced his Fiscal Year 2006 budget on February 7, 2005. The budget projected a deficit for the year of $390 billion, a reduction from the previous year. However, the budget did not include the cost of military operations in Iraq and Afghanistan and some other costs of the war on terrorism. The administration argued that it did not include these costs because it could not estimate them. One week later, however, it proposed an $81.9 billion supplemental appropriation for Fiscal Year 2005, most of which was devoted to these purposes. There was no doubt that a substantial supplemental appropriation would be needed for Fiscal Year 2006, but if the budget included a reasonable estimate of it, the projected deficit would have increased over 2005 rather than decreased. In the end, the administration requested about $120 billion for Fiscal Year 2006 for operations in Iran and Iraq.

---

[39] Andrew C. Revkin, "Editor of Climate Reports Resigns," *New York Times,* June 10, 2005.
[40] James Glanz, "Scientists Say Administration Distorts Facts," *New York Times,* February 19, 2004, p. A18.

Just as Congress was poised for a final vote on the energy bill in 2005, the EPA delayed the planned release of an annual report on fuel economy. The contents of the report showed that cars and trucks were significantly less fuel-efficient, on average, than they were in the late 1980s, and this information would not have been helpful in passing a bill that largely ignored mileage regulations. A spokeswoman for the EPA said the timing of the release of the report had nothing to do with the energy bill deliberations.[41]

DISTORTION. Distortion comes in many forms. One of the most common is to provide impressive statistics without going into the details of how they were compiled. In the selling of the 2003 tax cut, the catch phrase the George W. Bush administration used was that "92 million Americans will receive an average tax cut of $1,083." That sounded, and was intended to sound, as if every American family would get about $1,083. Although it was true that those who received tax cuts averaged about $1,100, the administration omitted the fact that 50 million citizens would receive no tax cut at all, and about half of those American families who would receive a tax cut would get less than $100. The $1,083 number was inflated by the very big tax cuts received by a relatively small number of wealthy people.

Similarly, the administration often referred to the need to eliminate the estate tax in order to save family farms or small businesses from what it termed the "death tax." Officials conveniently ignored the fact that fewer than 2 percent of estates actu-

---

[41] Danny Hakim, "E.P.A. Holds Back Report on Car Fuel Efficiency," *New York Times,* July 28, 2005.

ally pay a tax and that very few small business or farms have been lost as a result of the tax. Indeed, the White House had difficulty finding a single such farm.

Rhetoric can distort the truth in other ways. President Bush never publicly blamed Saddam Hussein or Iraq for the events of September 11, but he consistently used nuanced rhetoric that linked U.S. policy in Iraq to the 9/11 attacks and blurred distinctions between Saddam's support for other terrorist groups and his murky connections to al Qaeda and between his past use of weapons of mass destruction and his possession of them in 2003.[42] For example, on the March 19, 2005, the second anniversary of the U.S. invasion of Iraq, the president spoke to the nation in his Saturday radio address. "We knew of Saddam Hussein's record of aggression and support for terror. We knew of his long history of pursuing, even using, weapons of mass destruction, and we know that September the 11th requires our country to think differently." Thus in a few words the president juxtaposed allusions to Saddam Hussein, terrorism, weapons of mass destruction, and September 11. Although the president's statement was technically correct, it is likely that many listeners would infer a connection between Saddam Hussein and the 9/11 attacks and that he possessed weapons of mass destruction—and it is equally likely that the White House was well aware of this potential.

By November 2005, most people had concluded that the Bush administration had deliberately misled them to obtain support for invading Iraq. As we have seen, the White House struck back,

---

[42] See, for example, Amy Gershkoff and Shana Kushner, "Shaping Public Opinion: The 9/11-Iraq Connection in the Bush Administration's Rhetoric," *Perspectives on Politics* 3 (September 2005): 525–537.

arguing that charges that it had manipulated prewar intelligence were, in Vice President Cheney's words, "dishonest and reprehensible" and that critics were seeking a political advantage in the middle of a war and undermining the morale of U.S. troops in the process.[43] It also claimed that none of the investigations studying intelligence regarding the war on terrorism had found manipulation of information. Finally, administration officials used a number of venues, including the White House website, to distribute comments of critics showing that many of them had supported removing Saddam Hussein from power and voted to authorize the president to use force to do so. Thus, the officials claimed, their critics were hypocrites.

The president and other top officials did not note that none of the investigations related to the war on terrorism had focused on the manipulation of intelligence or that the White House had opposed efforts for them to do so. Nor did the administration point out that members of Congress and others were largely reliant on the information that the administration provided them and that none of the critics saw the raw intelligence available to the White House. Thus, critics' previous support of the war could not be evidence that the administration did not mislead the country about the nature of the threat Iraq posed to the United States.

PREVARICATION? There are times when the president and his administration make statements that are simply not true. After a cabinet meeting on November 13, 2002, Bush claimed that "the

---

[43] Michael A. Fletcher and Peter Baker, "Bush, Cheney Denounce Democratic Senators Critical of Iraq War," *Washington Post*, November 17, 2005, p. A8.

deficit would have been bigger without the tax relief package."[44] In other words, he claimed the tax cut had not only paid for itself but had actually increased the revenues for the federal government. Even his own Council of Economic Advisors disagreed.[45]

In the eight months before the United States invaded Iraq in March 2003, President George W. Bush and his administration made a series of arguments justifying going to war.[46] The reasons he advanced for going to war with Iraq ranged from the idealistic goal of bringing democracy to Iraqis and the humanitarian desire to rid them of a vicious tyrant to geo-strategic concerns about the future of the Middle East. By far the most compelling arguments to the American people, however, focused on the risks to the national security of the United States.

The core of the president's argument was that Saddam Hussein could cause grave harm to Americans. In his most comprehensive speech on the war, delivered October 7, 2002, Bush focused largely on the threat of banned weapons. Iraq, Bush said, had "a massive stockpile of biological weapons" and "thousands of tons of chemical agents" and was "reconstituting its nuclear weapons program." The president asked, "If we know Saddam Hussein has dangerous weapons today—and we do—does it make any sense for the world to wait to confront him as he grows even stronger and develops even more dangerous weapons?" In his March 17, 2003, speech on the eve of war, Bush declared, "Intelligence gathered by this and other governments leaves no

---

[44] *Remarks by the President after Meeting with the Cabinet*, White House, November 13, 2002.
[45] *Economic Report of the President*, February 2003 (Washington, D.C.: U.S. Government Printing Office, 2003), pp. 57–58.
[46] James P. Pfiffner, "Did President Bush Mislead the Country in His Arguments for War with Iraq?" *Presidential Studies Quarterly* 34 (March 2004): 25–46.

doubt that the Iraq regime continues to possess and conceal some of the most lethal weapons ever devised."

President Bush repeatedly claimed that Saddam Hussein had reconstituted his nuclear weapons program and was potentially "less than a year" away from possessing nuclear weapons, placing the United States in immediate peril. This allegation was a powerful argument that deposing Saddam Hussein was important for U.S. national security. However, the evidence upon which it was based was wrong. Even at the time the president made the claims, the evidence was questionable, including the assertion that Iraq had purchased uranium oxide, "yellowcake," from Niger, and that aluminum tubes shipped to Iraq were intended to be used as centrifuges to create the fissile material necessary for a nuclear bomb.

One of the keys to broad public support for an invasion of Iraq was the fear that Iraq could attack the United States mainland. Thus, the possibility of Iraq using unmanned, drone airplanes to deliver chemical or biological weapons—a possibility raised by President Bush in his important October 7, 2002, speech—provoked serious concern. However, the U.S. Air Force had discounted this possibility in its assessments of Iraq's capabilities.

The administration also repeatedly implied that there was a link between al Qaeda, the September 11 attacks, and Iraq. For example, on September 14, 2003, in an interview on *Meet the Press,* Vice President Cheney declared, "If we're successful in Iraq . . . then we will have struck a major blow right at the heart of the base, if you will, the geographic base of the terrorists who had us under assault now for many years, but most especially on 9/11." It was not until September 18, 2003—months after the war began—that President Bush conceded the United States had no evidence of any Iraqi involvement in the attacks.

Did the president and other administration officials tell outright lies about the nature and immediacy of the threat Iraq posed to the United States? Probably not. The president and other administration officials, most notably Vice President Cheney, certainly often made statements that in hindsight were wrong, but there is no evidence that they did not believe their statements to be true. For the most part they were sloppy analysts rather than mendacious advocates. The administration was cavalier in evaluating the basis for its conclusions. Officials, including the president, readily accepted information that supported their goal of removing Saddam Hussein from power while ignoring the often tenuous basis of this information. Similarly, they discounted challenges to supportive "facts." They did, of course, employ rhetoric to make connections that evidence did not support.

By not revealing—or perhaps recognizing—the tenuous basis for his conclusions about the threat Iraq posed to the United States or clarifying the lack of evidence of any role of Iraq in the September 11 attacks, the president exposed himself to conclusions that he had knowingly misled the public. As early as February 2004, a national poll found that a majority of Americans believed President Bush either lied (21 percent) or deliberately exaggerated (31 percent) evidence that Iraq possessed weapons of mass destruction in order to justify war.[47]

Questionable statements did not end with the end of major combat operations. In mid-April 2003, the United States found two trailers that appeared similar to mobile biological weapons production facilities that Colin Powell had cited in his prewar

[47] Richard Morin and Dana Milbank, "Most Think Truth Was Stretched to Justify Iraq War," *Washington Post*, February 13, 2004, p. A1. *Washington Post*/ABC News poll, February 10–11, 2004.

address to the United Nations. Most analysts concluded that the trailers were most likely *not* biological weapons labs. Nevertheless, Bush claimed that they were clear evidence of weapons of mass destruction, telling a Polish television interviewer, "We found the weapons of mass destruction. We found biological laboratories."[48]

Equally odd were the president's postwar claims that Saddam Hussein had not allowed weapons inspectors into Iraq. For example, on July 14, 2003, he declared that "we gave him a chance to allow the inspectors in, and he wouldn't let them in."[49] However, weapons inspectors were in Iraq from November 2002 until Bush gave them an ultimatum in March 2003 to leave for their own safety. Nevertheless, on January 27, 2004, during an informal press conference with Polish President Aleksander Kwasniewski, he again claimed that Saddam Hussein "did not let us [inspectors] in."[50]

SLIPPAGE

Despite the White House's commitment to a disciplined public relations effort and its skill in implementing such a policy, there were missteps, some of them glaring. An examination of the first half of 2004 provides useful illustrations.

In February 2004, the president's Council of Economic Advisors produced the annual *Economic Report of the President*. The report contained a passage that appeared to praise the movement

---

[48] Interview of the President by TVP, Poland, May 29, 2003.
[49] "Remarks by the President and United Nations Secretary General Kofi Annan in Photo Opportunity," The Oval Office, July 14, 2003.
[50] "President Bush Welcomes President Kwasniewski to White House," The Oval Office, January 27, 2004.

of U.S. service jobs to such low-wage countries as India: "When a good or service is produced more cheaply abroad, it makes more sense to import it than make or provide it domestically." This view may have represented good economics, but it demonstrated a tin ear when it came to politics. Adding fuel to the fire, N. Gregory Mankiw, chairman of the Council of Economic Advisors, angered manufacturers, software writers, and even radiologists by proclaiming that "outsourcing is just a new way of doing international trade. More things are tradable than were tradable in the past, and that's a good thing." Not everyone agreed.[51]

In addition, the report anticipated that 2004 employment would on average be 2.6 million jobs higher than last year. The secretaries of commerce and the treasury and the president had to separate themselves from such an optimistic projection. Finally, the report posed a rhetorical question: "When a fast-food restaurant sells a hamburger . . . is it providing a 'service' or is it combining inputs to 'manufacture' a product?" The point, the administration's economists said, was to question the practicality of congressional proposals to offer tax breaks to manufacturers. It did not take Democrats long to accuse the White House of wanting to reclassify burger flippers as holding manufacturing jobs.

On March 1, 2004, a host of U.S. industries began paying trade sanctions to Europe because Congress and the White House had not replaced illegal export subsidies with new aid for ailing manufacturers. In the following week, the president was to name an assistant commerce secretary for manufacturing and services,

---

[51] Jonathan Weisman and Mike Allen, "Missteps on Economy Worry Bush Supporters," *Washington Post*, March 13, 2004, p. A1.

showing his concern for employment in the process. This was supposed to be a good-news day for a White House struggling with its economic message. Instead, the upbeat photo-op fizzled when it came to light that a year earlier, Anthony F. Raimondo, Bush's choice for the job, had opened a major plant in Beijing. The president pulled the nomination.

In May, Attorney General John Ashcroft warned America of alarming intelligence that "indicates Al Qaeda's specific intention to hit the United States hard." He apparently never coordinated with Tom Ridge, secretary of homeland security. Ridge reassured interviewers that there really was not much new intelligence floating around, just a general concern that al Qaeda would try to influence the election or be tempted by a summer of big events, such as the Group of 8 summit in Sea Island, Georgia, or the national political party conventions. However, White House officials expressed their displeasure, and Ashcroft and Ridge issued a joint statement reassuring the country that they actually did cooperate.[52]

The president traveled throughout the spring to promote his domestic programs such as education and health care. The White House regularly provided fact sheets about how much spending had increased in these politically popular areas and the president regularly appeared at No Child Left Behind celebrations boasting about how much he had increased federal spending on education. The Office of Management and Budget missed the message, however, and in mid-May inconveniently produced a memo to government departments telling them to be prepared for a $1.5 billion

---

[52] David E. Sanger, "Discipline Takes a Break at the White House," *New York Times*, May 30, 2004.

cut in education spending in the next year and a $900 million cut in veterans' benefits.

Information about the torture and mistreatment of prisoners at Abu Ghraib prison also became public in the spring of 2004. Bush and the White House were slow to comprehend the full magnitude of the scandal and how it threatened the country's reputation in the Middle East. At one point, the public discourse revolved around when and whether Bush had issued an apology.

Following the president's reelection in November 2004, the administration's public relations effort slipped again. The White House badly mishandled the embarrassing nomination of Bernard Kerik to be secretary of the Department of Homeland Security, and it was awkward at first when it indicated that John Snow was expected to step down as secretary of the Treasury in the near future, only to reverse itself and declare that Snow would serve the entire second term. Secretary of Defense Donald Rumsfeld made insensitive and widely disseminated remarks to U.S. soldiers and marines in Iraq about the adequacy of the United State's preparation for war. The United States initially low-balled its pledge of relief funds for tsunami victims in Southeast Asia while Bush remained out of sight on his ranch. The president also slipped in a January interview when he declared that he would not be making much effort on behalf of a constitutional amendment barring gay marriage. Although the president correctly assessed that prospects for such an amendment were poor, his candid admission forced him to increase the visibility of a divisive issue as he reiterated his commitment to the amendment to please the religious right. Joking about senior citizens' faulty memories in a January 26, 2005, press conference did little to advance his efforts to reform Social Security.

In June 2005, *U.S. News and World Report* White House reporter Kenneth Walsh posted a story on the magazine's website that senior Republicans were concerned that the once-vaunted White House PR machine was misfiring or not firing at all. They felt that the president's senior aides, who used to deal directly with the media during his first term and the 2004 campaign, did not have much time to talk to reporters anymore. White House insiders said that new recruits to the West Wing were gun-shy about talking to reporters because they feared making a gaffe or having their colleagues accuse them of leaking to the media—a cardinal offense in the Bush White House. In the first term, a handful of senior White House and campaign officials divided up 50 influential reporters in Washington and took turns calling them—to keep the journalists up to date, give the administration's spin on events, and acquire intelligence on what the media were about to report. According to Walsh, that level of engagement was gone, and this made Republicans worry that the administration was losing valuable opportunities to spread its message.[53]

On October 13, the White House touched off a new controversy over Iraq. With Iraqis about to vote on a constitution, it staged a live videoconference between the commander in chief and U.S. troops in Iraq. The president's aides billed the event as a chance for the president to hear directly from the troops in Iraq. They also hoped to reinforce the president's upbeat view of the progress being made there. Before the event was broadcast live on cable TV, however, the satellite picture from Iraq was inadver-

---

[53] Kenneth T. Walsh, "White House Watch: Bush's Jammed PR Machine," *U.S. News and World Report,* June 23, 2005.

tently beamed to television newsrooms in the United States. It showed a full-blown rehearsal of the president's questions, along with the soldiers' answers and coaching from Allison Barber, a senior Pentagon official.[54] The rehearsal not only undermined the point of the event, but it also reinforced the growing cynicism about the White House's efforts to manipulate public opinion.

CINDY SHEEHAN. The White House suffered another public relations setback when the president went for his annual vacation at his ranch near Crawford, Texas, in August 2005. Cindy Sheehan, a California woman whose 24-year-old son, Army Spec. Casey Sheehan was killed in Iraq in 2004, set up "Camp Casey" on the road leading to the ranch and demanded to speak to the president. She wanted to tell him that he should end the war and stop using her son's sacrifice to justify continued killing. In this slow news period, Sheehan became the focus of substantial media attention. Undeterred by a truck-driving local who mowed down hundreds of small white crosses erected by her supporters in the encampment and a shot gun blast across the street, she continued her antiwar vigil, eventually moving her operation off the roadside and onto the property of a Bush neighbor. It was not long before she had appeared on every major television and radio network and in newspapers around the world.

Sheehan, with her peaceful vigil, her anguish, and her gentle way of speaking, became a rallying point for those disaffected by the war, galvanizing antiwar activists and providing a catalyst for a more aggressive antiwar movement. What began as a solitary

---

[54] Dan Froomkin, "Caught on Tape," *Washington Post*, October 14, 2005.

campaign to force a meeting with President Bush quickly took on the full trappings of a political campaign. Soon Sheehan was working with a political consultant and a team of public relations professionals, and then she was featured in a television ad. After 13 days, she had to leave for six days to care for her mother, who suffered a stroke in California. In the meantime, she had attracted activists from around the country to Crawford, who raised more than $100,000 and organized food and sleeping arrangements, to carry on the protest. When she returned she found her supporters had established "Camp Casey 2." It was a large tent complex with several portable toilets, a stage, a hot buffet, and parking attendants. The antiwar protesters held an emotional ceremony, carried live on national television, in which they presented Sheehan with the boots worn by her son before he was killed. She tearfully laid them before a small cross bearing her son's name, amid sobs from other women whose sons also were killed in Iraq.

Sheehan placed Bush in a difficult position. He did not want to meet with her and thus set a precedent (and he had already met with her the previous year), but he also did not want to publicly refute the mother of a soldier killed in Iraq. In the end, refusing to meet with her provided the media with the opportunity to fill a news hole and turn Sheehan's vigil into a continuing saga. Caught by surprise to the reaction to turning Sheehan away, the White House announced that the president would try to bolster support for his Iraq policy by giving three speeches in military settings over the last two weeks in August. In addition, stung by the ability of one grieving mother to inspire a growing antiwar movement, the White House found a military mom of its own to provide a counterpoint to Sheehan. CNN featured a story on

Tammy Pruett of Idaho, whose husband and five sons served or were serving in Iraq. The White House asked Pruett to attend a speech for Idaho National Guard members and air force personnel in Nampa, Idaho, where the president introduced her and then sent her out to talk to the press and to support staying the course in Iraq.[55] In addition, Bush supporters set up a counter-rally in Crawford, christening their spot "Camp Reality," adding to the circus atmosphere and attracting yet additional media attention.

HURRICANE KATRINA. On Monday, August 29, 2005, Katrina, a category 4 hurricane, hit New Orleans and the Mississippi and Alabama Gulf coast. By Tuesday, levees on Lake Pontchartrain had been breeched and 80 percent of the city was underwater. What followed may be the greatest natural disaster in U.S. history. Thousands of people drowned and tens of thousands of homes and businesses were ruined. Rescue and relief services took days to arrive as thousands of survivors suffered through fires, looting, and an absence of basic necessities such as food, water, and health care. Americans were riveted to their televisions as they witnessed scenes reminiscent of third world countries.

Despite the fact that New Orleans was filling up with water, the president did not break his regular schedule, and on Tuesday he flew to San Diego to commemorate the 60th anniversary of the Allied victory over Japan and was seen photographed strumming a guitar. On Wednesday, he finally cut short his vacation and flew over the devastated area on the way to Washington. He addressed

---

[55] Dan Froomkin, "War Mom vs. Peace Mom," *Washington Post*, August 25, 2005.

the nation in a terse statement from the Rose Garden late in the afternoon. It was one of the worst speeches of his presidency, failing to articulate the sense of grief of a distraught nation or to provide the reassurance it needed.

Over the next few days, the president continued to appear flatfooted, at times tentative and distracted. He did not visit the devastated area until Friday, and then he joked about youthful partying in New Orleans. More importantly, the president avoided the thousands of suffering people crowded into the New Orleans Superdome and Convention Center (reports indicated the White House feared the negative reaction he would receive there). In a defensive mode, Bush even claimed at one point that no one could have foreseen the levee breaking, a statement contradicted by a host of visible studies and reports in the previous few years and substantial discussion in the days before Katrina hit land. One reporter summed up the president's performance by noting that nine days after the United States was attacked on September 11, 2001, the president stood before a joint session of Congress and rallied the nation to a new mission. Nine days after Hurricane Katrina devastated New Orleans and much of the Gulf Coast, Bush stood in an auditorium across the street from the White House and directed storm victims to a website and a toll-free telephone number. Without an identifiable enemy to blame, the executive branch's own failures became the focus of attention as the president was groping to find his voice and set out a vision of how the government and the American people should respond.[56]

---

[56] Richard W. Stevenson, "Leader Who Rose in 9/11 Slips in Wake of Storm," *New York Times*, September 9, 2005.

In the meantime, the crisis in New Orleans deepened because of a virtual standoff between hesitant federal officials and besieged authorities in Louisiana. Normally placid TV reporters on the scene in New Orleans were openly deploring the government's failure to help the victims adequately. And their outrage, illustrated with hauntingly edited montages of weeping mothers, sickly children, and dead bodies rotting on the street, was seconded by complaints from state and local officials about the absence of federal help.

The deep gulf between the disturbing reality in the storm-ravaged South and the slow federal response detached from the desperation felt on the ground created a political crisis for the president, threatening to undermine his legislative agenda and push him even lower in the polls. In a belated realization of the situation's political ramifications, the White House developed a plan to contain the political damage from the administration's response to Hurricane Katrina by the weekend after the storm. It orchestrated visits by cabinet members to the region, including return visits by the president, directed administration officials to shift discussion to what the government was doing at the moment rather than respond to attacks from Democrats on the relief efforts, and sought to move the blame for the slow response to Louisiana state officials.[57] Finally, on September 13 the president accepted responsibility for some of the failure for dealing with the disaster and gave a nationally televised address two days later.

---

[57] Adam Nagourney and Anne E. Kornblut, "White House Enacts a Plan to Ease Political Damage," *New York Times,* September 5, 2005; Jim VandeHei, "Officials Deal With Political Fallout by Pointing Fingers," *Washington Post,* September 5, 2005, p. A17.

When a tremendously destructive tsunami hit East Asia in late 2004, many observers criticized Bush for his slow and modest initial response to send aid. In response, he asked former presidents Bill Clinton and George H. W. Bush to lead a drive to raise funds for the victims of the storm. He reprised this request a week after Katrina hit, but this time the victims were American citizens. The most the president could hope for was damage control.

Following the trend in the modern presidency, the Bush White House has engaged in a permanent campaign on behalf of the president and his policies. Indeed, going public has been at the core of its governing strategy. The White House, especially in the president's first term, has been skilled in adopting a strategic perspective and employing a range of public relations techniques. But has the White House been successful in persuading the public to support the president? Has there been a long-term political cost in its manipulation of information? Chapter 3 explores the answers to these questions.

CHAPTER 3

Persuading the Public

It is one thing to go public. It is something quite different to succeed in moving public opinion. How successful has George W. Bush been in his efforts to govern through a permanent campaign?

Given all the time and effort that the White House invests in attempting to persuade the public, it is especially interesting that presidential aides do not know how successful they have been. Martha Kumar found that communications staffers in both the Clinton and Bush White Houses agreed that their efforts to gauge the success of their salesmanship tended to be partial and impressionistic rather than comprehensive and scientific. Presidential Press Secretary Ari Fleischer attributed it to the fact that they had so little time to look back and take stock. "We move too fast to look back and have some type of empirical analysis or empirical accounting system like that. I think other than the use of your gut, you don't really do it."[1]

---

[1] Quoted in Martha Joynt Kumar, *Wired for Sound* (manuscript, 2006).

In this chapter, we examine the public's responsiveness to the president from a number of standpoints. First, we look at the president's success in obtaining support for himself through his nationally televised addresses. Then we investigate several key issue areas in the Bush presidency to learn whether public opinion moved in the president's direction. Finally, we analyze the results of the historic midterm elections of 2002 to see whether we can attribute the Republicans' success to the president's campaigning.

TELEVISED ADDRESSES AND PUBLIC APPROVAL

Perhaps the most potentially powerful tool for going public is the nationally televised address. These addresses represent the best opportunity for the president to reach the largest audience of his fellow citizens, because almost every American has access to television and most are accustomed to turning to it for news. In addition, when the president addresses the nation, he does so directly (and rapidly), without the mediation of the press. Moreover, in a televised address, the president does not appear as a partisan, but rather as a statesman, usually speaking from the dignified surroundings of the Oval Office or before a joint session of Congress.

George W. Bush delivered 25 nationally televised addresses through December 2005, several of which were quite short. He focused all but two of these speeches broadly or dealt with the war on terrorism or the war in Iraq. Only one dealt with legislation before Congress, the president's proposal to create a Department of Homeland Security. Table 3.1 shows the difference in presidential approval in the Gallup polls taken most closely before and after each of Bush's live televised address to the nation. (In comparing survey results of two samples such as those employed by Gallup, differences between the results must be about 6 percentage points before we can be reasonably sure that the results reflect a real difference.)

TABLE 3.1
Changes in George W. Bush Approval Ratings after National Addresses

DATE OF SPEECH	SUBJECT OF SPEECH	CHANGE IN APPROVAL IN PERCENTAGE POINTS
20 January 2001	Inaugural Address	NA
27 February 2001	Administration goals	+1
9 August 2001	Stem cell research	+2
11 September 2001	Terrorist attacks	+35
20 September 2001	Terrorist attacks	+4
7 October 2001 (afternoon)	War in Afghanistan	+2
8 November 2001	War on terrorism[a]	0
29 January 2002	State of the Union	−2
6 June 2002	Department of Homeland Security	+4
11 September 2002	Anniversary of terrorist attacks	+4
7 October 2002	War with Iraq[b]	−5
28 January 2003	State of the Union	+1
1 February 2003	*Columbia* space shuttle disaster	−2
26 February 2003	War with Iraq	+1
17 March 2003	War with Iraq	+13

continues

Table 3.1 continued

1 May 2003	War with Iraq	−1
11 September 2003	Reconstruction of Iraq	−7
14 December 2003	Capture of Saddam Hussein[c]	+7
20 January 2004	State of the Union	−4
20 January 2005	Inaugural Address	+6
2 February 2005	State of the Union	+6
28 June 2005	War with Iraq	+1
19 July 2005	Supreme Court Nominee	0
15 September 2005	Aftermath of Hurricane Katrina	−6
18 December 2005	War with Iraq	+2
31 January 2006	State of the Union	−1

SOURCE: Gallup polls, various dates.
[a] Broadcast by only ABC
[b] Broadcast only by Fox—not ABC, NBC, CBS, or PBS.
[c] Broadcast at 12 P.M., EST

The figures in the third column of the table show that a statistically significant change in Bush's approval following a televised presidential address occurred only three times. The first was an increase of 35 percentage points following the terrorist attack on September 11, 2001. Few would attribute the public's rallying around the commander in chief to the president's brief comments that evening. There was another rally, this time a 13-percentage-point increase, following the president's address on March 17, 2003, announcing the invasion of Iraq. Again, it would be stretching to attribute the rally to the president's short statement.

Gallup did not ask the approval question during a three-week period in the second half of January and early February 2005. The first Iraqi elections occurred during this period, a very favorable event for the president. Bush also delivered his second inaugural address and the State of the Union address during these weeks. It is impossible to isolate the impact of these high profile events, but Gallup found a 6-percentage-point increase in the president's approval during this time. However, the sample of this poll, taken February 4–6, overrepresented Republicans, and Gallup immediately took another reading on February 7–10. The latter poll found that the president had lost 8 percentage points in his approval ratings and had dipped to 49 percent approval. Since the president's approval leveled off for the following six weeks to what it had been in early January, it seems reasonable to conclude that his two televised addresses had little impact on his approval.

The president endured frustration in using his televised addresses to increase his support from the beginning of his tenure. His approval went up only 1 percentage point in the Gallup poll following his address to a joint session of Congress on February 27, 2001, and only 2 percentage points following his August 9, 2001, address on his decision regarding federal funding of stem cell research. In the months following September 11, 2001, when his approval was very high, there was less potential to increase his support. Yet even when his approval declined, televised addresses still made little impact on his public support.

GAINING THE PUBLIC'S ATTENTION

To be a useful tool for influencing public opinion, a televised address must first capture the public's attention. To the extent that the president fails to attract an audience, he loses the opportunity to influence public opinion. Scholars and other commentators have assumed that the president consistently draws a broad audience for his televised speeches.[2]

At first glance, it seems quite reasonable to assume that because the president is so visible and speaks on such important matters, he will always attract a large audience for his speeches. Wide viewership was certainly common during the early decades of television. Presidential speeches routinely attracted more than 80 percent of those watching television, an audience no one network could command.[3] A study by A. C. Nielsen analyzed ratings of 19 nationally televised appearances (12 in primetime) by President Ford. All but three of these appearances *raised* ratings over those of the normal entertainment offerings.[4]

Things have changed, however. When Ronald Reagan urged Congress to adopt his Contra-aid package in March 1986, more than half of the households watching TV viewed something else, the first time in history that a president failed to reach at least 50 percent of U.S. television households. More than 16 million households that would normally be watching network television defected to cable channels or simply turned off their sets.[5]

[2] John E. Mueller, *War, Presidents, and Public Opinion* (New York: Wiley, 1973); Lyn Ragsdale, "The Politics of Presidential Speechmaking, 1949–1980," *American Political Science Review* 78 (December 1984): 971–984; Roy L. Behr and Shanto Iyengar, "Television News, Real World Cues, and Changes in the Public Agenda," *Public Opinion Quarterly* 49 (Spring 1985): 38–57; Lyn Ragsdale, "Presidential Speechmaking and the Public Audience," *Journal of Politics* 49 (August 1987): 704–736; Dennis M. Simon and Charles W. Ostrom, "The Impact of Televised Speeches and Foreign Travel on Presidential Approval," *Public Opinion Quarterly* 53 (Spring 1989): 58–82; Paul Brace and Barbara Hinckley, "Presidential Activities from Truman through Reagan: Timing and Impact," *Journal of Politics* 55 (May 1993): 382–398; Jeffrey E. Cohen, *Presidential Responsiveness and Public Policy-Making* (Ann Arbor: University of Michigan Press, 1997).
[3] Joe S. Foote, "Ratings Decline of Presidential Television," *Journal of Broadcasting and Electronic Media* 32 (Spring 1988): 225.
[4] A. C. Nielsen, *Nielsen Newscast* (Northbrook, IL: Nielson, 1975).
[5] Foote, "Ratings Decline of Presidential Television," 227–229.

In addition, the White House is interested in reaching the entire public, not just those who might be watching television. The appropriate measure for audience penetration is the percentage of households *owning* televisions watching the president for an average minute of programming. Because virtually every household in the country owns a television, this measure is synonymous with the measuring the percentage of households watching the president.

Research has found that the percentage of households owning televisions who watched the president for an average minute decreased steadily from the Nixon administration through the Clinton years. By the late-1990s, the president was attracting less than a third of the homes to watch even his State of the Union message. Even the extraordinary interest in the President Clinton/Monica Lewinsky scandal and the media's frenzied treatment of it right before the 1998 State of the Union message created only a modest spike in viewer interest.[6]

Paradoxically, it was developments in technology that allowed the president to reach mass audiences, yet it has been further developments that have made it easier for these same audiences to avoid listening to the White House. Matthew Baum and Samuel Kernell argue persuasively that the root cause of this drop in viewership is access to alternatives to watching the president provided by cable television.[7] In 2000, 76 percent of all households received cable service, and 85 percent of households owned a VCR[8] (providing yet additional opportunities to avoid watching

---

[6] George C. Edwards III, *On Deaf Ears* (New Haven, CT: Yale University Press, 2003), 191.
[7] Matthew A. Baum and Samuel Kernell, "Has Cable Ended the Golden Age of Presidential Television?" *American Political Science Review* 93 (March 1999): 99–114.
[8] Nielsen Media Research, *2000 Report on Television*, 12–13.

the president). As cable becomes even more widely available and as the number of channels available to viewers increases, the president is likely to experience even more difficulty in attracting an audience for his addresses. New networks such as Fox, WB, and UPN provide yet additional distractions from the president.

The alternatives to network television make it easy to tune out the president. Thus, it is not surprising that the decline of watching the president has been more rapid than the erosion of the networks' share of the television audience. In a study of primetime addresses by Ronald Reagan, Joe Foote found that millions of people (representing on average 11 million households) turned away from the networks but not from viewing television when the president was speaking. Almost all of these people returned to watching the networks after the president finished his speech.[9] As former White House chief of staff Leon Panetta points out, presidents who wish to exploit the bully pulpit will have to learn to use the new multichannel system.[10]

Part of the reason for the modest response to Bush's early addresses may be that he drew equally modest audiences. A total of about 40 million viewers saw at least part of his nationally televised address in February 2001. This audience compares unfavorably with the 67 million viewers for Bill Clinton's first nationally televised address in 1993. Moreover, there was a substantial fall-off in viewership during the president's speech.[11] Only 32 million people saw his speech on stem cell research on August 9.[12]

---

[9] Foote, "Ratings Decline of Presidential Television," 228–229.
[10] Remarks made at a forum of chiefs of staff held on June 15, 2000, at the Woodrow Wilson Center in Washington, D.C.
[11] *Washington Post,* March 1, 2001, p. C1.
[12] Nielsen Media Research, Press Release, June 29, 2005.

The terrorist attacks on September 11, 2001, increased interest in the president's messages, however. About 82 million watched his address to a joint session of Congress on September 20, 2001, and his 2002 State of the Union message drew about 54 million viewers.[13] A live televised press conference on October 11, 2001, (his only one that year) drew 64.8 million viewers. The prospect of war with Iraq attracted viewers, as 62 million watched his State of the Union message in 2003 and an estimated 73.3 million people watched Bush deliver his February 26, 2003, speech demanding Saddam Hussein leave in 48 hours or face war. His May 1, 2003, speech from the deck of an aircraft carrier declaring an end to major combat operations in Iraq averaged about 49 million viewers. About 44 million viewers tuned in for the 2004 State of the Union, and an April 13, 2004, news conference that started with a Bush statement about the war, drew 41 million viewers.[14]

The steady decline in the size of audiences evident throughout 2003 and 2004 continued in Bush's second term. His 2005 State of the Union speech, which dwelled at length on his proposals to revamp the Social Security system, drew only 38.4 million viewers, the smallest TV audience to watch a president address a joint session of Congress in five years. Bush gave a nationally televised address on June 28, 2005, the first anniversary of the formal transfer of sovereignty to the Iraqis after the American-led invasion. It drew only about 24 million viewers. Even Bush's prime-time press conference on April 28, 2005, drew more viewers,

---

[13] Lisa de Moraes, "President Bush Has America Tuning In," *Washington Post*, January 21, 2002, p. C7.
[14] Nielsen Media Research.

about 33 million.[15] The extraordinary coverage of the devastation of Hurricane Katrina helped the president attract about 39 million viewers to his September 15, 2005, speech on rebuilding New Orleans and the Gulf Coast,[16] but this audience was a far cry from those earlier in his tenure. The president's speech on Iraq on December 18, the culmination of a several-week effort to bolster public support for the president's policy there, drew about 37 million viewers.[17]

The audience for the president's State of the Union message on January 31, 2006, reveals another frustration for the Bush White House. Not only did three-fourths of Americans not devote close attention to it, but most of those who did already supported the president. Bush was preaching to the choir, as Republicans were much more likely than Democrats or Independents to watch his speech[18]—making it more difficult to reach those who opposed him.

The president also schedules interviews with networks, which are always eager to have an exclusive story. For example, shortly after the capture of Saddam Hussein in December 2003, Bush granted a primetime interview to ABC's Diane Sawyer. ABC expected interest to be high in what the president had to say and moved up the interview by two days. More than 11 million people watched the president, a considerably larger audience than his interview with Tom Brokaw at the end of the fighting in the war in Iraq in April 2003 (8.8 million viewers), with Scott Pelley on the first anniversary of the September 11, 2001, terrorist attacks

---

[15] Nielsen Media Research, Press Release, June 29, 2005.

[16] Diego Vasquez, "Nearly 32 Million Catch Bush Speech," *Media Life*, September 16, 2005; Mike Reynolds, "Fox News Tops Bush Speech Ratings," *Media Life*, September 16, 2005.

[17] Bill Keveney, "Bush Speaks, Nation Listens," *USA Today*, December 20, 2005.

[18] Gallup poll, January 31, 2006; Pew Charitable Trust poll, February 1–5, 2006.

(9.6 million), or Brit Hume on the eve of Bush's address to the UN General Assembly in September 2003 (4.3 million). The bad news is that more people watched Paris Hilton star in an episode of the reality series *The Simple Life* than watched the president, and Bush only won the ratings war among viewers 50 and older.[19]

The White House not only has a problem in obtaining a receptive audience for the president's television appearances. In addition, it must face the obstacle of obtaining television coverage in the first place. Traditionally, presidents could rely on full network coverage of any statement they wished to make directly to the American people or any press conference they wished to be televised. Lyndon Johnson even insisted that the networks keep cameras hot in the White House so he could go on television on short notice. The president can no longer depend on access to network television, however.

As shown in Table 3.1, most of George W. Bush's primetime televised speeches focused on the September 11, 2001, terrorist attacks on the United States. His only primetime press conference during his first year in office (held October 11, 2001), received full network television coverage, as did his short presentations on September 11 and October 7, 2001. His major speech to a joint session of Congress on September 20, 2001, also received full network coverage. However, by November 8, 2001, most networks viewed the president's speech on the U.S. response to terrorism as an event rather than news. Perhaps knowing that the networks would refuse, the White House did not specifically request airtime. Instead, it informed the networks that the president's speech

---

[19] Lisa de Moraes, "Paris Outdraws the Prez," *Washington Post,* December 18, 2003, p. C1.

was available for broadcasting. Thus, CBS, NBC, and Fox chose not to carry the president's speech. Even in the face of terrorist attacks, presidents have no guarantee of airtime.

Nearly a year later, the president faced a similar problem. On October 7, 2002, he made his most comprehensive address regarding the likely need to use force against Saddam Hussein's regime in Iraq. The speech was strictly nonpartisan, and the White House had chosen the venue for the speech, Cincinnati, Ohio, because there was no statewide election in the midterm elections. The president's subject—going to war—focused on what is perhaps the most important decision a nation can make. Nevertheless, ABC, CBS, NBC, and PBS chose not to carry the president's speech. The White House was reluctant to make a special request for airtime out of concern for fanning fears of an imminent invasion, but it would have welcomed coverage. The networks argued that the president's speech contained little new information.[20] In the absence of breaking news, the commander in chief was unable to obtain airtime to discuss his thinking about going to war. As a result, the president's address on a possible war with Iraq achieved an audience of only 16.8 million.[21]

As shown in Chapter 2, Bush compensated for the increased difficulty of obtaining airtime and of gaining an audience when he had airtime, by traveling extensively around the country. The question is whether the increase in local appearances led to an increase in news coverage for the president and his policies. There is some

---

[20] Jim Rutenberg, "3 Networks Skip Bush's Talk, Citing Absence of Request, *New York Times,* October 8, 2002; David E. Sanger, "Bush Sees 'Urgent Duty' to Pre-empt Attack by Iraq," *New York Times,* October 8, 2002.
[21] Jim Rutenberg, "Speech Had Big Audience Despite Networks' Action," *New York Times,* October 9, 2002.

evidence that it did not. Figure 3.1 shows that a study of the news coverage of the first 60 days of the Clinton and George W. Bush presidencies found that there was a dramatic across-the-board drop-off in coverage on television, newspapers, and newsweeklies. Network television coverage was down 42 percent and newspaper coverage (*New York Times* and *Washington Post*) was off 38 percent. *Newsweek* magazine had 59 percent fewer stories about Bush in its pages than it carried about Clinton eight years earlier.

Although the president was still a dominant figure on op-ed and editorial pages, he was less visible on the front pages, financial pages, and in newscasts.[22] This lower profile was not an asset in advancing the president's agenda, and talk of the disappearing presidency began to be heard inside the Beltway.

FIGURE 3.1
Media Coverage of the President in the First 60 Days

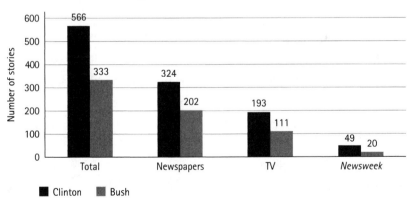

Source: The Project For Excellence in Journalism, *The First 100 Days: How Bush Versus Clinton Fared In the Press.*

---

[22] The Project For Excellence in Journalism, *The First 100 Days: How Bush Versus Clinton Fared In the Press*, 2001.

The presidency reappeared in force following the terrorist attacks of September 11, 2001. The prominence of the commander in chief in wartime and the nation's need for reassurance and action against terrorists compelled the media to cover his words and actions and allowed him to dominate the news.

Related to gaining the public's attention is educating it about accomplishments. This is not easy to do, however. For example, despite three tax cuts in as many years, in the fall of 2003, only 19 percent said Bush's policies made their taxes go down. Forty-seven percent noticed no effect, while 29 percent perceived that their taxes had gone up.[23] Similarly, in the summer of 2004 as the president's reelection campaigned heated up, most Americans did not recognize that the nation had been gaining jobs over the previous six months.[24]

TAXES

No policy has been more central to the George W. Bush presidency than tax cuts. They have been the answer to every economic situation. If the federal government is running a surplus, cut taxes. If the economy is stagnant, cut taxes. If the economy requires more investment, cut taxes on investments, savings, and estates.

The president made tax cuts the centerpiece of his campaign in 2000, and he wasted no time in proposing substantial tax cuts after his inauguration. He advocated them both frequently and

---

[23] CBS News/*New York Times* poll, September 28–October 1, 2003.
[24] AP/Ipsos poll, June 7–9, 2004.

forcefully. Often Bush's travels seemed motivated more by demonstrating his preexisting public support in states where he ran well in the election than in convincing more skeptical voters of the soundness of his proposals. He did not travel to California until May 29 and visited New York even later. Instead, the White House gave priority to states that Bush had won and that were represented by Democratic senators, including Georgia, Louisiana, Arkansas, Missouri, North and South Dakota, Montana, and North Carolina.

Table 3.2 shows responses to Gallup Poll questions on the president's 2001 tax cut proposal. The results show that public opinion did not change in response to the president's efforts.

Whatever the president's motivations for the venues of his speeches, he obtained the support of only one Senate Democrat (Zell Miller of Georgia, who announced his support of the tax cut before Bush's inauguration) on the April 4 bellwether vote for his full tax cut. The fact that the public did not rally behind the president may explain at least part of the lack of Democratic support.

TABLE 3.2
Public Support for Bush 2001 Tax Cut

POLL DATE	FAVOR	OPPOSE	NO OPINION
9–11 February 2001	56%	34%	10%
19–21 February 2001	53	30	17
5–7 March 2001	56	34	10
20–22 April 2001	56	35	9

SOURCE: Gallup poll, "Based on what you have read or heard, do you favor or oppose the federal income tax cuts George W. Bush has proposed?"

In 2003, the president proposed a fundamental change in the tax structure, one that would eliminate taxes on most stock dividends and capital gains and allow people to establish tax-free savings accounts. The policy did not gain traction with the public, however. The Pew Research Center for the People and the Press found that only 42 percent of the public approved of Bush's handling of taxes despite a high-profile White House campaign on behalf of its policy.[25] At the beginning of May, Pew found that only 40 percent of the public favored the president's tax cut.[26] Most respondents to a CBS/*New York Times* poll in early May said they did not think it was important to cut taxes or that doing so would stimulate the economy.[27] Similarly, the *Washington Post*/ABC News poll found that tax cuts were of low importance to the public and that when pollsters offered the choice between tax cuts and increased domestic spending, the public favored the latter by 67 percent to 29 percent.[28] Shortly before the president signed the truncated bill that eventually passed, Gallup found that more people felt the tax cuts were a bad idea than thought they were a good idea.[29]

The president originally requested a ten-year total of $726 billion in tax cuts. He repeatedly railed against the strategy of making tax cuts temporary and phasing them in over time. At the center of his proposal was the elimination of taxes on stock divi-

---

[25] Pew Research Center for the People and the Press poll, February 12–18, 2003.

[26] Pew Research Center for the People and the Press poll, April 30–May 4, 2003.

[27] CBS News/*New York Times* poll, May 9–12, 2003.

[28] Dana Milbank and Dan Balz, *Washington Post*, May 11, 2003 (website).

[29] Gallup poll, May 19–21, 2003. These results are based on a question asked of half the sample (N = 509). Forty-six percent responded that the tax cuts were a bad idea, 1 percent more than that thought they were a good idea.

dends. In the end, the president signed a tax bill that cut taxes $320 billion, that was temporary and phased in, and that did not eliminate the dividend tax.[30]

Four republican senators refused to support the full package: John McCain (Arizona), Lincoln Chafee (Rhode Island), Olympia Snowe (Maine), and George Voinovich (Ohio). The administration did not even try to pressure McCain and Chafee, knowing that they would not budge on the issue, but it did target Voinovich and Snowe. In addition, the White House did not object when the Club for Growth ran advertisements aimed at these two senators in their home states. The administration also targeted conservative Democrats John Breaux (Louisiana), Blanche Lincoln (Arkansas), and Ben Nelson (Nebraska).

The White House staged dozens of events around the country with administration officials and mobilized friendly interest groups to pressure senators. Sometimes these efforts seemed to equate tax cuts with patriotism. More importantly, the president took to the road, attempting to exploit his 70 percent approval ratings following the cessation of fighting in Iraq. In Ohio, the home of Republican holdout Voinovich, the president derided the Senate bill that provided $350 billion in tax cuts as "a little bitty" tax relief package and insisted that senators who did not support him "might have some explaining to do."

In the end, the efforts had little impact and may even have backfired. Ben Nelson was the only Democrat (aside from long-time tax cut supporter Zell Miller) who supported even the

---

[30] It is possible, of course, that the tax cuts would be made permanent in the future. The point here is the contrast between what the president wanted and what he got.

$350-billion tax cut bill the Senate passed. Of the four Republican opponents, only Voinovich voted for the final bill—after holding out for $32 billion of relief for the states and insisting that leaders subtract it from even the scaled-down Senate bill. The White House declared victory, of course, but in reality Bush concluded that it was more important to have a tax cut than to stand on principle over its size and content.[31] The lack of success of his strategy of going public had left him no choice.

THE WAR WITH IRAQ

The president's most important initiative in 2002 was preparation for war with Iraq. In the late summer, the White House decided it should move on regime change in Iraq and sought the public's backing. The context in which Bush sought this support was certainly favorable. In surveys conducted over the previous ten years, stretching back to the end of the Gulf War, majorities had generally supported U.S. military action in Iraq to remove Saddam Hussein from power. The American public has long held strongly negative perceptions of Iraq and its leader. In a December 1998 poll, Saddam Hussein received the worst rating of any public figure tested in Gallup Poll history—1 percent positive and 96 percent negative.[32] In early 2002, the country of Iraq received a 6 percent favorable and 88 percent unfavorable rating, the worst of any of the 25 countries tested in that poll.[33] Since 1991,

---

[31] Dana Milbank and Jim VandeHei, "Bush Retreat Eased Bill's Advance," *Washington Post,* May 23, 2003, p. A5.
[32] Gallup poll, December 28–29, 1998.
[33] Gallup poll, February 4–6, 2002.

Iraq had never received even a 10 percent favorable rating.[34] Asked in February 2001 what country was America's worst enemy, Americans named Iraq significantly more often than any other country.[35]

In September 2002, most Americans felt that Iraq had developed or was developing weapons of mass destruction. Many Americans felt that if left alone, Iraq would use those weapons against the United States within five years. Most Americans felt that Saddam Hussein sponsored terrorism that affected the United States. A little more than half of Americans took the additional inferential leap and concluded that Saddam Hussein was personally and directly involved in the September 11, 2001, terrorist attacks.[36]

On August 26, 2002, Vice President Cheney delivered a hard-hitting speech laying out the administration's case for invading Iraq, and then, on the anniversary of the terrorist attacks, the president delivered a nationally televised address. The next day he addressed the United Nations, demanding that it take action to disarm Iraq. Later, he asked Congress to pass a resolution authorizing him to use force against Iraq. On October 7, Bush addressed the nation again, delivering his most comprehensive presentation regarding the likely need to use force against Saddam Hussein's regime in Iraq. On February 26 and March 17, 2003, the president again made national addresses on Iraq.

Figure 3.2 shows public support for the invasion of Iraq. Public opinion did not change in response to the administration's

---

[34] Chris Chambers, "Americans Most Favorable Toward Canada, Australia and Great Britain; Iran, Libya and Iraq Receive the Lowest Ratings," Gallup Poll News Release, February 16, 2001.
[35] Gallup poll, February 1–4, 2001.
[36] Frank Newport, "Public Wants Congressional and U.N. Approval before Iraq Action," Gallup Poll, News Release, September 6, 2002.

blitzkrieg. Gallup used the phrase "sending American ground troops" in the question about invading Iraq. Some other polling organizations simply asked about "military action"—an easier threshold—and found higher levels of support. The president, of course, sought support for the use of ground troops as well as other means of projecting force. Nevertheless, surveys by the Pew Research Center and the CBS/*New York Times* poll found little or no change in public support for invading Iraq since the summer and before the White House's public relations effort. Indeed, Pew found that between mid-August and the end of October support for taking military action in Iraq to end Saddam Hussein's rule decreased by 9 percentage points.[37]

Furthermore, Americans expressed reservations and conditions to their support. They had a strong preference for both a congressional authorization for the use of force and securing the participation of allies.[38] They also preferred to wait for weapons inspectors to attempt to disarm Iraq before the United States took military action. At the same time, respondents said they were more concerned with the economy than with Iraq and 69 percent (including 51 percent of Republicans) complained that Bush should be paying more attention to the economy.[39]

As shown in Figure 3.2, public support for invading Iraq with ground troops stayed within a narrow range throughout the fall and winter until early February 2003. At that point, it increased

---

[37] Pew Research Center survey report, October 30, 2002.
[38] Editors of the Gallup Poll, "Nine Key Questions about Public Opinion on Iraq," Gallup Poll, News Release, October 1, 2002; Lydia Saad, "Top Ten Findings about Public Opinion and Iraq," Gallup Poll, News Release, October 8, 2002. Right up until the eve of the war, the public preferred to have UN approval of an invasion. The Gallup poll of February 24–26, 2003, found that only 38 percent of the public supported an invasion without UN approval.
[39] CBS/*New York Times* poll, October 3–5, 2002.

FIGURE 3.2
Public Support for Invasion of Iraq

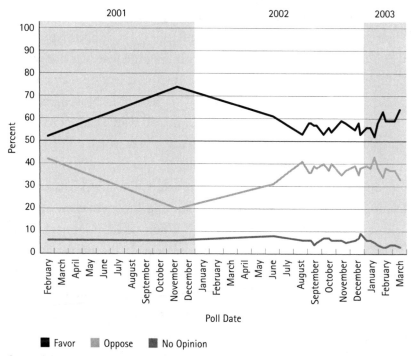

Poll Date

■ Favor ■ Oppose ■ No Opinion

Source: Gallup Poll question: "Would you favor or oppose sending American ground troops to the Persian Gulf in an attempt to remove Saddam Hussein from power in Iraq?"

5 percentage points. This increase was not in response to the president, however, but to Secretary of State Colin Powell's presentation of evidence against Iraq to the UN. In the month following Powell's speech, support for an invasion drifted downward until the middle of March, when the president issued the final ultimatum to Saddam Hussein that marked the beginning of a rally in support of war.

The war itself was over in a matter of weeks, but the pacification, reconstruction, and democratization of Iraq was to take much longer. The president needed to sustain support for his policy, especially as he sought reelection, and the administration devoted enormous time and energy to obtaining the public's support. As Figure 3.3 shows, however, the public was *less* supportive of the war after a year, with a majority concluding the war was not worth fighting. This low level of support for the president's policy continued throughout 2005, dipping below 40 percent in November.

Partisanship polarized views about the war. Democrats were much less likely than Republicans to say it was worth going to war in Iraq. In April 2005, for example, 79 percent of Republicans responded that it was worth going to war, while only 17 percent of Democrats held the same opinion. Among Independents, 36 percent said it was worth going to war.[40] When asked in January 2006 if the war had been a mistake, 51 percent of the public agreed, including 76 percent of Democrats and 63 percent of Independents. Only 14 percent of Republicans shared that view, however.[41]

There are two ways of interpreting the decline in support for the war. On the one hand, public support eroded more quickly than for the wars in Korea and Vietnam. On the other hand, one might view the public support the war did receive as surprisingly high, given the absence of weapons of mass destruction and the lack of connection between Saddam Hussein and international terrorism—the main justifications for the war. This support may be the result of the White House's success in connecting it in some people's minds with the broader war on terrorism.[42]

---

[40] Gallup poll, April 1–2, 2005.
[41] Gallup poll, January 20–22, 2006.
[42] John E. Mueller, "The Iraq Syndrome," *Foreign Affairs* (November/December 2005): 45.

FIGURE 3.3
Support for War with Iraq

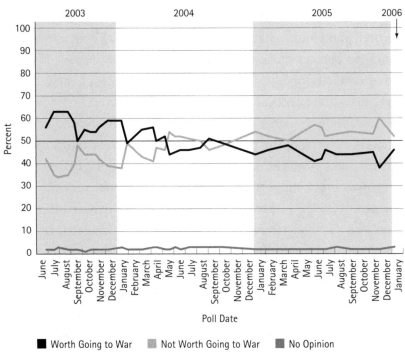

Worth Going to War   Not Worth Going to War   No Opinion

Source: Gallup Poll question: "All in all, do you think it was worth going to war in Iraq, or not?"
(Through 2003: "All in all, do you think the situation in Iraq was worth going to war over, or not?")

In a paradoxical twist, it is possible that the public was not even harsher in its judgments about the war with Iraq because of widespread ignorance regarding central justifications for the war. Long-standing negative views of Saddam Hussein predisposed Americans to believe the worst. Before the war with Iraq in 2003, two-thirds of the public expressed the belief that Iraq played an important role in the September 11 terrorist attacks. After the war, substantial percentages of the public believed that the United

States had found clear evidence that Saddam Hussein was working closely with al Qaeda, that the United States had found
weapons of mass destruction in Iraq, and that world opinion
favored the United States going to war in Iraq.[43] In the fall of
2003, 43 percent of the public still believed that Saddam Hussein
was personally involved in the 9/11 attacks.[44] All of these beliefs
were inaccurate, as even the White House admitted.[45]

Even more striking, two years after the United States-led invasion, 56 percent of the public thought Iraq had weapons of mass
destruction before the start of the war and 6 in 10 believed Iraq
provided direct support to the al Qaeda terrorist network.[46] At
the end of 2005, 41 percent of U.S. adults still believed that Saddam Hussein had strong links to al Qaeda; 22 percent believed
that Saddam Hussein helped plan and support the hijackers who
attacked the United States on September 11; 26 percent believed
that Iraq had weapons of mass destruction when the United
States invaded; and 24 percent believed that several of the hijackers who attacked the United States on September 11 were Iraqis.[47]
As shown in Chapter 2, the administration's rhetoric may well
have contributed to the public's confusion. The president's refusal
to admit mistakes publicly also may have encouraged his supporters to hold to their original—although incorrect—beliefs.

---

[43] Steven Kull, Clay Ramsay, and Evan Lewis, "Misperceptions, the Media, and the Iraq War," *Political Science Quarterly* 118 (Winter 2003–2004): 569–598.
[44] CBS News/*New York Times* poll, September 28–October 1, 2003.
[45] Dana Milbank, "Bush Disavows Hussein-September 11 Link," *Washington Post,* September 18, 2003, p. A18.
[46] Dan Balz and Richard Morin, "Years After Invasion, Poll Data Mixed: Doubts About War, Optimism for Iraqis," *Washington Post,* March 16, 2005, p. A1. ABC News/*Washington Post* poll, March 10–13, 2005.
[47] Harris poll, December 8–14, 2005.

Partisanship polarized views about the rationales for the war as well as about the war itself. Gary Jacobson has shown that Republicans' initial high regard for the president and trust in his honesty encouraged acceptance of his original case for war. When these premises proved faulty, Republicans either failed to notice or decided it was irrelevant and continued to support the war, accepting the administration's claim that it was integral to the war on terrorism and thus to the security of the United States. Their capacity to get the facts wrong, even when they were aware of official reports that challenged their views and even after the administration had abandoned some of its original rationales for the war, was extraordinary. Jacobson concludes that the widespread resistance to information suggests that, particularly among Republicans, support for the war came first and the specifics of the factual case for it were of much less importance. It was loyalty to the president, most tenaciously among white conservative Christians, that sustained at least a base of support for the president and his policy in Iraq. Bush's bonding with conservative Christians had a significant payoff, as many of them appeared to believe that Bush was God's chosen instrument to lead a global war pitting good against evil and gave him unwavering, unquestioning support.[48]

Democrats, on the other hand, generally did not trust Bush, so their support for the war depended crucially on belief in its necessity. The lack of evidence of weapons of mass destruction or Hussein's complicity in the 9/11 attacks—which they *did* notice—

---

[48] Gary C. Jacobson, *A Divider, Not a Uniter: George W. Bush and the American People* (New York: Longman, 2006), chaps. 5–6.

confirmed their distrust and their support for the president's policy in Iraq collapsed. As Jacobson put it, "Consistent with the theories of cognitive dissonance and mass opinion formation,
partisan differences in prior beliefs were thus reinforced by partisan differences in reactions to events and revelations in Iraq."[49] It
is possible that the inadvertent or intentionally misleading nature
of some of the president's arguments on behalf of the war and the
U.S. performance in the war's aftermath contributed to the alien-
ation of Democrats and many Independents.

Another way of examining the president's ability to obtain
public support for the war with Iraq is to examine opinion regarding his handling the situation there. Figure 3.4 shows that public
approval of the way President Bush handled the situation in Iraq
rose to an impressive 76 percent near the end of the fighting in
April 2003. However, it quickly diminished in the face of widespread looting and other lawless behavior by Iraqis and the beginning of the insurgency. By October, less than half the public
approved of his performance, and, for the first time, more of them
disapproved than approved. The president continued to receive
only minority approval of his handling of the situation in Iraq for
the next two years as the death toll of both Americans and Iraqis
continued to rise. By September 2005, his approval rating on this
policy had fallen to 32 percent while fully two-thirds of the public
disapproved of his performance.[50]

By June 2005, the president was losing the middle of the electorate. Especially troubling for the president was the fact that
more than half of the American public believed that the war in Iraq

[49] Gary C. Jacobson, "The Public, the President, and the War in Iraq" (paper presented at the annual meeting of the American Political Science Association, Washington D.C.), September 1–4, 2005, p. 35.
[50] Gallup poll, September 16–18, 2005.

FIGURE 3.4
Bush's Handling of Iraq

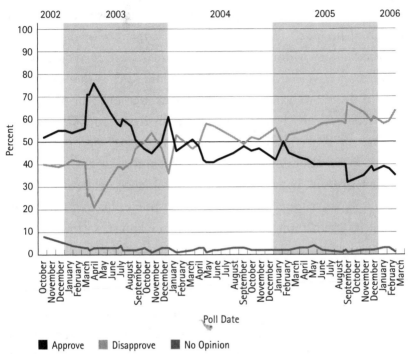

Source: Gallup poll question: "Do you approve or disapprove of the way George W. Bush is handling the war in Iraq?"

had not made the United States safer, undermining the principal rationale for the war. Nearly six in ten said the war was not worth fighting. Only Republicans maintained their support of Bush's policies.[51] Gallup found that 59 percent of the public opposed the war.[52] Numerous lawmakers, including some Republicans, accused him of not offering honest assessments about the strength of the insurgency and the slow pace of training battle-ready Iraqi

[51] *Washington Post*/ABC News poll, June 2–5, 2005.
[52] Gallup poll, June 16–19, 2005.

forces. "The war has gone on longer and more violently than people envisioned," declared Senator Lindsey Graham, Republican of South Carolina. "We always accentuated the positive and never prepared the public for the worst. . . . People are dying in larger numbers than we thought, and the insurgency seems to be growing stronger, not weaker." The result, Graham said, is that Bush "ill-prepared the public for the trial and tribulations" of planting a new democracy in the heart of the Middle East.[53]

Bush had hoped the successful January 2005 elections in Iraq would boost the popularity of the conflict and allow him to distance himself from it. But the strength and violence of the insurgency eroded support for the president. In response, he met with Iraqi Prime Minister Ibrahim Jafari at the White House for the first time and devoted several speeches to the war, including a major address on the first anniversary of Iraq's sovereignty. Bush's new approach was mostly rhetorical, however, as the White House did not change its basic policy or time frame for bringing home the 140,000 U.S. troops.[54] On the bright side for the White House, public support for staying the course in Iraq, now that the United States was there, declined less slowly than support for the war itself or the president's performance as commander in chief. Nevertheless, support for options to withdraw U.S. troops slowly increased.[55]

By January 2006, opinion about the president's handling of Iraq was extraordinarily polarized. The overall approval level of 39 percent masked the fact that, on the one hand, 82 percent of Republicans supported his stewardship but, on the other hand,

---

[53] Jim VandeHei, "Bush Is Expected to Address Specifics on Iraq," *Washington Post,* June 16, 2005, p. A8.
[54] VandeHei, "Bush Is Expected to Address Specifics on Iraq."
[55] Mueller, "The Iraq Syndrome," pp. 45–46.

only 28 percent of Independents and nearly no Democrats— 7 percent—agreed with this evaluation.[56]

TERRORISM

The president has done better at obtaining public approval for his handling terrorism. As Figure 3.5 shows, until November 2005, a majority of the public had always approved of his performance in this area. Although his approval rating was extraordinarily high following the September 11, 2001, terrorist attacks and during the war with Afghanistan, he has maintained support for his handling of terrorism throughout most of his tenure. It is not surprising, then, that he chose to focus his reelection campaign around the war on terrorism rather than specific stands on domestic policy such as Social Security or the war in Iraq and its aftermath.

However, approval of the president's handling of terrorism drifted down. Actually, in a June CBS News/*New York Times* poll, only 50 percent of the public approved of Bush's handling of the campaign against terrorism. The drop in approval occurred disproportionately among Independents.[57] Perhaps one reason for this diminished support was that by July 2005, nearly half (47 percent) of the public said that the war in Iraq had *hurt* the war on terrorism and 45 percent felt it had increased the chances of terrorist attacks in the United States.[58] Thus the president was losing what had been his strongest suit. By November 2005, less than half the public approved of his performance on terrorism,

---

[56] Gallup poll, January 20–22, 2006.
[57] Dana Milbank and Claudia Deane, "Poll Finds Dimmer View of Iraq War," *Washington Post*, June 8, 2005.
[58] Pew Research Center for the People and the Press poll, July 13–17, 2005.

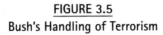

FIGURE 3.5
Bush's Handling of Terrorism

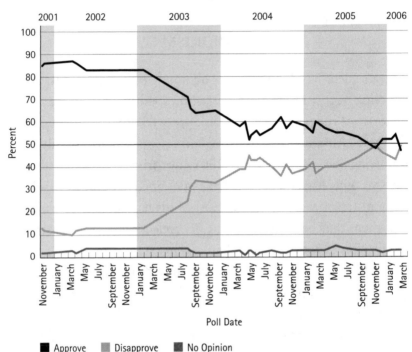

Poll Date

■ Approve   ■ Disapprove   ■ No Opinion

Source: Gallup Poll question: "Do you approve or disapprove of the way George W. Bush is handling terrorism?" (November 2001 and March 2002: "Do you approve or disapprove of George W. Bush's efforts to prevent future terrorism in the U.S.?" November 2002 through August 2003, except for January–February: "Do you approve or disapprove of George W. Bush's handling of U.S. military action abroad to fight terrorism?")

and despite an intensive public relations effort, Bush has not regained his lost support.

MIDTERM ELECTIONS

Modern presidents typically have taken an active role in midterm congressional elections. Despite their efforts, presidents are usually disappointed in the results of midterm elections. Even George

Washington's Federalists lost seats in the House in the first midterm election, in 1790. A recurring feature of American politics is the *decrease* in representation of the president's party in Congress in midterm congressional elections (see Table 3.3). In 1986, the Republicans lost eight seats in the Senate, depriving President Reagan of a majority. In 1994, the Democrats lost eight Senate seats and 52 House seats, losing control of both houses of Congress in the process. The 1998 election was an exception: the Democrats gained five seats in the House.

One might think that during a war, such as the war on terrorism that began in the fall of 2001, voters would be less likely to

TABLE 3.3

Gains or Losses for the President's Party in Midterm Elections

YEAR	PRESIDENT	HOUSE	SENATE
1954	Eisenhower (R)	−18	−1
1958	Eisenhower (R)	−47	−13
1962	Kennedy (D)	−4	+3
1966	Johnson (D)	−47	−4
1970	Nixon (R)	−12	+2
1974	Ford (R)	−47	−5
1978	Carter (D)	−15	−3
1982	Reagan (R)	−26	0
1986	Reagan (R)	−5	−8
1990	G. Bush (R)	−9	−1
1994	Clinton (D)	−52	−8
1998	Clinton (D)	+5	0
2002	G. W. Bush (R)	+6	+2
	Average	−21	−3

support opposition party candidates. This would be incorrect, however. Lincoln's Republicans lost seats in 1862 during the Civil War. More dramatically, in 1918, only days before the Allies' victory in World War I, Woodrow Wilson's Democrats lost 19 seats in the House and six in the Senate. This loss cost the Democrats control of both houses of Congress and was an embarrassment for the president, who had appealed for Democratic victories. In 1942, less than a year after the Japanese attack on Pearl Harbor, the Democrats under Franklin D. Roosevelt lost 50 seats in the House and nine in the Senate. Eight years later, in 1950, the United States was fighting the Korean War. The Democrats under Harry S. Truman lost 29 seats in the House and six in the Senate. Things did not get any better for the president's party in the midterm elections during the Vietnam War (1966 and 1970) or the buildup for the Gulf War in 1990.

No sooner did people change their calendars to 2002, than political discussion focused on the upcoming midterm elections. The big question was whether the president would be able to leverage his personal approval ratings into votes for Republican candidates in the 2002 midterm elections. President Bush faced a quandary, however. He had had success operating as a wartime president above the political fray. Yet he was also the leader of his party in a very closely divided Congress, and he wanted to pass legislation. The president resolved this tension by putting off partisan politics for a time, but in the end, he actively raised funds and campaigned for Republican candidates for Congress.

In the month following the president's October 7, 2002, speech on possible war with Iraq, Bush engaged in the most active midterm campaigning of any president in history. In the end, the

Republicans gained seats in both houses of Congress, maintaining the majority in the House and regaining it in the Senate. The historic nature of these gains (exceeded only once—in 1934—during the previous century) generated considerable commentary about the president's public leadership.

Bush campaigned relentlessly, covering 15 carefully chosen states in the last five days of the campaign alone, and he rallied his party. The most significant fact of the Republican success in the elections was the heavy turnout in Republican base, not Democratic abstentions. A Gallup poll taken the weekend before the election found that 64 percent of Republicans were "more enthusiastic" about voting than in the past, while only 51 percent of Democrats responded that way.[59] On the other hand, the Democrats failed to rally—they had little to rally around, lacking both a message and a messenger. Voters did not necessarily support the Republicans on the issues, but the White House succeeded in turning the election into a referendum on a popular president.[60]

Most people who entered the booths did not have terrorism on their minds. More were concerned about the economy and the prospect of war with Iraq. But the minority who did have terrorism on their minds was overwhelmingly Republican, and the Democrats were not able to position themselves well on enough of the other issues to counter this strong GOP advantage. The war on terrorism had shifted the public debate to national security

---

[59] William Schneider, "The Bush Mandate," *National Journal,* November 9, 2002, 3358; Adam Nagourney and Janet Elder, "Positive Ratings for the G.O.P., If Not Its Policy," *New York Times,* November 26, 2002, pp. A1, A 22.
[60] William Schneider, "A Popularity Contest," *National Journal,* November 16, 2002, 3346.

issues that favored the Republicans and shielded the president from criticism on domestic issues that favored the Democrats.

Despite the Republican success, perspective is important. The election was very close. The *Washington Post* reported that a change of 41,000 votes in only two states out of 77 million cast nationwide would have kept the Senate in Democratic hands. As political analyst Charlie Cook put it, "This was a year of very close races that, for the most part, broke toward Republicans but in no way reflected a significant shift in the national direction."[61]

In addition, the Republicans enjoyed several advantages. Because the president had lacked coattails in 2000, there was less chance for setbacks in the midterm elections. Few Republicans held seats that lacked a substantial Republican base. In fact, since Al Gore received the most votes in 2000, we would have expected the Democrats to lose seats.

The Republicans also had gained as a result of redistricting following the 2000 census. Both the *National Journal* and *Congressional Quarterly Weekly Report* concluded that the Republican gains in the House almost exactly matched these territorial gains.[62] (The Republicans were successful, however, in boosting the security of representatives who had won narrowly in 2000.)

Democrats also had to play on Republican turf, trying to pick up seats in traditionally Republican areas. For example, 26 out of the country's 45 competitive House seats were in districts in which Al Gore received less than 50 percent of the vote in 2000.[63]

[61] Charlie Cook, "Off to the Races: So Much for the GOP Sweep," December 10, 2002, Washington, D.C.
[62] Richard E. Cohen, "New Lines, Republican Gains," *National Journal,* November 9, 2002, 3285; Gregory L. Giroux, "Redistricting Helped GOP," *Congressional Quarterly Weekly Report,* November 9, 2002, 2934–2935.
[63] Charlie Cook, "A Landslide? That Talk is Mostly Just Hot Air," *National Journal,* November 9, 2002, 3346–3347.

The Democrats' seven strongest bids to take over Republican-held seats were in states Bush had won in 2000, and four of the six vulnerable Democratic seats were in states Bush won while Gore had only narrowly carried the other two, Minnesota and Iowa.

The Republicans raised more money than the Democrats did (although not in Georgia), and in a handful of hotly contested races, the money helped. Having more money also allowed the Republicans to concentrate their funding in battleground states and districts.[64]

The Republicans also enjoyed an advantage with candidates. The White House actively recruited quality candidates, including Senate winners Norman Coleman (Minnesota), James Talent (Missouri), and Saxby Chambliss (Georgia). The Democrats, on the other hand, had a weak cohort of challengers to Republican incumbents.[65] The memorial service for Minnesota Senator Paul Wellstone a few days before the election turned into a political rally that alienated some voters in a closely contested election and gave Coleman an excuse to resume his campaign.

Charlie Cook found no Republican wave except perhaps in Georgia. Instead, he concluded that the basics of getting out the vote decided the midterm elections in 2002.[66] Indeed, the Republicans operated a finely engineered voter-mobilization effort. In Georgia, the state with the biggest Republican successes, the party implemented a meticulous organizational plan that included computer analysis, training programs for volunteers, and a voter

---

[64] Bob Benenson, "GOP Won Midterm by Winning Series of Small Battles," *Congressional Quarterly Weekly Report,* November 9, 2002, 2890. See also Jim VandeHei and Dan Balz, "In GOP Win, a Lesson in Money, Muscle, Planning," *Washington Post,* November 10, 2002, pp. A1, A6, A7.
[65] Gary C. Jacobson, "Terror, Terrain, and Turnout: Explaining the 2002 Midterm Election," *Political Science Quarterly* 118 (Spring 2003): 1–22.
[66] Cook, "A Landslide? That Talk is Mostly Just Hot Air," 3346–3347.

registration drive followed by massive mailing, telephone, and neighborhood canvasses in the closing days of the campaign. The president visited as late as November 2 to energize the Republican ranks. Aiding this grassroots mobilization were the National Rifle Association and United Seniors (an organization heavily under-written by the drug industry).[67]

The Bush administration has invested extraordinary time and energy attempting to obtain the public's support, and it has demonstrated both skill and discipline in its efforts. Nevertheless, the public has been largely unresponsive to the White House. As shown in Chapters 6 and 7, this scenario reoccurred regarding the president's efforts to reform Social Security. These results raise serious questions about the efficacy of the permanent campaign. But perhaps Bush was more successful in obtaining support for himself than for his policies. Chapter 4 addresses this question.

[67] Peter H. Stone and Shawn Zeller, "Business and Conservative Groups Won Big," *National Journal,* November 9, 2002, 3355.

CHAPTER 4

Public Opinion About the President

Certainly one of the highest priorities of presidents is to obtain the public's support for themselves. Presidents believe that public approval increases the probabilities of obtaining the passage of legislation in Congress, positive coverage in the press, and even responsiveness in the bureaucracy. As a result of their belief in the importance of public approval, they devote an impressive amount of time, energy, and money to obtaining it.

As shown in Chapter 2, the George W. Bush White House has been no exception to this pattern. But as we learned in Chapter 1, an unprecedented level of partisan polarization has marked the Bush presidency. This chapter focuses on examining how the public has evaluated the president and identifying the most important influences on these appraisals.

THE "HONEYMOON" PERIOD

The unusual nature of George W. Bush's election had a substantial potential to weaken the start of his presidency—and eliminate any potential for a honeymoon. The vagaries of the electoral college elected him with fewer popular votes than his principal opponent. Receiving neither a majority nor even a plurality of the vote, the new president could not credibly claim a mandate from the people. Moreover, the Republicans lost seats in both houses of Congress, undermining any claim to presidential coattails.

Many (mostly Democrats) saw his victory as illegitimate, because he received more than a half-million fewer votes than Al Gore and because of the peculiar circumstances surrounding the determination of the winner of Florida's electoral votes. A Gallup poll taken just before the inauguration found that 31 percent of Americans thought Bush "won on a technicality" and 24 percent thought he "stole the election," while 45 percent said he "won fair and square." Thirty-eight percent of Americans still considered Gore to be the "real winner of the election."[1]

Nevertheless, Americans were optimistic that the new president would succeed in the core activities of the presidency (see Table 4.1). In addition, the public had confidence that the president would make progress on important issues such as improving the country's security and education and keeping America prosperous.

The public was less sanguine regarding other specific policy accomplishments, however. Most people did not feel that the president would succeed at improving race relations, the environment,

---

[1] Gallup poll, January 15–16, 2001.

TABLE 4.1
Early Expectations of President George W. Bush

CONFIDENT THAT THE PRESIDENT CAN:

Set a good moral example	81%
Use military force wisely	78
Prevent major scandals in his administration	77
Manage the executive branch wisely	77
Work effectively with Congress to get things done	74
Fulfill the proper role of the United States in world affairs	72
Handle an international crisis	71

SOURCE: CNN/*USA Today*/Gallup poll, January 15–16, 2001.

or conditions for the poor; reducing crime; or healing the country's political divisions. A plurality did not anticipate that the president would succeed in improving the healthcare system, and majorities did not believe the president could deliver on a tax cut, ensuring the long-term health of the Medicare and Social Security systems, or keeping the federal budget balanced (see Table 4.2). Indeed, only 46 percent of the public felt the country would be better off in four years.[2]

There were forces working in the new president's favor, however. The "positivity bias," the tendency to evaluate positively public figures and institutions, has the greatest potential for influence in ambiguous situations, such as the beginning of a president's term, when the new occupant of the Oval Office is unknown to the public as chief executive. There tends to be a

---

[2] Gallup poll, January 15–16, 2001.

TABLE 4.2

Expectations of the George W. Bush Administration

Do you think the Bush administration will or will not be able to do the following?

NOT	WILL	WILL
Improve military security for the country	81%	16%
Improve education	66	32
Keep America prosperous	63	33
Increase respect for the presidency	61	36
Improve respect for the United States abroad	58	38
Improve moral values in the United States	55	41
Keep the federal budget balanced	50	46
Ensure the long-term strength of the Social Security system	50	44
Cut your taxes	49	46
Ensure the long-term strength of the Medicare System	49	44
Improve the healthcare system	46	49
Improve race relations	44	51
Reduce the crime rate	44	50
Improve conditions for the disadvantaged and the poor	44	51
Improve the quality of the environment	42	52
Heal political divisions in this country	41	53

SOURCE: Gallup poll, January 15–16, 2001.

---

national consensus following a presidential campaign: People want their new president to succeed and usually give him the benefit of the doubt.

In addition, as people have little basis on which to evaluate the president, they may turn elsewhere for cues. The press generally treats a new chief executive favorably. Moreover, there is excitement and symbolism inherent in the peaceful transfer of power, the inaugural festivities, and the prevalent sense of "new beginnings." All this creates a positive environment in which initial evaluations of elected presidents take place, buttressing any tendency toward the positivity bias.

Bush may have lost the popular vote for president, but he received positive reviews immediately after taking office. Although he only won 48 percent of the vote the previous November, 57 percent of the public approved his performance in the first two polls taken after his inauguration (see Table 4.3). Bill Clinton began his tenure with a similar 58 percent approval rating. As is typically the case in presidential approval polls, party identification was the best predictor of approval. For example, in the February 9–11 Gallup poll, the president received approval from 88 percent of Republicans, 54 percent of Independents, but only 31 percent of Democrats. The president's approval level held reasonably steady, and had increased slightly to 62 percent near the symbolic 100-day mark.

Another advantage for Bush was that at the beginning of his term, 65 percent of the public approved of him as a person. This aggregate figure represented 91 percent of Republicans, 63 percent of Independents, and 40 percent of Democrats. However, perhaps reflecting the acrimony of the election controversy, 49 percent of Democrats disapproved of Bush as a person.[3]

Bush also enjoyed positive evaluations on a number of personal character dimensions, particularly as someone with a vision for the country's future and who was strong and skilled enough to

---

[3] Gallup poll, February 9–11, 2001.

TABLE 4.3
George W. Bush Job Approval

DATE	APPROVE %	DISAPPROVE %	NO OPINION %
2001			
February 1–4	57	25	18
February 9–11	57	25	18
February 19–21	62	21	17
March 5–7	63	22	15
March 9–11	58	29	13
March 26–28	53	29	18
April 6–8	59	30	11
April 20–22	62	29	9
May 7–9	53	33	14
May 10–14	56	31	13
May 18–20	56	36	8
June 8–10	55	35	10
June 11–17	55	33	12
June 28–Jul 1	52	34	14
July 10–11	57	35	8
July 19–22	56	33	11
August 3–5	55	35	10
August 10–12	57	35	8
August 16–19	57	34	9
August 24–26	55	36	9
September 7–10	51	39	10
September 14–15	86	10	4
September 21–22	90	6	4
October 5–6	87	10	3
October 11–14	89	8	3
October 19–21	88	9	3
November 2–4	87	9	4
November 8–11	87	9	4
November 26–27	87	8	5
December 6–9	86	10	4
December 14–16	86	11	3
2002			
January 7–9	84	12	4
January 11–14	83	13	4
January 25–27	84	13	3
February 4–6	82	14	4

Table 4.3 continues

Table 4.3 continued

DATE	APPROVE %	DISAPPROVE %	NO OPINION %
February 8–10	82	14	4
March 1–3	81	14	5
March 4–7	77	18	5
March 8–9	80	14	6
March 18–20	79	16	5
March 22–24	79	17	4
April 5–7	76	19	5
April 8–11	75	20	5
April 22–24	77	17	6
April 29–May 1	77	20	3
May 6–9	76	19	5
May 20–22	76	17	7
May 28–29	77	17	6
June 3–6	70	23	7
June 7–8	74	18	8
June 17–19	74	20	6
June 21–23	73	21	6
June 28–30	76	19	5
July 5–8	76	18	6
July 9–11	73	21	6
July 22–24	69	24	7
July 26–28	69	26	5
July 29–31	71	23	6
August 5–8	68	26	6
August 19–21	65	28	7
September 2–4	66	29	5
September 5–8	66	30	4
September 13–16	70	26	4
September 20–22	66	30	4
September 23–26	68	26	6
October 3–6	67	28	5
October 14–17	62	31	7
October 21–22	67	28	5
October 31–November 3	63	29	8
November 8–10	68	27	5
December 5–8	64	29	7
December 9–10	63	32	5
December 16–17	63	33	4
December 19–22	61	32	7

Table 4.3 continues

Table 4.3 continued

DATE	APPROVE %	DISAPPROVE %	NO OPINION %
2003			
January 3–5	63	32	5
January 10–12	58	37	5
January 13–16	61	34	5
January 23–25	60	36	4
January 31–February 2	61	35	4
February 3–6	59	35	6
February 7–9	61	34	5
February 17–19	58	37	5
February 24–26	57	37	6
March 14–16	58	38	4
March 22–23	71	25	4
March 24–25	69	27	4
March 29–30	71	26	3
April 5–6	70	27	3
April 7–9	69	26	5
April 14–16	71	24	5
April 22–23	70	26	4
May 5–7	69	28	3
May 19–21	66	30	4
May 30–June 1	64	32	4
June 9–10	62	34	4
June 12–15	63	33	4
June 27–29	61	36	3
July 7–9	62	34	4
July 18–20	59	38	3
July 25–27	58	38	4
August 4–6	60	36	4
August 25–26	59	37	4
September 8–10	52	43	5
September 19–21	50	47	3
October 6–8	55	42	3
October 10–12	56	40	4
October 24–26	53	42	5
November 3–5	54	43	3
November 14–16	50	47	3
December 5–7	55	43	2
December 11–14	56	41	3
December 15–16	63	34	3

Table 4.3 continues

Table 4.3 continued

DATE	APPROVE %	DISAPPROVE %	NO OPINION %
2004			
January 2–5	60	35	5
January 9–11	59	38	3
January 12–15	53	44	4
Jan. 29–Feb. 1	49	48	3
February 6–8	52	44	4
February 9–12	51	46	3
February 16–17	51	46	3
March 5–7	49	48	3
March 8–11	50	47	3
March 26–28	53	44	3
April 5–8	52	45	3
April 16–18	52	45	3
May 2–4	49	48	3
May 7–9	46	51	3
May 21–23	47	49	4
June 3–6	49	49	2
June 21–23	48	49	3
July 8–11	47	49	4
July 19–21	49	47	4
July 30–August 1	48	49	3
August 9–11	51	46	3
August 23–25	49	47	4
September 3–5	52	46	2
September 13–15	52	45	3
September 24–26	54	44	2
October 1–3	50	48	2
October 9–10	47	49	4
October 11–14	48	49	3
October 14–16	51	47	2
October 22–24	51	46	3
October 29–31	48	47	4
November 7–10	53	44	3
November 19–21	55	42	3
December 5–8	53	44	3
December 17–19	49	46	5
2005			
January 3–5	52	44	4
January 7–9	52	44	4

Table 4.3 continues

Table 4.3 continued

DATE	APPROVE %	DISAPPROVE %	NO OPINION %
January 14–16	51	46	3
February 4–6	57	40	3
February 7–10	49	48	3
February 25–27	52	45	3
March 7–10	52	44	4
March 18–20	52	44	4
March 21–23	45	49	4
April 1–2	48	48	4
April 4–7	50	45	5
April 18–21	48	49	3
April 28–May 1	48	49	3
May 2–5	50	45	5
May 20–22	46	50	4
May 23–26	48	47	5
June 6–8	47	49	4
June 16–19	47	51	2
June 24–26	45	53	2
June 29–30	46	51	3
July 7–10	49	48	3
July 22–24	49	48	3
July 25–28	44	51	5
August 5–7	45	51	4
August 8–11	45	51	4
August 22–25	40	56	4
August 28–30	45	52	3
September 8–11	46	51	3
September 12–15	45	52	3
September 16–18	40	58	2
September 26–28	45	50	5
October 13–16	39	58	3
October 21–23	42	55	3
October 24–26	41	56	3
October 28–30	41	56	3
November 7–10	40	55	5
November 11–13	37	60	3
November 17–20	38	57	5
December 5–8	43	52	5
December 9–11	42	55	3
December 16–18	41	56	3
December 19–22	43	53	4

Table 4.3 continues

Table 4.3 continued

2006

January 6–8	43	54	3
January 9–12	43	53	4
January 20–22	43	54	3
February 6–9	42	55	3
February 9–12	39	56	3
February 28–March 1	38	60	2

Source: Gallup Poll.

achieve this vision (see Table 4.4). The public's image of Bush seemed consistent with the image of a straight-talking chief executive officer that he tried to project during the campaign. Contrary to the views of his most vocal detractors, majorities of the public felt that Bush understood complex issues, and only 26 percent of the public felt he was not working hard enough to be an effective president.[4] In light of the public's evaluations of his predecessor, it is worth noting that large majorities saw the new president as honest and trustworthy.

Positive evaluations of the president's personal characteristics proved to be important, because the April 20–22, 2001, Gallup poll showed that 52 percent of Americans considered leadership skills and vision to be the most important criterion for evaluating the president's job performance—compared to 36 percent who felt that the president's stance on issues was the most important criterion. Gallup found that a plurality of all key subgroups, including Bush's natural opponents of Democrats and liberals,

---

[4] Gallup poll, April 20–22, 2001.

TABLE 4.4

Evaluations of George W. Bush Characteristics and Qualities, First Two Years

Thinking about the following characteristics and qualities, please say whether you think it applies or doesn't apply to George W. Bush. How about [ROTATED]?

CHARACTERISTIC	2/9–11/01	4/20–22/01	10/5–6/01	4/29–5/1/02	7/26–28/02	1/10–12/03
			% SAYING APPLIES			
Is honest and trustworthy	64	67		77	69	70
Is a strong and decisive leader	61	60	75	77	70	76
Is tough enough for the job		68	68			
Can manage the government effectively	61		79	75	66	67
Shares your values	57	58		67	60	54
Inspires confidence	57	55	75		66	65
Cares about the needs of people like you	56	59	69	66	60	56
Understands complex issues	55	56	69	68	60	
Generally agrees with you on issues you care about	53		60	64		
Is a person you admire	49			64		
Keeps his promises		57				
Is sincere in what he says			84	76		
Provides good moral leadership				84		
Puts the country's interests ahead of his own political interests				72		
Is not a typical politician				54		

SOURCE: Gallup Poll.

assigned more importance to leadership skills and vision than to agreement on issues. The importance the public accorded the president's personal characteristics may partly explain why his overall job approval rating was higher than support for his job performance in the more specific policy-related areas.

Shortly after September 11, 2001, the public was even more positive about Bush as a person, and these evaluations held—even after two years of his presidency. Large majorities saw him as honest and trustworthy, strong and decisive, an effective manager, inspiring confidence, caring about average people and sharing their values, and as having a vision for the country.

Bush's overall approval also exceeded his approval on many specific issues. Table 4.5 presents results of four Gallup polls taken during his presidency. Focusing on the two polls in the pre-September 11, 2001, period, we see that the public rated the president most highly on the issues that were his highest priorities: taxes, education, and defense. It is reasonable to conclude that these issues were the most salient to the public in the early months of the Bush administration. Conversely, less than 50 percent of the public approved of his performance on Social Security, unemployment, abortion, the environment, and energy. These issues evidently were less salient in evaluations of the president.

Thus, President Bush appeared to be well positioned in his relations with the public early in his term. The public accorded him reasonably high levels of approval for his job performance, liked him as a person, and perceived him as having a wide range of positive personal characteristics that it valued in a chief executive. Ratings of his performance on issues were more mixed, but were positive on his priority issues.

TABLE 4.5
Issue Approval for George W. Bush, First Two Years

			% APPROVE		
ISSUE	4/20–22/01	7/10–11/01	3/22–24/02	7/26–28/02	1/10–12/03
Overall	62	57	79	69	58
Economy	55	54	65	52	53
Foreign Affairs	56	54	71	63	48
Defense	66		80		63
Education	62	63	63	62	57
Taxes	54	60	64		49
Budget deficit	52		51		43
Unemployment	47		57		
Environment	46	46	53		
Abortion	43		49		39
Energy	43	45	57		
Social Security		49	47		
Health Care			52	47	41

SOURCE: Gallup Poll.

As presidents perform their duties, citizens obtain more information and thus a more comprehensive basis for judging them. Moreover, as time passes, people may begin to perceive greater implications of presidential policies for their own lives. Overall, the president's approval held reasonably steady in the mid-50s, but had dipped to 51 percent in the Gallup poll that concluded on September 10, 2001 (Bill Clinton was at 47 percent approval at this point in his tenure). Things were not going well for the president.

As Congress resumed its session following its summer recess, Democrats were beginning to blame the president's tax cut for "defunding" the federal government and forcing Congress to spend the surplus provided by Social Security contributions. Policymakers were to have placed these funds in a "lock box," off limits for paying current expenses. At the same time, unemployment was climbing and news about the country's economic recession was more prominent in the media. The president's initiatives on education and funding for faith-based charities were stalled, and stories were circulating that opponents were thwarting Secretary of Defense Donald Rumsfeld's efforts to reform the U.S. defense posture.

The public was also giving the president low marks on the environment and energy (see the July 10–11, 2001, Gallup poll in Table 4.5). In March, the president made a series of environmental decisions that were widely viewed as pro-industry, including reversing a campaign pledge to seek a reduction in carbon dioxide emissions from power plants, rescinding Bill Clinton's regulations lowering level of arsenic acceptable in drinking water, rejecting the Kyoto accords, withdrawing the ban on building roads in 60 million acres of federal forests and limits on logging in those areas, and canceling higher efficiency standards for air conditioners. The White House also sought to permit drilling for oil in the Arctic National Wildlife Refuge. Then the administration launched a national energy policy that most commentators saw as emphasizing exploration and production rather than conservation and the development of alternative energy sources. The president played into stereotypes of conservative Republican former energy company executives being too cozy with special interests. In April, Gallup found that 63 percent of the public felt that big business had too much influence over the administration's decisions.[5]

THE RALLY

As Table 4.3 shows, the president stood at an unimpressive 51 percent approval in the Gallup poll that concluded on September 10, 2001. The terrorist attacks the next day provided the president an opportunity to remake his image and build a new relationship with the American people.

Within days (perhaps hours) of the attack, questions of the president's legitimacy or competence disappeared for most Americans in the outburst of patriotism for which the commander in chief served as the focal point. In a poll on September 11, *prior* to Bush's short nationwide address, a Gallup poll found 78 percent of Americans expressing confidence in Bush's ability to handle the situation. The September 14–15 Gallup poll showed 91 percent of Americans approving of the way the president was handling the response to the terrorist attacks—nearly a week *before* his address to a joint session of Congress. The ABC News/*Washington Post* poll on September 13 found the same level of approval.

Equally important, Americans overwhelmingly saw the president as rising to the occasion. After a shaky start, he performed well, confident, reassuring, and resolute. As R. W. Apple Jr., wrote

---

[5] Gallup poll, April 20–22, 2001.

in the *New York Times,* Bush "sought to console the bereaved, comfort the wounded, encourage the heroic, calm the fearful, and . . . rally the country for the struggle and sacrifices ahead."[6] There was no more talk of a stature gap in the presidency.

Following the September 11 terrorist attacks, approval of Bush's job performance soared to 86 percent (see Figure 4.1). This increase of 35 percentage points represents the largest rally effect ever recorded by the Gallup Poll. The second highest jump Gallup recorded in the past half-century was during the Gulf War, when approval of the president's father, George H. W. Bush, jumped by 20 percentage points after he launched Operation Desert Storm in January 1991.

The surge in support was not limited to the president's overall approval. In addition to the 91 percent approval of the way Bush was handling the events surrounding the terrorist attacks, almost nine in ten Americans expressed confidence in the U.S. government's ability to protect its citizens from future attacks. The administration also benefited in another way from the rally around the president. Although Americans overwhelmingly blamed Osama bin Laden and other countries for the terrorist attacks, a majority also blamed airport security, the CIA, and the FBI. Forty-five percent blamed the Clinton administration, but only 34 percent blamed the Bush administration.[7]

Shortly after September 11, the public saw Bush in a new light. Large majorities saw him as sincere, strong and decisive, an

---

[6] R. W. Apple Jr., "After the Attacks: Assessment: President Seems to Gain Legitimacy," *New York Times,* September 16, 2001, p. A1.
[7] Gallup poll, September 14–15, 2001.

FIGURE 4.1

George W. Bush Job Approval

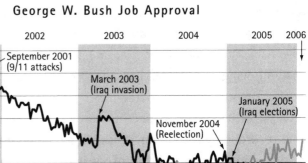

Source: Gallup Poll.

effective manager, inspiring confidence, caring about average people, and understanding complex issues (see Table 4.4). The following spring, the public still saw his personal characteristics and qualities in a very positive light.

The president's overall job approval level rose another 4 percentage points in the September 21–22, 2001, Gallup poll, reaching 90 percent. This approval rating was one point higher than the previous high point, registered by his father at the end of hostilities in the Persian Gulf War.[8]

---

[8] Gallup poll, February 28–March 3, 1991.

The rally for Bush was based on changes in the evaluations of Democrats and Independents. Republicans have accorded the president strong support from his first days in office, typically providing more than 90 percent approval. Thus, there was little potential for Republicans to rally.[9] The potential was much greater for Democrats and Independents, only a minority of whom (44 percent for Independents and 27 percent for Democrats) approved of his performance before the terrorist attacks. Immediately afterwards, their approval levels rose to more than 80 percent.

Between September 11, 2001, and the end of March 2002, the president maintained the approval of more than 79 percent of the public, a level unprecedented in the past half century. High evaluations of his performance on defense and foreign policy issues undoubtedly drove the president's high overall approval. However, his impressive approval levels seem to have had a halo effect, increasing his support on unrelated issues as well. The results of the March 22–24, 2002, Gallup poll (see Table 4.5) show that the public's evaluation of Bush's handling of issues rose substantially not only for defense and foreign affairs, but also for the economy, unemployment, energy, and the environment. He maintained the strong support he had previously achieved on education and taxes. In that same poll, the president received 86 percent approval for his performance on preventing terrorism in the United States and also for fighting terrorism abroad. Seventy-two percent of the public approved of his handling of the Middle East.

---

[9] On this point, see George C. Edwards III and Tami Swenson, "Who Rallies? The Anatomy of a Rally Event," *Journal of Politics* 59 (February 1997): 200–212.

The terrorist attacks and the resulting war on terrorism's dominance of the public agenda, then, had the perverse consequence of solving several intractable problems facing the president. After September 11, the recession gave way as a news story to terrorism and preparation to wage war in Afghanistan. Later, the president could lay blame for economic problems at the feet of Osama bin Laden and his supporters. Everyone seemed to forget about the Social Security lock box, as Congress raced to provide whatever was needed to aid the victims of terrorism and to fight terrorists abroad. When consensual policy dominates the political landscape, presidents do well in the polls.

The president's approval ratings may have also inoculated Bush from the public blaming him for bad news. For example, in January 2002, only 20 percent of the public blamed the Bush administration "a lot" or "fairly much" for the current recession.[10] In May 2002, most people agreed with the administration's contention that the information available to it prior to September 11 was not sufficient to prevent the terrorist attacks on the World Trade Center and Pentagon.[11] Bush's defense of his failure to file notification of his sale of Harken stock on time and of the accounting practices at Harken seemed to put the story to rest.

AFTER THE RALLY

Although the rally that began on September 11, 2001, was the most sustained in modern times, its decay was inevitable. Bush's approval ratings gradually declined, remaining above 80 percent

[10] Gallup poll, January 11–14, 2002.
[11] Gallup poll, May 20–22, 2002.

until March 2002, above 70 percent until July 2002, and above 60 percent until January 2003. Americans seemed to be growing uneasy amid terrorism warnings, a stagnant economy, and the failures of prominent institutions, including the FBI, CIA, major corporations, and the Catholic Church.

The Gallup poll of June 3–6, 2002, found that the president's approval had dropped 7 points in a week, and its poll of June 21–23 showed only one-third of the public believed the United States was winning the war on terrorism. The drop in the public's approval of the president's performance on foreign affairs, the economy, and health care reflected these concerns.[12] We saw in Chapter 2 that the president suffered serious declines in the percentage of the public who felt he possessed strong leadership qualities, could deal wisely with international crises, or could negotiate effectively with world leaders.[13] Clear majorities of the public also viewed business as having too much influence on Bush and his administration and the administration as more interested in protecting the interests of large corporations than those of ordinary Americans. The public was split on whether the president or his aides were in charge of the White House.[14] As in the previous summer, the administration seemed to be adrift.

The decline in Bush's overall job approval rating during this period was the result in large part in his losses among those who had rallied earlier: Democrats and, to a lesser degree, Independents. By the end of the summer, the president had fallen to 50 percent approval among Democrats and 56 percent among

---

[12] Gallup poll, July 26–28, 2002.
[13] CBS News/*New York Times* poll, June 14–18, 2002.
[14] CBS News/*New York Times* poll, July 13–16, 2002.

Independents. On the other hand, the president's ratings among Republicans remained in the 90s.[15]

In August, the drift continued. The administration was finding it difficult to recruit allies for fighting Saddam Hussein and faced vocal criticism in the United States and abroad for its unilateral approach to Iraq. After the president asked both the UN and Congress for backing to use force to change the Iraqi regime, the public began moving behind the president and his approval ratings reversed some of the losses sustained over the summer.

In sum, having drifted down in the Gallup Poll as far as 65 percent in August (lower in the polls of a number of other organizations), Bush's overall approval ratings increased slightly in September. As the spotlight turned from the economy, corporate malfeasance, and failures in the intelligence community to responses to the Iraqi threat against the United States, the president's approval ratings stabilized and even increased slightly. They remained in the high 50s and 60s until the president announced the commencement of the Iraq war.

A SECOND RALLY

Following the onset of U.S. military action in Iraq in March 2003, Bush experienced another approval rally, as the public rallied behind the commander in chief. His 58 percent mid-March job approval rating increased to 71 percent a week later. This

---

[15] Gallup poll, August 19–21, 2002.

rally did not have the staying power of the post-September 11 rally, however.

Widespread looting and chaos occurred in the immediate aftermath of the U.S. victory in Iraq. Then terrorist incidents and a broader insurgency in Iraq accelerated through the summer of 2003. In addition, it became increasingly clear that the Iraqis had no weapons of mass destruction. Bush's approval rating dropped to a low of 50 percent in September 2003, shortly after his nationally televised address in which he reported on the difficulty of the situation in Iraq, and asked Congress to support an additional $87 billion in funding for the U.S. efforts there and in Afghanistan. This was the first time he had fallen below his approval level of 51 percent on September 10, 2001.

On December 13, 2003, the U.S. military captured former Iraqi dictator Saddam Hussein, who had fled Baghdad at the start of the military action. This success buoyed the president's approval and he jumped to 63 percent. However, by the end of January 2004, when the Democratic presidential nomination contests dominated the news, Bush's approval hit a new low of 49 percent. The highly charged partisanship of the presidential election year kept Bush around the 50 percent mark during 2004, ranging from a low of 46 percent in May, following reports of Iraqi prisoner abuse, to 54 percent in September, just prior to the presidential debates. Bush had a 48 percent job approval rating as he was reelected, and got a slight "victory bounce" to 53 percent (and subsequently to 55 percent) after he defeated John Kerry.

Not only did the president receive much less of a bounce in his overall approval ratings following the war in Iraq than following the September 11 attacks, but his role as commander in chief also had less of a halo effect on evaluations of his performance in other presidential roles. By the fall of 2003, the public's evaluations of his handling the economy and foreign affairs reached the lowest levels of his presidency to that time. A CBS/*New York Times* poll found that only 45 percent of the public had confidence in his ability to deal with an international crisis and only 40 percent had confidence in his economic decisions. Half the public thought the administration's policies had made employment worse, and more than half thought the nation's economy and U.S. relations with its allies were worse than when he took office. Only 41 percent thought the war was worth the cost.[16]

Bush's overall approval continued to exceed his approval on many specific issues. Comparing the figures in Table 4.6 with those in Table 4.5 shows that in general, approval of the president's performance in specific policy areas fell over his tenure. Shortly before his second inauguration in January 2005, most people did not approve of his performance in foreign affairs, taxes, the deficit, the environment, Social Security, health care, and Iraq. He achieved only a 50 percent approval rating on the economy. Only on the issues of terrorism (58 percent) and education (52 percent) did the president obtain the approval of a majority of the public.

In the nearly two years remaining in his first term following the war in Iraq, the public also evaluated the president's personal characteristics more critically (Table 4.7). It was less likely to view him as honest and trustworthy, as strong and decisive, or as sharing its values—although majorities still held these perceptions.

---

[16] CBS News/*New York Times* poll, September 28–October 1, 2003.

TABLE 4.6
Issue Approval for George W. Bush, 2003–2005

ISSUE	8/25–26/03	1/2–5/04	6/3–6/04	1/7–9/05	6/24–26/05	9/16–18/05
	% APPROVE					
Overall	59	60	49	52	45	40
Economy	45	54	41	50	41	35
Foreign Affairs	55	58	44	47		38
Education	52	56		52		
Taxes	52	57		49		
Budget deficit	39			32		
Environment				49		
Energy	47		33		36	
Social Security				41	31	
Health Care	43	43		40	34	
Iraq	57	61	41	42	40	32
Terrorism	66		56	58	55	

SOURCE: Gallup Poll.

TABLE 4.7

Evaluations of Bush Characteristics and Qualities, 2003–2004

Thinking about the following characteristics and qualities, please say whether you think it applies or doesn't apply to George W. Bush. How about [ROTATED]?

			% SAYING APPLIES	
CHARACTERISTIC	4/5–6/03	6/27–29/03	11/14–16/03	2/16–17/04
Has clear plan for solving country's problems		50		42
Is honest and trustworthy	73	65	59	55
Is a strong and decisive leader	80	75	66	65
Shares your values			53	52
Inspires confidence	70			
Cares about the needs of people like you	65	57	49	
Generally agrees with you on issues you care about			48	47
Is a person you admire		54	50	

SOURCE: Gallup Poll.

Worse for Bush was the fact that majorities of the public did not admire him or believe he cared about typical people, had clear plans for solving the country's problems, or agreed with them on issues they cared about.

BUSH FIRST TERM IN HISTORICAL PERSPECTIVE

George W. Bush's first-term approval ratings were of historical proportions. According to the Gallup Poll's calculations, Bush's 67 percent average approval in his first year in office is second only to Kennedy's and Eisenhower's for a complete first year in office among presidents since Truman (see Table 4.8).

TABLE 4.8
First Year Average Job Approval Ratings, Truman to G. W. Bush

PRESIDENT	DATES	AVERAGE APPROVAL
Truman*	4/20/45–1/19/46	77 %
Kennedy	1/20/61–1/19/62	76
Johnson*	11/22/63–1/19/64	76
Eisenhower	1/20/53–1/19/54	69
George W. Bush	1/20/01–1/19/02	67
George H. W. Bush	1/20/89–1/19/90	66
Carter	1/20/77–1/19/78	62
Nixon	1/20/69–1/19/70	61
Reagan	1/20/81–1/19/82	57
Ford*	1/20/74–1/19/75	51
Clinton	1/20/93–1/19/94	49

* Substantially abbreviated first year because of the death or resignation of predecessor.
SOURCE: Gallup Poll.

The 67 percent job approval rating for his first year in office and the 71 percent rating in his second year were also among the highest for any year, as is shown in Table 4.9. Since the tenure of John F. Kennedy, only the president's father, with a 70 percent approval rating in his third year in office, had a better full year than did George W. Bush in 2001; and no president during that period had higher approval than Bush had in his second year. Bush's

TABLE 4.9
Top Yearly Averages of Presidential Job Approval

PRESIDENT	DATE	AVERAGE APPROVAL
Truman*	4/12/45–1/19/46	77%
Kennedy	1/20/61–1/19/62	76
Johnson*	11/22/63–1/19/64	76
Johnson	1/20/64–1/19/65	73
Eisenhower	1/20/55–1/19/56	72
Kennedy	1/20/62–1/19/63	72
Eisenhower	1/20/56–1/19/57	72
G. W. Bush	1/20/02–1/19/03	71
G. Bush	1/20/91–1/19/92	70
Eisenhower	1/20/53–1/19/54	69
G. W. Bush	1/20/01–1/19/02	67
G. Bush	1/20/90–1/19/91	67
G. Bush	1/20/89–1/19/90	66
Eisenhower	1/20/54–1/19/55	65
Johnson	1/20/65–1/19/66	65
Eisenhower	1/20/59–1/19/60	64

* Substantially abbreviated first year because of the death or resignation of predecessor.
SOURCE: Gallup Poll.

second-year average was easily the highest, since Truman, for any president's second year in office. The previous best second years were his father's 67 percent average in 1990–1991, Eisenhower's 65 percent in 1954–1955, and Johnson's 65 percent in 1965–1966.

Only Harry S Truman's 87 percent in the spring of 1945 following Franklin D. Roosevelt's death bettered the approval rating of 86 percent for the fourth quarter of Bush's presidency (extending from October 20 to January 19). In recent times, only the president's father's 83 percent rating for the first quarter of 1991, which coincided with the successful conclusion of the Persian Gulf War, comes close to Bush's fourth quarter average.

Overall, Bush averaged a 62 percent job approval rating during his first term, the fourth best among recent presidents, and the second best for a full term, behind Eisenhower's 70 percent for 1953–1957 (see Table 4.10). Gallup has approval data for 62 presidential "years." Bush's 67 percent in his first year rates as the eleventh best yearly average, his second year average of 71 percent is the eighth best, and his third year score of 60 percent is the twenty-seventh best. His 50 percent average for his fourth year ranks only thirty-ninth, however.[17]

THE SECOND TERM

George W. Bush began his second term with considerably less popular support than other recent incumbent presidents did after their reelection. Although Bush received a modest five-point

---

[17] Jeffrey M. Jones, "Bush Averages 62% Approval in First Term," *Gallup News Service,* January 19, 2005.

TABLE 4.10
Approval Averages for Presidential Terms

PRESIDENT	TERM (DATES)	AVERAGE APPROVAL
Lyndon Johnson	First (1963–1965)*	74.2%
John Kennedy	First (1961–1963)*	70.1
Dwight Eisenhower	First (1953–1957)	69.6
George W. Bush	First (2001–2005)	62.1
George H. W. Bush	First (1989–1993)	60.9
Bill Clinton	Second (1997–2001)	60.7
Dwight Eisenhower	Second (1957–1961)	60.5
Harry Truman	First (1945–1949)*	56.9
Richard Nixon	First (1969–1973)	55.8
Ronald Reagan	Second (1985–1989)	55.3
Lyndon Johnson	Second (1965–1969)	50.3
Ronald Reagan	First (1981–1985)	50.3
Bill Clinton	First (1993–1997)	49.5
Gerald Ford	First (1974–1977)*	47.2
Jimmy Carter	First (1977–1981)	45.5
Harry Truman	Second (1949–1953)	35.4
Richard Nixon	Second (1973–1974)*	34.4

* Partial term
SOURCE: Jeffrey M. Jones, "Bush Averages 62% Approval in First Term," *Gallup News Service*, January 19, 2005.

bounce in his approval rating after his election in 2004, his 53 percent rating was actually the lowest of any of the last seven presidents who won election while serving as president in the first poll conducted after their elections (see Table 1.1).

The president also began his second term in office without a clear mandate to lead the nation. Only 45 percent of respondents in a January 2005 *Washington Post*/ABC News poll said they preferred that the country go in the direction that Bush wanted to lead it. Fifty-eight percent of the public disapproved of his handling of the situation in Iraq, and only 44 percent said the war was worth fighting. A majority of Americans expressed disapproval of Bush on other key issue areas. A slight majority, 52 percent, disapproved of the way he was handling the economy, and half or more were also dissatisfied with the way Bush dealt with the budget deficit (58 percent disapprove), immigration (54 percent), and health care (51 percent). The president received higher marks on the key issue of terrorism, where a 61 percent majority approved of the job he was doing. In addition, 56 percent expressed satisfaction with his education policies. The public was divided on the president's handling of environmental issues, foreign affairs, and taxes.[18]

The first poll after the president's inauguration in January 2005 showed him at 57 percent, perhaps with some help from the successful Iraqi elections that month. However, approval dropped 8 percentage points in a Gallup poll taken in the next four days (see Chapter 3). Two months after the inauguration, his approval stood at 45 percent, possibly as a result of the public's disapproval of his support for intervening in the Terri Schiavo case. Polls found large majorities of Americans opposed to the intervention by Congress and the president, and the Gallup poll found 53 percent of Americans disapproved of the way Bush has handled the Schiavo situation.[19]

---

[18] Richard Morin and Dan Balz, "Political Divisions Persist After Election," *Washington Post,* January 18, 2005. *Washington Post*/ABC News poll, January 12–16, 2005.
[19] Gallup poll, April 1–2, 2005.

The public was also harsh in its evaluation of Bush as a person. When asked in a February 16–21 Pew Research Center poll to describe the president in one word, 42 percent of the respondents chose a negative term like "arrogant," "incompetent," or "idiot." Thirty-four percent chose a positive term like "honest," "integrity," or "leader."

By May, the president was doing even worse. Pew found Americans critical of the president's job performance in many policy areas, but negative opinions of his handling of the economy and Iraq were doing the most damage to his overall approval rating, which now stood at only 43 percent. Just 35 percent of the public approved of Bush's handling of the economy, and only 37 percent approved of his handling of Iraq and 38 percent his handling of foreign policy. His positive ratings on energy and Social Security were even lower, at 31 and 29 percent, respectively. Only for his handling of terrorists threats did a majority (57 percent) of the public approve of his job performance.[20]

In June, the disjuncture between the administration's upbeat rhetoric on Iraq and the realities of months of turmoil, insurgent attacks, and casualties took a serious toll on the public's support for the president, especially among Independents. A major poll found for the first time that more than half of the American public believed that the war in Iraq had not made the United States safer. In addition, nearly three-quarters of Americans said the number of casualties in Iraq was unacceptable, while two-thirds said the U.S. military was bogged down and nearly six in ten said the war was not worth fighting. Barely half the public approved of Bush's

---

[20] Pew Research Center for the People and the Press poll, May 11–15, 2005.

handling of the campaign against terrorism, which had been his strongest suit. Fewer than four in ten Americans approved of the president's handling of Iraq, foreign policy, and the economy.[21] In addition, partisan polarization hit a new high. Although 89 percent of Republicans approved of Bush's handling of his job as president—and just 10 percent disapproved—only 11 percent of Democrats approved of his performance in office and 88 percent disapproved. Among Independents, 37 percent approved and 58 percent disapproved.[22]

Things did not improve by August 2005, despite the president's success with the congressional passage of a comprehensive energy bill and the Central American Free Trade Agreement. The president's approval ratings reached a new low, 40 percent, weighed down by anger over Iraq and concerns about lackluster wage increases and stubbornly high gasoline prices. Gallup found that 57 percent of the public felt that the war in Iraq made the United States *more* vulnerable to terrorism—directly contrary to the president's main justification for the war—and 56 percent thought the United States occupation was going badly.[23]

To make matters worse for the president, Hurricane Katrina hit the Gulf Coast at the end of August. Natural disasters and other tragedies offer both opportunities and risks for a president. They offer the opportunity to articulate the nation's sense of loss, reflect its innate compassion, provide reassurance, and demonstrate decisive leadership. If the leader fails to rise to the occasion, a national spotlight illuminates the failure for all to see—and judge.

---

[21] *Washington Post*/ABC News poll of June 2–5, 2005; CBS News/*New York Times* poll of June 10–15, 2005.
[22] Gallup poll, June 24–26, 2005.
[23] Gallup poll, August 5–7, 2005.

Americans were not satisfied with the response of the federal government to the tragic lose of life and property resulting from Katrina. We saw in Chapter 1 how the White House mishandled both the implementation of disaster assistance and the public relations surrounding it. Despite five trips to the hurricane-ravaged Gulf Coast, a nationally televised speech on the subject, and pledges of billions of dollars to help Louisiana, Mississippi, and Alabama recover from Hurricane Katrina, Gallup found that in mid-September, only 41 percent of the public approved of Bush's response to Hurricane Katrina, and only 42 percent felt that his efforts were motivated by sincere concern for the victims whereas 56 percent viewed his response as motivated by political reasons.[24]

The slow federal response to the hurricane also increased—or confirmed—public doubts about the Bush administration's capacity to deal with pressing problems. Later in September, 56 percent of Americans said they were now less confident about the government's ability to respond to a terrorist attack or natural disaster, and 63 percent said they were uneasy about his ability to make the right decisions about the war in Iraq.[25] Only 47 percent of the public felt the president was a person who displayed good judgment in a crisis.[26] It is ironic that by February 2006 the public had slightly more confidence in the UN than in the president's ability to deal with the issue of Iran's nuclear aspirations.[27]

Those general impressions of ineffectiveness extended across the board to the appraisal of Bush's handling of particular issues. As Table 4.6 shows, by September only 38 percent of the public

[24] Gallup poll, September 16–18, 2005.
[25] *New York Times*/CBS News poll, September 9–13, 2005.
[26] Gallup poll, September 8–11, 2005.
[27] Gallup poll, February 9–12, 2006.

approved of his handling of foreign affairs, 35 percent approved of his handling of the economy, and 32 percent approved of his handling the situation in Iraq. Only 22 percent approved of his handling of gas prices.[28]

By January 2006, nearly two-thirds of Americans said things had gotten worse in the country during Bush's tenure, and only 35 percent were satisfied with the way things were going in the United States.[29] Table 4.11 shows that Bush had regained the approval of a slim majority of the public on his handling of terrorism, but he was nowhere close to enjoying majority approval on a range of other important issues.

Bush's image among Americans suffered not only in evaluations of the way he handled his job, but in his personal characteristics as well. Perhaps the most positive image of the president has been that of a strong and decisive leader. By mid-September 2005, only 49 percent of the public agreed with this characterization, only 47 percent said he was honest and trustworthy, and only 42 percent said he cared about people like them (Table 4.12). Despite a sustained public relations effort, he made little headway in improving these perceptions by the following January.

The issue of honesty was especially troubling for the White House, because Bush had campaigned on a platform of restoring integrity to the presidency. However, by the end of October 2005, amid a growing focus on alleged ethical lapses in the administration, most notably the indictment of Vice President Cheney's chief of staff, "Scooter" Libby, 43 percent of the public felt that the level of ethics and honesty in the federal government had *fallen*

---

[28] Gallup poll, September 8–11, 2005.
[29] Gallup poll, January 20–22, 2006.

TABLE 4.11

Issue Approval for George W. Bush, 2006

ISSUE	% APPROVE	
	1/20–22	2/6–9
Overall	43	42
Terrorism	52	54
Problems Caused by Hurricane Katrina	41	
Economy	39	40
Foreign Affairs		39
Iraq	39	38
Energy		30
Corruption in Government	28	
Health Care	31	27
Immigration	25	

SOURCE: Gallup Poll.

during Bush's presidency. A majority of the public said the administration deliberately misled the country in making its case for war with Iraq,[30] and nearly two-thirds (including 91 percent of Democrats, 73 percent of Independents, and 28 percent of Republicans) declared that the Bush administration "generally misleads the American public on current issues to achieve its own ends."[31] It

[30] *Washington Post*/ABC News poll, October 30–November 2, 2005. At about the same time, a Pew Research Center poll (November 3–6, 2005) found that 43 percent of the public thought that the United States and British leaders were mostly lying when they claimed that Iraq possessed weapons of mass destruction; and a Gallup poll (October 28–30, 2005) found that 53 percent of the public felt Bush "definitely misled" the public about weapons of mass destruction. See also the *Washington Post*/ABC News poll, December 2–6, 2005, and Gallup poll of January 20–22, 2006.
[31] Harris Interactive poll, November 8–13, 2005, reported in "Majority Believe White House Misleads Public, Poll Shows," *Wall Street Journal Online*, November 23, 2005.

TABLE 4.12

Evaluations of Bush Characteristics and Qualities, 2005–2006

Thinking about the following characteristics and qualities, please say whether you think it applies or doesn't apply to George W. Bush. How about about [ROTATED]?

| | % SAYING APPLIES | | | | | | |
CHARACTERISTIC	1/14–16/05	4/1–2/05	7/22–24/05	8/28–30/05	9/16–18/05	1/20–22/06
Is honest and trustworthy	56	56	54	51	47	49
Is a strong and decisive leader	61		62	60	49	51
Shares your values		55	50	46		44
Inspires confidence	50			47		
Cares about the needs of people like you	45	53		44	42	44
Is a person you admire	45			43		

SOURCE: Gallup Poll.

is not surprising that the president's overall approval level fell to 37 percent in mid-November.[32]

The White House responded to the president's fall in the polls with an aggressive public relations effort, but by March 2006, he was only at 38 percent approval. Although 82 percent of Republicans approved of his performance as president, only a fourth (27 percent) of Independents and hardly any Democrats (a mere 10 percent) did so.[33] Once having lost the trust of the American people, it is difficult to regain it.

The tragic events of September 11, 2001, propelled George W. Bush to levels of public approval unmatched in the lifetimes of most Americans. However, the insurgency in Iraq, stagnant wages, and high gasoline prices, reinforced by mishandling relief efforts in the wake of Hurricane Katrina and a series of ethical issues, undermined public confidence in the president and his policies and brought the president down in the polls. He averaged only 46 percent approval in the first year of his second term.

The ultimate goal of obtaining the public's approval is moving Congress to support the president's legislative program. In Chapter 5, we examine Bush's relations with Congress and the impact his approval levels have on Congress.

[32] Gallup poll, November 11–13, 2005.
[33] Gallup poll, February 28–March 1, 2006.

CHAPTER 5

Leading in Congress

Richard Neustadt focused his landmark work on *Presidential Power* on the strategic level of power. As he put it,

> *There are two ways to study "presidential power." One way is to focus on the tactics . . . of influencing certain men in given situations. . . . The other way is to step back from tactics on those "givens" and to deal with influence in more strategic terms: what is its nature and what are its sources? . . . Strategically, [for example] the question is not how he masters Congress in a peculiar instance, but what he does to boost his chance for mastery in any instance . . .* [1]

This chapter follows Neustadt's lead in focusing on the Bush administration's political strategy with respect to its relations with Congress. The forty-third president, more than most of his predecessors, has focused on developing and implementing a strategy

---

[1] Richard E. Neustadt, *Presidential Power and the Modern Presidents* (New York: Free Press, 1990), 4.

for governing. We have already seen that the White House's core governing strategy has been to go public, with the goal of obtaining public support to use to persuade Congress to support its initiatives. In this chapter, I focus on the impact of this strategy as well as other key elements of the administration's relations with Congress. Because the president's terms occurred in quite different contexts, I focus separately on the second term at the end of the chapter.

ASSESSING STRATEGIC POSITION

The early months of a new presidency represent the most important period for establishing the tone and character of the White House's relationship with Congress. It is the time of closest scrutiny and the greatest vulnerability to making major mistakes. Taking the right steps early and avoiding errors can lay the foundation for a productive working relationship. Actions taken early create lasting impressions.

The first step a new administration should take to ensure success with Congress is to assess accurately its strategic position so it understands the potential for change and will not overreach or underachieve. Presidents must largely play the hands that the public deals them through its electoral decisions on the presidency and Congress and its evaluations of the chief executive's handling of his job.[2] Presidents are rarely in a position to augment substantially their political capital, especially when just taking office.

---

[2] See George C. Edwards III, *At the Margins: Presidential Leadership of Congress* (New Haven, CT: Yale University Press, 1989).

The early periods of new administrations most clearly etched on our memories as notable successes are those in which presidents properly identified and exploited conditions for change. When Congress first met in special session in March 1933 after Franklin D. Roosevelt's inauguration, it rapidly passed the new president's request for bills to control the resumption of banking, repeal Prohibition, and effect government economies. This is all FDR originally planned for Congress to do; he expected to reassemble the legislature when permanent and more constructive legislation was ready. Yet the president found a situation ripe for change, and he decided to exploit this favorable environment and strike repeatedly with hastily drawn legislation before sending Congress home. This period of intense activity came to be known as the Hundred Days.

Lyndon Johnson also knew that his personal leadership could not sustain congressional support for his policies. He realized that the assassination of President Kennedy and the election of 1964 provided him a unique chance to pass his Great Society legislation and moved immediately to exploit it. Similarly, the Reagan administration recognized that the perceptions of a mandate and the dramatic elevation of Republicans to majority status in the Senate provided it with a window of opportunity to effect major changes in public policy, but that it had to concentrate its focus and move quickly before the environment became less favorable. Moreover, within a week of the March 30, 1981, assassination attempt on Reagan, Michael Deaver convened a meeting of other high-ranking aides at the White House to determine how best to take advantage of the new political capital the shooting had created.

If the White House misreads its strategic position, the president may begin his tenure with embarrassing failures in dealing with Congress. Moreover, the greater the breadth and complexity of the policy change a president proposes, the more opposition it is likely to engender—and thus the stronger the president's strategic position must be to succeed. In an era when a few opponents can effectively tie up bills, the odds are clearly against the White House.

Bill Clinton overestimated the extent of change that a president elected with a minority of the vote could make, especially when the public is dubious and well-organized interest groups are fervently opposed. Nevertheless, the president proposed without Republican support perhaps the most sweeping, complex prescriptions for controlling the conduct of state governments, employers, drug manufacturers, doctors, hospitals, and individuals in American history. There was insufficient foundation for change of this magnitude. The consequences of the bill's failure were greater than disappointment, however. Because Clinton declared health care reform to be the cornerstone of his efforts to change public policy, his handling of the bill became a key indicator of the administration's competency at governing. The bill's death throes occurred only a few months before the 1994 elections, the greatest midterm electoral disaster for the Democrats since the Truman administration.

George W. Bush took office after one of the closest elections in American history. The highly unusual, protracted denouement of the election and the truncated transition period of only 38 days between the resolution of the election and the inauguration—

about half the normal time for a shift in power—had the potential to turn the transition into a circus and undermine the new president's chances of success.

Bush received neither a majority nor even a plurality of the vote, and many (mostly Democrats) saw his victory as illegitimate, because he received more than a half-million fewer votes than Al Gore and because of the peculiar circumstances surrounding the determination of the winner of Florida's electoral votes. A Gallup poll taken just before the inauguration found that 31 percent of Americans thought Bush "won on a technicality" and 24 percent thought he "stole the election," while 45 percent said he "won fair and square." Thirty-eight percent of Americans still considered Gore to be the "real winner of the election."[3]

In light of the election results, the new president could not credibly claim a mandate from the people. Moreover, the Republicans lost seats in both houses of Congress, undermining any claim to presidential coattails. After the election, Republicans found themselves with only a very narrow majority in the House and required the vice president to break a 50-50 split in the Senate.

It is not difficult to imagine a president elected in such circumstances to move cautiously, seeking first to increase his legitimacy with the majority of the public who did not support him for president. Some commentators saw the potential for paralysis in Washington, and others (again, mostly Democrats) urged the president to act as if he were indeed paralyzed, proposing only policies that enjoyed bipartisan support.

---

[3] Gallup poll, January 15–16, 2001.

Neither the narrowness of his election nor the nature of its resolution intimidated Bush, however. Although his tone was one of reconciliation, he ignored those who urged him to strike a bipartisan posture and hold off on his major initiatives. According to author Bob Woodward, Vice President Dick Cheney remembered that "a notion of sort of a restrained presidency because it was such a close election, that lasted maybe 30 seconds. . . . We had an agenda, we ran on the agenda, we won the election—full speed ahead."[4] Reflecting a strategic perspective, Bush concluded that he would receive the same criticism from opponents regardless of the scope of his proposals, so he might as well make big demands and compromise only when necessary. "Big steps get more followers than small steps," said Ari Fleischer, the president's press secretary.[5]

The White House correctly understood that the one policy that both unified and energized Republicans was tax cuts. Although most congressional Democrats would oppose the cuts, a majority of the public, including Independents and even some Democrats, would support or at least tolerate them. Equally important, Congress could consider tax cuts, unlike most other major policies, under rules that prohibited a filibuster. Thus, a united, although slender, majority could prevail, and the president moved immediately to lower taxes dramatically.

In addition, congressional Republicans, who had not enjoyed unified control of the presidency and Congress for nearly half a century, were eager to govern. The overwhelmingly conservative

---

[4] Quoted in Bob Woodward, *Plan of Attack* (New York: Simon and Schuster, 2004), 28.
[5] Dana Milbank, "Bush Goes With the Bold Stroke: Outsize Proposals Key to Strategy—but Not Without Risk," *Washington Post*, January 9, 2003, p. A1.

ideology of members of the Republican caucus, especially in the House, made it easy for them to agree on shifting policy to the right, and they saw no reason to compromise with the Democrats if they did not have to. This attitude was consistent with Bush's, whose basic leadership strategy was to press for policies as close to his preferred outcomes as possible and only negotiate when absolutely necessary.

ACTING STRATEGICALLY

In addition to its core governing strategy of going public and its assessments of its strategic position, the Bush White House has been attentive to other key strategic elements in its relations with Congress. Among the most important are focusing on priorities, moving rapidly to exploit opportunities, setting the national agenda, and displaying tactical flexibility.

Setting Priorities

New presidents are wise to resist the temptations to try to deliver on all their campaign promises immediately following their elections and to accede to the many demands that interests make on a new administration. Instead, it is important to establish priorities among legislative proposals. In addition, because the Washington community pays disproportionate attention to the first major legislative initiatives, it is especially critical to choose early battles wisely.

If the president is not able to focus Congress's attention on his priority programs, they may become lost in the complex and overloaded legislative process. Congress needs time to digest what the president sends, to engage in independent analyses, and to schedule hearings and markups. Unless the president clarifies his priorities, Congress may put the proposals in a queue.

Setting priorities is also important because presidents and their staff can lobby effectively for only a few bills at a time. The president's political capital is inevitably limited, and it is sensible to focus on the issues he cares about most. Setting priorities early also can reduce intra-administration warfare over the essence of the administration.

President Carter was widely criticized for failing to set legislative priorities, especially in light of the scale, diversity, complexity, and controversial nature of his initial legislative program. Conversely, the Reagan administration knew it lacked the political capital to pass a broad program that would include divisive social issues. Thus, it enforced a rigorous focus on the president's economic plan, its priority legislation. By focusing its resources on its priorities, the administration succeeded in using the budget to pass sweeping changes in taxation and defense policy.

Karl Rove, the president's wide-ranging senior advisor, maintained that Bush campaigned on six key issues: tax cuts, education standards, military upgrades and a missile defense shield, federal support for faith-based charities, partial privatization of Social Security, and Medicare reforms and prescription drug coverage for seniors.[6] If these were Bush's priorities, he did a good job of focusing on them.

---

[6] Alexis Simendinger, "The Report Card They Asked For," *National Journal*, July 21, 2001, 2335.

First, the Bush White House made a clear choice of a large income tax cut as its highest legislative priority. This made good strategic sense for a conservative administration. The president and his advisors felt that the notable victory of enacting a major tax cut early in the administration would signal the administration's competence in governing while unifying the Republican party for the more difficult issues ahead. Equally important, by severely limiting the government's resources, cutting taxes would set the terms of debate for nearly all the policy debates that would follow and restrain the Democrats' ability to use the budget surplus for expansion of social welfare policies. Of course, engaging in a highly partisan fight over taxes early in the administration while simultaneously seeking bipartisan support on other issues may have had counterproductive consequences for future coalition building.

Tax cuts were not the administration's only priorities. Education reform, an overhaul of defense policy, and greater federal support for faith-based social welfare programs were also high on the list. The president not only spoke extensively about each initiative, but also went to considerable lengths to focus attention on each proposal in the early weeks of the administration. The faith-based initiative received attention in the week after the inauguration, followed in successive weeks by education, tax cuts, and defense.

In general, the George W. Bush White House rarely sends detailed legislation to Congress and takes clear stands only on a select group of issues. For example, in 2000, the last year of Bill Clinton's tenure, the Office of Management and Budget (OMB) issued formal statements of administration policy on 142 bills and resolutions. In 2004, OMB issued just 61 statements for Bush, and the White House took a stand on only 11 contentious issues that did not involve nominations and that the Senate decided on roll-call votes (and two of these were votes on ending debate). Thus, Bush saved his intervention for the issues he found most important for spending his time, energy, and political capital. In addition, by keeping a low profile, Bush avoided appearing overbearing to congressional Republicans. According to Rob Portman, who headed George H. W. Bush's congressional lobbying team from 1989 to 1991, the president "uses his direct influence selectively. I think that's important—you can wear out your welcome on the Hill."[7] Table 5.1 shows the number of presidential stands on roll-call votes in each house in Bush's first term.

As *Congressional Quarterly* reported at the end of his first term, "Overall, Bush's formula of remaining disengaged from Congress on many issues and using his political capital sparingly—but aggressively—has proven advantageous, allowing him to minimize his defeats."[8] In his first term, the president won more than 80 percent of the roll-call votes on which he took a stand in both the House and the Senate.

Even when he has taken stands, Bush typically has not taken a personal role in negotiating details of legislation until late in the consideration of a bill. On his priority issues, he has tended to focus on a few essentials, cede ground when necessary to reach his

---

[7] Joseph J. Schatz, "With a Deft and Light Touch, Bush Finds Ways to Win," *Congressional Quarterly Weekly Report*, December 11, 2004, 2900, 2903.
[8] Schatz, "With a Deft and Light Touch, Bush Finds Ways to Win," 2900.

TABLE 5.1
Nonunanimous Votes on which Bush Took a Stand

	NUMBER OF VOTES*	
YEAR	HOUSE	SENATE
2001	35	29
2002	32	18
2003	47	66
2004	27	17
2005	42	30

*On roll-call votes on which the winning side was supported by fewer than 80 percent of those voting.

ultimate objective, and rely on Republican leaders to keep the troops in line. The president was most involved with his major tax cut bills in 2001 and 2003 and the 2002 No Child Left Behind Act, all of which the White House largely initiated. On energy and a prescription drug benefit under Medicare, he provided encouragement to act while steering clear of details. Indeed, he backed away from the Medicare debate after facing criticism early in 2003 when a leak showed he was considering proposing that only seniors who moved to privately sponsored health care plans would get a drug benefit. The White House only made real push on Medicare in the final moments, and kept the president out of the process until the very end. It left the heavy lifting to the Republican leadership, who wanted to keep the president inoculated from conservative Republicans agitated over the huge expense of the bill. The president also stayed at the periphery of House-Senate negotiations on the 2004 intelligence bill for months and only intervened in the final weeks when success seemed attainable and after Republican leaders told him it was necessary.[9]

Moving Rapidly

Presidents must not only recognize the opportunities in their environment, devise a strategy for governing, and set priorities. To succeed with Congress, they must also move rapidly to exploit those opportunities. First-year proposals have a better chance of passing Congress than do those sent to the Hill later in an administration. Thus, the White House should be ready to send its priority legislation to Capitol Hill.

The failure to be ready to propose priority legislation may be costly. A policy vacuum existed in the approximately ten months between Bill Clinton's inauguration and the arrival of a complete health care reform proposal on Capitol Hill. In this vacuum, issues of relatively low priority, such as the gays in the military, received disproportionate attention in the press and may have cost the administration vital goodwill that it would need in its search for support for its cornerstone policy. In addition, the delay in producing a health care reform bill forced the president to raise it in the context of major expenditures of political capital in battles on behalf of his budget and NAFTA.

Despite a severely truncated transition, the Bush administration lost no time in sending priority bills to Congress. Proposals

---

[9] Richard E. Cohen, "Where's the Beef?" *National Journal,* September 20, 2003, 2866–2870; Elisabeth Bumiller, "Sharply Split House Passes Broad Medicare Overhaul; Forceful Lobbying by Bush," *New York Times,* November 23, 2003, 21; Schatz, "With a Deft and Light Touch, Bush Finds Ways to Win," 2903; Marilyn Werber Serafini, "A Prescription for Defeat," *National Journal,* August 30, 2003, 2612–2613.

for a large cut in income taxes, education reform, and increased support for faith-based charities went to Congress in short order. Specific changes in defense policy would take longer, but the White House launched an extensive review of the nation's defense posture.

The administration was not ready with proposals for all its priority issues, however. It deferred two very important items on the "big six" list. The White House delegated Social Security reform to a commission and postponed consideration of Medicare and a prescription drugs benefit. Given the disappearance of the general revenue budget surplus, the lack of consensus on these issues, and the president's limited political capital, the delays appear to be sensible strategic choices rather than evidence of disorganization or lethargy.

Influencing the Agenda

A major goal of every administration is dominating the political agenda. Usually this means focusing public attention on its priority issues and, if possible, keeping lower priority and potentially politically damaging issues off the agenda. The efforts of the White House to set priorities and focus on them helped to secure them a place on the national agenda. A study of the first 60 days of news coverage of the Bush and Clinton administrations found that Bush was more successful than Clinton was in focusing attention on his message. Each of the five major stories about Bush was on his priority initiatives, amounting to more than a third of all stories.[10]

---

[10] The Project For Excellence in Journalism, *The First 100 Days: How Bush Versus Clinton Fared In the Press*, 2001.

Setting priorities in the early weeks of a new administration is also important because during the first months in office the president has the greatest latitude in focusing on priority legislation. After the transition period, other interests have more influence on the White House agenda. Congress is quite capable of setting its own agenda and is unlikely to defer to the president for long. In addition, ongoing policies continually force decisions to the president's desk.

The Bush presidency was no exception to the challenge of controlling the national agenda. At the same time that the president was seeking support for his priority items, he had to engage in legislative battles on important issues such as campaign finance reform and a patients' bill of rights, and make a highly visible decision on stem cell research. In fact, he had to devote one of only two nationally televised addresses (scarce presidential resources) of his first seven months in office to the latter. Bush also inevitably became embroiled in the issue of U.S. Navy practice bombings in Vieques, Puerto Rico. More damaging were his responses to the unexpected energy shortage in California and potential environmental regulations, many of which his predecessor proposed. His and Vice President Cheney's energy plan was widely viewed as a sop to the oil and gas industry the two served, and many people saw the administration as having a weak commitment to environmental protection.

Responding to the terrorist attacks of September 11 immediately dominated the president's agenda. The emphasis on national unity in the weeks that followed the tragedy and the inevitable focus of the president's energies on national security limited the opportunities for him to push hard for his most contentious proposals.

At the same time, the terrorist attacks and the resulting war on terrorism's dominance of the public agenda had the perverse consequence of solving several intractable problems facing the president. As Congress resumed its session following its summer recess in 2001, Democrats were beginning to blame the president's tax cut for "defunding" the federal government and forcing Congress to spend the surplus provided by Social Security contributions. Congress was to have placed these funds in a "lock box," off limits for paying current expenses. At the same time, unemployment was climbing and news about the country's economic recession was becoming more prominent in the media. Opponents in Congress had stalled the president's initiatives on education and funding for faith-based charities, and the media was reporting stories that recalcitrants in the Pentagon were rolling Secretary of Defense Donald Rumsfeld in his efforts to reform the U.S. defense posture. After September 11, the media focused on terrorism and preparation to wage war in Afghanistan rather than the recession and the Social Security lock box. The attacks also allowed the president to blame economic problems on the terrorists.

When the president proposed a Department of Homeland Security on June 6, 2002, and when he made his case for regime change in Iraq later that summer, he had no difficulty dominating the nation's agenda. Issues dealing with the security of Americans, recently shocked by terrorist attacks, easily captured the media's and the public's attention. Even a looming war with Iraq, however, could not stop people from placing the sagging economy at the forefront of their concerns.[11]

The day after the president landed on the carrier *Abraham Lincoln* on May 1, 2003, under a banner proclaiming "Mission Accomplished," the White House began an effort to refocus its message—and thus the public's agenda—to domestic concerns, starting with the economy but extending to other issues such as tax cuts, health care, energy, and limits on lawsuit awards. As part of this effort, the president visited Oregon to promote his plan to expand logging as a way to thin forests and reduce the risk of fire. As the *New York Times* reported, "With two big forest fires darkening the skies near here, President Bush could hardly have had a more compelling setting today to promote his approach to reduce the risk of devastating blazes. He even took a bumpy helicopter ride for a close-up look, providing another of the made-for-television images that the White House used skillfully."[12] However, with television images and newspaper headlines focused on violence overseas and its implications for his leadership, the president's efforts to burnish his environmental credentials, court moderate voters, and focus the nation on domestic matters struggled for traction. The attention of the news media and much of the world remained riveted by the Middle East violence and the growing terrorist threat in Iraq. Thus, Bush was in many ways a hostage to his foreign policy and events abroad.

In the election year of 2004, the White House did not have a substantial legislative agenda, and Republicans in Congress felt it

---

[11] See, for example, Gallup polls, January 13–16, 2003; February 3–6, 2003; and March 3–5, 2003.

[12] Richard W. Stevenson, "Bush Tries to Put Focus on Domestic Policy, but Events Conspire Against Him," *New York Times*, August 22, 2003.

was better to coast and avoid prolonged contentious debates that might backfire. The agenda was reelection. Following the election, however, the president announced plans for a bold and large agenda for his second term, including reforming Social Security, tort litigation, and the tax code.

Once again, a range of large and small matters provided distractions from the president's agenda. In the spring of 2005, the fight over the Democrats' use of the filibuster to block judicial nominees threatened to overshadow Social Security reform, the centerpiece of the president's domestic agenda. Top Republicans recognized that partisan rancor and Democratic threats to slow the Senate's business to a crawl could make the already tense climate less conducive to a deal on Social Security. It also could divert the public's attention from the president's efforts to obtain their support. Nevertheless, Bush was committed to a fight over judicial nominees, on principle and because he was intent on making sure that Democrats could not use the filibuster to block Supreme Court nominations he expected to be making, so he could not downplay the issue.[13]

Bush had hoped to spend the summer of 2005 focusing on Social Security. Instead, he was forced to defend his economic record and war policies in the face of growing uneasiness among the public and Republicans in Congress. His poll numbers on his handling of Iraq had dropped to all-time lows (see Chapter 4), forcing him to take a more assertive and public role to reassure nervous Americans and Republican lawmakers about the White

---

[13] Richard W. Stevenson, "Fight on Judges Obscures Social Security," *New York Times,* May 20, 2005.

House plan for victory. Bush felt he needed to show voters he had a plan to lower gasoline prices and prevail in Iraq. "In the coming weeks, the president will sharpen his focus on the two big issues facing the American people: growing our economy and winning the war," announced White House Director of Communications Dan Bartlett.[14] Later in the summer, Washington fixated on the president's Supreme Court nomination and the controversy over whether White House deputy chief of staff and political director Karl Rove was the source of the leak to columnist Robert Novak that revealed a CIA operative's identity.

On a smaller scale, Bush had to rearrange his schedule from focusing on Social Security when he felt he needed to fly from Crawford to Washington to sign legislation affecting Terri Schiavo and later flying to Rome for the funeral of Pope John Paul II. When he held his monthly press conference on May 31, in which he hoped to focus on his agenda, Mark Felt revealed that he was the Deep Throat who provided crucial information regarding the Watergate cover-up to *Washington Post* reporter Bob Woodward. Naturally, this revelation became the lead story for the next day's news.

Displaying Tactical Flexibility

The Bush White House has displayed tactical flexibility when political momentum has moved against it. When public opinion

---

[14] Jim VandeHei, "Bush Is Expected to Address Specifics on Iraq," *Washington Post*, June 16, 2005, p. A8.

regarding the administration's performance in the war on terrorism declined in the late spring of 2002 (discussed in Chapter 3), the White House shifted gears quickly on the Democrats' proposal for a Department of Homeland Security. Instead of opposing it, the president announced an even more extensive reorganization of government. When public opinion clearly supported seeking the support of both Congress and the United Nations for an invasion of Iraq, the White House put aside its claims of executive authority for unilateral action and asked the UN for multilateral action and Congress for a resolution authorizing force.

When the administration received low marks for its response to the corporate fraud and accounting practices scandals that came to light in 2002, the president embraced an accounting regulation measure far stronger than the one he proposed. When campaign finance reform passed, and proved to be popular, the president signed it. Similarly, when a farm bill passed in 2002 that substantially exceeded the president's budget proposal, he signed it to shore up Republican support in farm belt constituencies for the upcoming midterm elections.

As shown in Chapter 1, George W. Bush won several major changes in domestic policy. Often the president did not secure all that he sought, however. In 2001, for example, he embraced a reconciliation law that, although delivering the deepest tax cut in two decades, came up $290 billion short of the mark he wanted. In 2003, his tax cut was less than half of what he sought. The 2002 No Child Left Behind Act did not include vouchers for use for private schools. Nevertheless, after concluding that he had achieved the best outcome possible given the will of Congress, the president typically proclaimed the final compromise a notable victory.

THE IMPACT OF HIGH APPROVAL
ON CONGRESS

One of the perennial questions about presidential-congressional relations is the impact of the president's public approval on the support he received in Congress. This question is especially pertinent because of the administration's choice of going public as its core governing strategy. Did George W. Bush's extraordinarily high approval ratings following the terrorist attacks provide him a significant political resource in his attempts to obtain congressional support for his policies? Did the patriotic response to the attacks help him to mobilize the public on behalf of his programs? Bush certainly seemed aware of the potential advantages of public support—as well as its ephemeral nature. As the president put it, "It is important to move as quickly as you can in order to spend whatever capital you have as quickly as possible."[15]

Where the public supported his policies—on fighting the war on terrorism abroad, on investigating and prosecuting terrorism at home, and in reorganizing the government to enhance domestic security—the president ultimately won most of what he sought. Even on security issues, however, the going was not always easy. He lost on the issue of privatizing airport security workers, although Congress considered the bill in the immediate aftermath of the September 11 attacks. The president also faced a protracted battle over the new Department of Homeland Security when his proposal for additional flexibility in personnel pol-

---

[15] Quoted in Dana Milbank, "Bush Popularity Isn't Aiding GOP Domestic Agenda," *Washington Post*, June 16, 2002, p. A4.

icy in the department infuriated labor unions, a core Democratic constituency.

Passing legislation was even more difficult on the divisive domestic issues that remained on Congress's agenda, including health care, environmental protection, energy, the economy, government support for faith-based social programs, corporate malfeasance, judicial nominees, and taxes. The politics of the war on terrorism did not fundamentally alter the consideration of these issues, which continued to divide the public and their representatives in Congress as they had before. The inevitable differences between the parties predictably emerged, exacerbated by the narrow majorities in each chamber and the jockeying for advantage in the midterm elections.

Bipartisanship in one arena (the war on terrorism) does not necessarily carry over in another. As the parties in Congress have become more homogeneous over time and as the number of competitive seats has shrunk, especially in the House, the differences between the parties have increased. The opposition party does not offer very fertile ground for presidents on most issues—even during wartime. Thus, the president failed to obtain many of his top-priority items in 2002, including making the 2001 tax cuts permanent and passing his fiscal stimulus program, providing government funding for a robust faith-based initiative, and obtaining drilling rights in the Arctic National Wildlife Refuge. He made no progress on partially privatizing Social Security, banning cloning and certain kinds of abortion, or passing private-school tax credits, and the president experienced plenty of frustration on obtaining confirmation of his judicial appointees. He also had to sign a farm bill that was much more costly than he wanted.

In December 2001, the president concluded quiet negotiations with the Democrats led by Senator Edward Kennedy and signed a bill on education reform. The president was able to claim a victory on one of his top-priority issues, even though he had given up many of the most controversial elements of his original proposal. It is significant that to accomplish even this much, the president chose to negotiate in private rather than to go public.

In 2003, following the historic results of the 2002 midterm elections, many observers predicted that the president would be more successful in Congress. In addition, the White House hoped to parlay the victory in Iraq in the spring into support for his legislative plans. His aides did not think public backing for the war could automatically transfer to an unrelated domestic policy, but they did believe that success breeds success and that a lionized wartime leader could be a leader to whom people would listen. A swell of public support, in turn, could inject some much-needed adrenaline into the president's domestic efforts,[16] or so they hoped.

Such predictions were illusory, however. With Bush focused mostly on the war in Iraq, a small but crucial number of Republican moderates in the Senate broke ranks and dealt significant blows to several of his highest-profile policies, slicing in half the president's $726 billion tax cut proposal and defeating his plan for oil drilling in the Arctic National Wildlife Refuge in Alaska. Democrats were no easier to deal with, forcing the president to accept a faith-based plan stripped of its essential features and to

---

[16] Richard E. Cohen and Alexis Simendinger, "Like Father, Like Son?" *National Journal*, March 29, 2003, 991, 993.

put on hold his proposal for capping medical malpractice lawsuit damages. The opposition also continued to oppose effectively his nominations to appellate courts.

The president won on a prescription drug plan under Medicare, a tax cut, and a large appropriation for the wars in Iraq and Afghanistan, and he supported the successful Republican-led effort to ban partial birth abortions. But in each case, the White House had to lobby hard to win, and even then, it obtained less than half of its tax cut proposal. In addition, separate houses of Congress also took action that the White House opposed. The Senate voted to block the administration's proposed changes in overtime regulations and to overturn a Federal Communications Commission rule that would let large media conglomerates consolidate, and the House voted to lift the ban on most travel to Cuba and repeal a provision of the USA Patriot Act that lets police conduct searches and seizures without advanced notice. Both houses voted to limit the president's initiative on privatizing federal jobs. However, the president was able to use support in one chamber or the power of the party leadership in conference committees to kill each of these policies.

The modest impact of Bush's high approval ratings is not surprising. The president's public support must compete for influence with other, more stable factors that affect voting in Congress, including members' ideologies, party affiliations, personal views and commitments on specific policies, and constituency interests. Although constituency interests may seem to overlap with presidential approval, we should view them as distinct forces. It is quite possible for constituents to approve of the president but oppose him on particular policies, and it is opinions on these policies that will ring most loudly in congressional ears. Members of Congress are unlikely to vote against the clear interests of their constituents or the firm tenets of their ideologies solely in deference to a widely supported chief executive.[17]

It is interesting that at the beginning of his term, Bush's travels seemed motivated more by demonstrating his support in states where he ran well in the election than in convincing more skeptical voters of the soundness of his proposals. He did not travel to California until May 29 and visited New York even later. Instead, the White House gave priority to states that Bush had won and that were represented by Democratic senators, including Georgia, Louisiana, Arkansas, Missouri, North and South Dakota, Montana, and North Carolina. The goal of these trips seemed to be to demonstrate preexisting public support in the constituencies of members of Congress who were potential swing votes. Whatever the president's motivations, he obtained the support of only one Senate Democrat (Zell Miller of Georgia, who announced his support of the tax cut before Bush was inaugurated) on the April 4 bellwether vote for his full tax cut. In 2003, the president seemed to be following the same strategy as he campaigned for his tax cut proposal. His travel seemed designed to work at the margins to convince moderate senators of both parties that his tax cut proposal enjoyed public support in their states. The president's efforts on behalf of his proposals to reform Social Security are discussed in Chapter 7.

---

[17] On the question of the impact of presidential approval on presidential support in Congress, see Edwards, *At the Margins;* and George C. Edwards III, "Aligning Tests with Theory: Presidential Approval as a Source of Influence in Congress," *Congress and the Presidency* 24 (Fall 1997): 113–130.

PARTY SUPPORT OF THE PRESIDENT

Representatives and senators of the president's party are almost always the nucleus of coalitions supporting the president's programs. No matter what other resources presidents may have, without seats in Congress held by their party, they will usually find it very difficult to move their legislative programs through Congress. Thus, leading their party in Congress is the principal task of all presidents as they seek to counter the tendencies of the executive and legislative branches toward conflict inherent in the system of checks and balances.

Table 5.2 shows the support members of each party gave Bush on roll-call votes on which he took a stand in his first term. Clearly, there was a substantial difference between the levels of support the president received from members of the two parties, with the gap averaging 62 percentage points in the House and 69 in the Senate in his first term.

TABLE 5.2
Support for Bush's Stands, First Term*

| | HOUSE | | | | SENATE | | |
YEAR	ALL	DEMOCRATS	REPUBLICANS	ALL	DEMOCRATS	REPUBLICANS
2001	52%	19%	84%	51%	14%	89%
2002	55	24	84	54	23	87
2003	54	16	89	56	21	81
2004	54	23	82	50	11	87

*On roll-call votes on which the winning side was supported by fewer than 80 percent of those voting.

With a president of their own in the White House, party members in Congress may alter their voting tendencies.[18] For example, Republicans have a tendency to be more supportive of internationalist foreign policies and are more likely to accept governmental economic activity when a Republican is president. Democrats, on the other hand, have a tendency to move in the opposite direction when there is a Republican in the White House. In 2001, with a Republican as president, many Republicans in Congress shifted to supporting foreign aid and increasing the national debt ceiling, even though they had opposed these policies under the previous Democratic administration of Bill Clinton.

Despite the proclivity of members of Congress to support presidents of their party, the White House may also experience substantial slippage in party cohesion in Congress. This slippage forces the White House to adopt an activist orientation toward party leadership and sometimes devote as much effort to converting party members to support them as to mobilizing members of their party who already agree with them.

Members of the same party share many policy preferences and have similar electoral coalitions supporting them. These members are also more open to presidential influence. Members of the president's party typically have personal loyalties or emotional commitments to their party and its leader, which the president can often translate into votes when necessary. Thus, members of the

---

[18] See Terry Sullivan, "Bargaining with the President: A Simple Game and New Evidence," *American Political Science Review* 84 (December 1990):1167–1196; and Glen Biglaiser, David J. Jackson, and Jeffrey S. Peake, "Back on Track: Support for Presidential Trade Authority in the House of Representatives," *American Politics Research* 32 (November 2004): 679–697, concerning party members switching to support the president of their party.

president's party vote with him when they can, thereby giving him the benefit of the doubt, especially if their own opinion on an issue is weak. Moreover, this proclivity for supporting the president increases the effectiveness of other sources of party influence.

One of these sources is the desire of members of the presidential party to avoid embarrassing "their" administration. This attitude stems from two motivations. The first is related to the sentiments already discussed, but the second is more utilitarian. Members of the president's party have an incentive to make the president look good because his standing in the public may influence their own chances for reelection. They also want a record of legislative success to take to the voters. In 2003, Republicans overcame their distaste for social welfare programs and supported a prescription drug program under Medicare to show that they could deliver when they had power and to give President George W. Bush a victory to aid his reelection in 2004.

Each party has a set of floor and committee leaders in the House and Senate who, in theory, should be a valuable resource for their party's leader in the White House. The president needs both their advice and their resources for making head counts and other administrative chores. Because of their role perceptions, because their reputations for passing legislation give them a clear stake in the president's success, and because they are susceptible to the same sentiments and pressures toward party loyalty as are other members of Congress, floor leaders of the president's party in Congress are usually very supportive of the White House. Committee leaders of the president's party typically have a similar orientation.

Speaker of the House Dennis Hastert has been quite effective in supporting Bush's program. The increasing uniformity of views within the Republican members of the House has facilitated the Speaker's ability to develop and enforce a party stance on policy— and to work on behalf of the president. According to Vice President Dick Cheney, the Speaker is good at telling White House what will fly in the House and thus it helps shape what the White House proposes.[19] In addition, the rules in the House make control of the agenda by the majority party much easier than in the more decentralized Senate.

We saw earlier that Bush has adopted a selective approach to legislative activity, taking stands on relatively few issues and often intervening late in the legislative process. The White House has also typically articulated general goals for legislation and then stepped aside as the president's allies crafted the details and pushed the bill through. At the core of this strategy have been Republican majorities in both houses of Congress (except for part of 2001 and all of 2002 in the Senate) and a like-minded Republican leadership bent on avoiding vetoes and willing to twist arms so the president could win and preserve his political capital for when he needed it most. Moreover, the Republican House whip operation is so good that president did not need to do much. As we have seen, even when the president lost on a vote in one of the chambers, the Republican leadership was often able to remove the offending provisions in the conference committees, which they controlled. For example, both chambers of Congress passed limitations on the privatization of government services that the White House supported. Nevertheless, the Republican leadership

---

[19] Jonathan Frazen, "The Listener," *New Yorker,* October 6, 2003, 94.

removed the provisions in the conference committee. According to one House Republican aide, "If you had divided government, we wouldn't have done that."[20]

There are limits to relying on party leaders to do the difficult work, however. In 2004, following his reelection, the president faced an embarrassing situation in the House on his proposal to reform the structure of intelligence in the U.S. government. As *Congressional Quarterly* put it,

> *After four years of twisting arms to move the president's top priorities while he mostly stayed out of the fray, House leaders, facing discord in their own ranks, refused to put the intelligence overhaul measure . . . on the floor unless the White House applied its own muscle.*[21]

The scars of the battle for the prescription drug benefit bill were evident and House Republican leaders did not want to split their conference. It took several weeks and a heated exchange between House Majority Leader Tom DeLay and the White House's top lobbyist on Capitol Hill, David W. Hobbs, for the message to sink in. At that point, the White House launched a more aggressive, and ultimately successful, campaign for Republican support.[22]

Observers have given the president mixed marks in his dealings with his party. On the one hand, the president has been a very successful and active fundraiser for his party's congressional

---

[20] Schatz, "With a Deft and Light Touch, Bush Finds Ways to Win," 2901–2904.
[21] Robert Novak, "Bush's Problem with Congress," *Washington Post*, June 6, 2005, p. A19.
[22] Jonathan Allen and John M. Donnelly, "From Impasse to Enactment": How a Deal Is Brokered," *Congressional Quarterly Weekly Report*, December 11, 2004, 2938.

candidates. And, as discussed below, he has campaigned actively for them. Yet in June 2005, conservative columnist Robert Novak wrote that, "in nearly 4 1/2 years, President Bush has not progressed in handling Congress. He seems at as much of a loss in dealing with the legislative branch as the day he entered the White House." Novak claimed that Bush was not adept at turning around Republican strays. "When the House Republican leadership on occasion has given the president a list of recalcitrant members to rope in on a specific bill, he has never delivered."[23] Although this criticism may have been a bit harsh, there were other reports of the president's difficulties of convincing skeptical Republicans to support him.[24]

Bush suffered a major embarrassment when Republican Senator James Jeffords of Vermont left the party and became an Independent in the middle of 2001. Because Jeffords caucused with the Democrats, his move gave them a majority in the Senate for the rest of the congressional term. Jeffords was disappointed with the White House's refusal to support increased spending for education and other social welfare programs, and he resented the pressure it put on him to toe the party line.

Increasing the Partisans

Members of Congress who are of the president's party are more likely to support the president than are members of the opposition party, and presidents do their best to exploit this potential of partisan support. Nevertheless, such actions are inevitably at the

---

[23] Novak, "Bush's Problem with Congress."
[24] See, for example, Sheryl Gay Stolberg, "Instead of Dialogue, Bush Gives Senators Bottom Line," *New York Times*, October 18, 2003, p. A6.

margins of coalition building because they take place within the confines of the partisan balance of the Congress. To exploit the benefits of party leadership fully, presidents need as many of their fellow partisans in Congress as possible. Once members of Congress have been elected, they rarely change their party affiliation, and the few instances when they have changed have not resulted from presidential persuasion. Thus, if presidents are to alter the party composition of Congress, they must help to elect additional members of their party. One way to try to accomplish this goal is to campaign for candidates in midterm congressional elections.

In 2002, Republicans made small gains in both houses. In this election, George W. Bush engaged in the most active midterm campaigning of any president in history. The Republican gains were the result of both favorable redistricting following the 2000 Census and a heavy turnout among Republicans, who responded to the president, who was extraordinarily popular in the face of the 9/11 attacks (see Chapter 3).

Another potential way in which presidents may influence the partisan composition of Congress is through their coattails. Presidential coattails are part of the lore of American politics. Politicians project them in their calculations, journalists attribute them in their reporting, historians recount them, and political scientists analyze them. However, we have limited understanding of how they affect the outcomes in congressional elections. (A coattail victory is a victory for a representative of the president's party in which presidential coattail votes provide the increment of the vote necessary to win the seat.)

Coattail victories, whether they bring in new members or preserve the seats of incumbents, can have significant payoffs for the president in terms of support for the administration's programs.

Those members of the president's party who won close elections may provide an extra increment of support out of a sense of gratitude for the votes they perceive they received due to presidential coattails or out of a sense of responsiveness to their constituents' support for the president.

However, research has found that presidential coattails determine the outcomes of very few congressional races.[25] George W. Bush's Republicans lost two seats in the House in the elections of 2000. The net gain of three Republican House seats in 2004 was the result of a redistricting effort in Texas led by House Majority Leader Tom DeLay. Most House seats are too safe for a party, and especially for an incumbent, to have the election outcome affected by the presidential election. The president's standing with the public is more likely to affect Senate elections, but the president's party typically gains no seats at all in a presidential election year.[26] Reflecting this average, the Republicans lost four seats in the Senate in 2000, while they gained that many in 2004.

Bipartisanship

Despite the advantage that presidents have in dealing with members of their party in Congress, they must often solicit bipartisan support. The opposition party may control one or both houses of Congress. Thus, even if all members of the president's party supported the administration on its key initiatives, that would not be

---

[25] George C. Edwards III, *The Public Presidency* (New York: St. Martin's, 1983), 83–93; Gregory N. Flemming, "Presidential Coattails in Open-Seat Elections," *Legislative Studies Quarterly* 20 (May 1995): 197–212.

[26] James E. Campbell and Joe A. Sumners, "Presidential Coattails in Senate Elections," *American Political Science Review* 84 (June 1990): 513–524; Alan I. Abramowitz and Jeffrey A. Segal, *Senate Elections* (Ann Arbor: University of Michigan Press, 1992), 121, 233, 238.

sufficient. George W. Bush enjoyed Republican party control of both houses of Congress for less than five months in 2001 before the Democrats gained a majority in the Senate. Republicans gained majorities in each chamber for the remainder of the president's tenure, however.

In addition, we have seen that the president cannot depend on all the members of his party to support him on all issues. The primary obstacle to party cohesion in support of the president is lack of a consensus among members of the president's party on policies. Although in recent years the parties in Congress have become more homogeneous—as conservative constituencies increasingly elect Republicans and liberal constituencies elect Democrats, especially in the House[27]—there is still a range of opinion within each party. When constituency opinion and the president's proposals conflict, members of Congress are more likely to vote with their constituencies, to whom they must return for reelection.

At other times, catering to the constituencies of fellow partisans requires trade-offs with other policies. On the night before a pivotal and known-to-be-close vote on the president's desire to begin energy exploration in the Arctic National Wildlife Refuge, freshman Republican Senator Mel Martinez told the director of the White House congressional liaison operation, Candida Wolff, that he was much more concerned with expanding a no-drilling zone of the coast of his home state of Florida. "This is something that I have to have." A few hours before the vote, Wolff's team made sure he received a letter from Interior Secretary Gale Norton

---

[27] David W. Rohde, *Parties and Leaders in the Postreform House* (Chicago: University of Chicago Press, 1991).

promising that the administration planned to extend current coastal drilling restrictions.[28]

Not only do partisan strategies often fail, but they also may provoke the other party into a more unified posture of opposition. When there is confrontation there can be no consensus, and consensus is often required to legislate changes on important issues. Presidents are also inhibited in their partisanship by pressures to be "president of all the people" rather than a highly partisan figure. Thus, presidents cannot ignore the opposition party and even a few votes may be enough to bring them a majority.

Despite the frequent necessity of a bipartisan strategy, its utility is usually limited. The opposition party is generally not a fertile ground for obtaining policy support. Few Democrats supported George W. Bush's tax cut proposals or the budget of which they were a part. Moreover, the president's efforts to exploit bipartisan support for the war on terrorism to increase support for his domestic policies have generally been unsuccessful.

When he was governor of Texas, Bush worked with both Democratic leaders, especially Lieutenant Governor Bob Bullock, and the Democratic rank and file in the state legislature. At the beginning of his presidency, Bush invited Democratic congressional leaders to the White House but quickly found the process unproductive and awkward. Apparently, Bush expected that as president he could work with Democratic leaders in Congress in the same way and was surprised when he could not. "It was one of the biggest eye openers of his first year," reported a White House aide. "He thought the meetings were a waste of everyone's

---

[28] "A 'Superstar' Negotiator Takes Hill for President," *Congressional Quarterly Weekly Report*, April 4, 2005, 824.

time," a former White House staffer said. "Plus, it was uncomfortable for everyone concerned to sit around a table and pretend to be friendly, and then they would go back to the Hill and blast us." As a result, the White House has spent little time trying to woo or negotiate with Democratic congressional leaders, especially those in the House.[29]

Cultivating rank-in-file Democrats was not much more effective. Because of the polarized partisan divide—and thus a dwindling number of moderate-to-conservative Democrats—there were few Democrats who were potential supporters of the White House. During George H. W. Bush's administration, the White House would routinely lobby 25–40 Democrats, depending on the issue. During the Reagan administration, that number was even higher. "We're lucky if we have 10–15 Democrats on our list today," a White House official reported.[30]

The president could usually afford to ignore Democrats in the House, because Republicans in that chamber were united and the party leadership effective in enforcing party unity. On the prescription drug bill, for example, there was virtually no Democratic input on the bill and Republicans essentially excluded them from conference committee meetings. The Republicans passed the bill by a 216-215 vote after the leadership kept the vote open for 173 minutes (instead of the usual 15) until 2:45 A.M. while it pressured a handful of their own troops to switch their votes and put the measure over the top.[31] Of course, the administration's

---

[29] Gary Andres, "Polarization and White House/Legislative Relations: Causes and Consequences of Elite-Level Conflict," *Presidential Studies Quarterly* 35 (December 2005): 763–764.
[30] Andres, "Polarization and White House/Legislative Relations," 763.
[31] Serafini, "A Prescription for Defeat," 2612–2613. The president did work with George Miller of California, the ranking member of the House Committee on Education and the Workforce on the No Child Left Behind legislation.

reluctance to compromise further alienated the Democrats. In the case of the prescription drug program, the White House won the votes of only nine House Democrats.

The Senate presented a different situation, however. "I think we had mixed success," declared a Bush White House lobbyist. "But we certainly spent a lot of time and attention working those Democratic Senators. We could afford to ignore the Democrats in the House . . . not so in the Senate." A former White House lobbyist said, "From the very beginning this was the place President Bush thought he could foster bipartisan agreements." The White House worked hard to cultivate Democratic support in the Senate, focusing early on Ted Kennedy of Massachusetts for the No Child Left Behind Act and Max Baucus of Montana on issues like tax and Medicare reform.[32] Sometimes the president was able to compromise enough with the Democrats to prevent a successful filibuster, as in his 2001 tax cut bill, or to appeal in a bipartisan way, as on the prescription drug bill. Many other times, as we have seen, the president could not prevail.

The White House had some self-inflicted wounds in wooing Senate Democrats, however. For example, Ben Nelson of Nebraska was a centrist and frequent swing voter. When it came to the president's proposal for a tax cut in 2003, Nelson was ready from the start to reach a compromise that could win his vote. He wanted $20 billion in aid to the states for his vote. However, before he could consummate such a deal, Bush went to Nebraska to generate support for his bill and called for prominent Republicans in the state to try to pressure the senator. "It's pretty

---

[32] Andres, "Polarization and White House/Legislative Relations," 764.

hard to make peace and war at the same time," said Nelson.[33] Similarly, Mary L. Landrieu of Louisiana, another centrist, said she would have to think long and hard before working with the president again. He targeted her for defeat in the 2002 election although in 2001 she voted for his tax cut and education plans.[34] Not unexpectedly, Harry Reid of Nevada, the Senate Democratic whip and then majority leader, found Bush difficult to work with and did not trust him.[35]

Initially the White House resisted the Democrats' proposal for a Department of Homeland Security, but in June 2002 it not only embraced the idea but also maneuvered Democrats into a standoff over proposed labor rules for the new department's employees. The president and Republican candidates then successfully used the issue against Democrats in the 2002 midterm elections, questioning their patriotism. Democrats were infuriated by what they viewed as a low blow, especially when the issue was successful against triple-amputee Vietnam veteran Max Cleland of Georgia.

THE SECOND TERM: A MANDATE FOR CHANGE?

On November 4, 2004, two days after the presidential election, George W. Bush offered his view of the political landscape during a press conference at the White House:

I feel it is necessary to move an agenda that I told the American people I would move. Something refreshing about coming

---

[33] Elsa Walsh, "Minority Report," *New Yorker,* August 8 and 15, 2005, 47–48.
[34] "Another Shot at His Legacy," *Congressional Quarterly Weekly Report,* August 28, 2004, 1953.
[35] Walsh, "Minority Report," 47–48.

off an election . . . you go out and you make your case, and you tell the people this is what I intend to do. And after hundreds of speeches and three debates and interviews and the whole process, where you keep basically saying the same thing over and over again, that when you win, there is a feeling that the people have spoken and embraced your point of view, and that's what I intend to tell the Congress, that I made it clear what I intend to do as the President, . . . and the people made it clear what they wanted, now let's work together.

. . . I earned capital in the campaign, political capital, and now I intend to spend it. It is my style. . . . I've earned capital in this election—and I'm going to spend it for what I told the people I'd spend it on, which is . . . Social Security and tax reform, moving this economy forward, education, fighting and winning the war on terror.

The president painted his second-term vision in bold, aggressive strokes: He would reform Social Security, keep reshaping the nation's education system, and accomplish other important goals. Moreover, he truly believed that the American people had given him a mandate for change—his political capital. He felt he had taken his case to the people, and they had clearly endorsed his policies. As a result, he argued, Congress should listen to the will of the people.

The Making of a Mandate

The Constitution's requirement that the entire nation participate in electing the president provides the White House the potential to claim a public mandate for the president's policies. An electoral mandate—the perception that the voters strongly support the president's character and policies—can be a powerful symbol in American politics. It can accord added legitimacy and credibility to the newly elected president's proposals. Concerns for representation and political survival encourage members of Congress to support the president if they feel the people have spoken.[36] And members of Congress are susceptible to such beliefs. According to David Mayhew, "Nothing is more important in Capitol Hill politics than the shared conviction that election returns have proven a point."[37] Members of Congress also need to believe that voters have not merely rejected the losers in elections but positively selected the victors and what they stand for.

More important, mandates change the premises of decision. Following the presidential election of 1932, the essential question became how government should act to fight the Depression rather than whether it should act. Similarly, following the election of 1964 the dominant question in Congress was not whether to pass new social programs, but how many to pass and how much to increase spending.

In 1981, the tables were turned. Ronald Reagan's victory placed a stigma on big government and exalted the unregulated marketplace and large defense budgets. More specifically, the terms of the debate over policy changed from which federal programs to expand to which ones to cut; from which civil rights

---

[36] Edwards, *At the Margins: Presidential Leadership of Congress*, chap. 8; David Peterson, Lawrence J. Grossback, James A. Stimson, and Amy Gangl, "Congressional Response to Mandate Elections," *American Journal of Political Science* 47 (June 2003): 411–426.
[37] David R. Mayhew, *Congress: The Electoral Connection* (New Haven, CT: Yale University Press, 1974), 70–71.

rules to extend to which ones to limit; from how much to regulate to how little; from which natural resources to protect to which to develop; from how little to increase defense spending to how much; and from how little to cut taxes to how much.

Such mandates are rare, however. Merely winning an election does not provide a president with a mandate. Every election produces a winner, but mandates are much less common. When asked about his mandate in 1960, John F. Kennedy reportedly replied, "Mandate, schmandate. The mandate is that I am here and you're not."[38]

The question is whether there was reason to believe that Bush had received a mandate for the American people. Just what political capital did Bush have? Was his analysis an accurate assessment of leverage he had gained from his election, or was it self-congratulatory and tinged with second-term hubris?

There is more to perceptions of mandates than a straightforward summing of the presidential election results. Even presidents who win election by large margins often find that perceptions of support for their proposals do not accompany their victories. In the presidential elections held between 1952 and 2000, most of the impressive electoral victories (Richard Nixon's 61 percent in 1972, Ronald Reagan's 59 percent in 1984, and Dwight Eisenhower's 57 percent in 1956) did not elicit perceptions of mandates. In 1984, Reagan won a great electoral victory with 59 percent of the vote. Public opinion polls at the time of the election showed that the voters viewed him in a very positive light as a strong, effective leader and accorded him high marks for his per-

---

[38] Quoted in Everett Carll Ladd, *The Ladd Report #1* (New York: W. W. Norton, 1985), 3.

formance on the economy and national security policy.[39] Moreover, the first Gallup poll after the inauguration found that Reagan enjoyed an approval rating of 62 percent. Yet the president immediately faced strong opposition in Congress to his proposals on domestic and foreign policy. As an example, in the Congress of 1985–1986 the president won no real increase at all in his cherished defense budget. Much of the time he was on the defensive, as in his embarrassing defeat on sanctions against South Africa.

Bush won reelection with less than 51 percent of the vote—the smallest percentage of any reelected president in more than half a century. In Chapter 1, we saw that the president's 53 percent approval rating following the election was the lowest of any of the last seven presidents who won election while serving as president in the first poll conducted after their elections. We have also seen that the first poll after Bush's inauguration in January 2005 showed him at 57 percent, perhaps with some help from the successful Iraqi elections that month, but also that his approval dropped 8 percentage points, to 49 percent, four days later (see Chapter 3). In sum, the public's show of support for the president was modest.

Why do election victories not automatically translate into perceptions of mandates for the newly elected president? The most straightforward explanation of perceptions of a mandate is that a clear majority of the populace has shown through its votes that it supports certain policies proposed by the winning candidate. Yet by their very nature, elections rarely provide clear indications of the public's thinking on individual proposals.

---

[39] See, for example, CBS News/*New York Times* poll, News Release, January 21, 1985, tables 1–3; "Opinion Roundup," *Public Opinion,* December-January 1985, 37.

If presidential elections are to provide majority support for specific policies, the following conditions must be met: (1) voters must have opinions on policies; (2) voters must know candidates' stands on the issues; (3) candidates must offer voters the alternatives the voters desire; (4) there must be a large turnout of voters; (5) voters must vote on the basis of issues; and (6) one must be able to correlate voter support with voters' policy views. These conditions are rarely met, if ever.[40] For this reason, it is very difficult to discern the relationship between voters' policy preferences and a president's victory at the polls.

Even landslide elections are difficult to interpret. For example, political scientist Stanley Kelley found that in Lyndon Johnson's victory in 1964, issues gave the president his base of support, and concerns over the relative competence of the candidates won the swing vote for him. In 1972, however, the question of competence dominated the election. Although traditional domestic issues associated with the New Deal were salient, they actually favored George McGovern, not the landslide winner, Richard Nixon.[41]

In addition, voters may be concerned with several issues in an election, but they have only one vote with which to express their views. Citizens may support one candidate's position on some issues yet vote for another candidate because of concern for other issues or general evaluations of performance. When they cast their ballots, voters signal only their choice of candidate, not their choice of the candidates' policies. One should be cautious in inferring support for specific policies from the results of this process,

---

[40] See for example Edwards, *The Public Presidency*, 18–23.
[41] Stanley Kelley, Jr., *Interpreting Elections* (Princeton, NJ: Princeton University Press, 1983), 72–125.

for the vote is a rather blunt instrument for expressing one's views. A postelection survey in December 2004 asked respondents whether Bush had won a mandate for his Social Security and tax proposals. Only 33 percent agreed that he had received a mandate for private accounts within Social Security, and only 38 percent agreed that he had secured a mandate to change the tax structure.[42]

In January 2005, at the time of the president's inauguration, a *Washington Post*/ABC News poll found that Bush received high marks on the key issue of terrorism, where a 61 percent majority approved of the job he was doing. However, only 45 percent of respondents said they preferred that the country go in the direction that Bush wanted to lead it. Fifty-eight percent of the public disapproved of his handling of the situation in Iraq, and only 44 percent said the war was worth fighting. A slight majority, 52 percent, disapproved of the way he was handling the economy, and half or more were also dissatisfied with the way Bush dealt with the budget deficit (58 percent disapprove), education (56 percent), immigration (54 percent), and health care (51 percent). The public was divided on the president's handling of environmental issues, foreign affairs, and taxes.[43]

The addition of a large number of new seats for the president's party in Congress is an indicator used by commentators, and certainly by members of Congress, in evaluating the significance of a president's electoral victory. If observers attribute long coattails to the president, they are likely to see the election as especially

[42] *Time Magazine*/SRBI poll, December 13–14, 2004.

[43] Richard Morin and Dan Balz, "Political Divisions Persist After Election," *Washington Post*, January 18, 2005; *Washington Post*/ABC News poll, January 12–16, 2005.

meaningful, because the people appear to be sending strong signals of support for the chief executive. In contrast, the absence of notable gains for the president's party in Congress detracts from the euphoria of victory and inserts an unsettling element into analyses that follow the election. If the president's party gains few seats, it makes it easy to conclude that the voters were sending mixed signals on election day and that the basis of the president's victory was more personal than political. The results of such congressional elections may also demonstrate to members of Congress that their electoral fortunes are not connected with the president's.

In 2004, the Republicans gained only three seats in the House, all of which were the result of an unusual redistricting in Texas that carved up previously Democratic seats. More impressively, the Republicans gained a net of four Senate seats. This gain was the result of winning open seats in the increasingly solid Republican South. Republicans defeated only one incumbent Democratic Senator, Tom Daschle of South Dakota, making it difficult to infer a change in public opinion.

The winning candidate's inclination to present policy alternatives during the campaign may also affect perceptions of a mandate. Often, in the interests of building a broad electoral coalition, a candidate avoids specifics to such a degree that he undercuts future claims of policy mandates. In American politics the electoral and governing processes are often quite separate. The figures in Table 5.3 show the victory percentages of winning presidential candidates since 1952. All four of the elections listed in the table in which the winner obtained more than 55 percent of the vote (1956, 1964, 1972, and 1984) were races in which the incumbent won reelection. With the exception of Lyndon Johnson, who had

TABLE 5.3
Presidential Election Results, 1952–2004

YEAR	WINNING CANDIDATE	PERCENTAGE OF POPULAR VOTE	ELECTORAL VOTE
1952	Eisenhower	55.1	442
1956	Eisenhower	57.4	457
1960	Kennedy	49.7	303
1964	Johnson	61.0	486
1968	Nixon	43.4	301
1972	Nixon	60.7	520
1976	Carter	50.1	297
1980	Reagan	50.7	489
1984	Reagan	58.8	525
1988	Bush	53.4	426
1992	Clinton	43.0	370
1996	Clinton	49.2	379
2000	G. W. Bush	47.8	271
2004	G. W. Bush	50.8	286

been in office only a year, the presidents used their campaigns to appeal as broadly as possible and run up the score. Yet in producing impressive personal victories they undermined their ability to govern after the election. Eisenhower, Nixon, and Reagan each experienced considerable difficulties with Congress in the two years immediately following their landslide victories.

George W. Bush's reelection campaign emphasized the war on terror, moral values, and his personal leadership qualities, and he referred to a range of policy goals he wanted to achieve in his second term. What he did not do was specify his plans for reforming the tax system, Social Security, education, or other new proposals. As we will see, the lack of attention to Social Security compromised Bush's ability to govern after the election, because his claims of a mandate for his reform proposals lacked credibility.

Related to the orientation of the campaign is the relative impact of continuity and change on perceptions of the outcome of the election. The results in 2004 reinforced the status quo. Continuity has considerably less psychological impact than change, especially if the change appears to be substantial. Members of Congress are more responsive to perceptions of changing public preferences than they are to the president's claims of a mandate.[44]

Overreaching?

David Broder, the dean of Washington columnists, reported that he found in January 2005 that Bush had instilled a belief among his close associates that the bigger and bolder the goals they set for themselves, the more they would accomplish. The way to avoid the "second-term curse," they argued, was to have a clear and ambitious agenda. They thought that things had gone downhill for Dwight Eisenhower, Ronald Reagan, and Bill Clinton because those presidents had largely used up their "big ideas" in their first terms. This lack of initiatives left them adrift, without much sense of purpose, and thus vulnerable to their enemies, in their final four years. Thus, Bush offered an ambitious set of

---

[44] Lawrence J. Grossback and David A. M. Peterson, "Comparing Competing Theories on the Causes of Mandate Perceptions," *American Journal of Political Science* 49 (April 2005): 406–419.

goals, ranging from the overhaul of American high schools to the achievement of democracy in the Middle East, and including a new energy policy and reforming Social Security, the tax system, the Senate's consideration of judicial nominations, and the tort system.[45]

As we have seen, however, it is difficult to interpret Bush's reelection as a mandate for change. We have also seen in Chapters 1 and 4 that Bush remained the most polarizing president in the history of polling and struggled to obtain the approval of even half the people. According to scholar Charles O. Jones, it was particularly striking to see "a second-term president with the smallest electoral college majority since Wilson in 1916 undertake the most ambitious agenda since Roosevelt in 1936."[46] Democrat John Podesta added that Bush made the mistake of trying to turn a successful election strategy of catering to his base into a governing philosophy that excluded Democrats.[47]

The president's party had majorities in both houses of Congress, and the House was under the tight control of the leadership. Moreover, the president's popularity among Republicans in the public made him an asset in getting out the vote in the 2006 midterm elections. Without the incentive of positioning Bush as a successful incumbent for reelection purposes, however, Republicans in both chambers were getting restless. The president would find it more difficult to unify the party if its members did not already agree with him.

---

[45] David S. Broder, "Paying a Price for Overreaching," *Washington Post,* April 28, 2005, p. A23.

[46] Quoted in Broder, "Paying a Price for Overreaching."

[47] Peter Baker and Jim VandeHei, "Bush's Political Capital Spent, Voices in Both Parties Suggest Poll," *Washington Post,* May 31, 2005, p. A2.

Chapter 7 shows that Bush rapidly became a victim of over-reach, overestimating his political capital and losing badly on the issue to which he devoted the most time and effort: Social Security. This chapter briefly reviews the president's experience on other legislation.

Before the Fall

The president received an early warning of problems to come when shortly after the 2004 election the House considered an intelligence reform bill that would have enacted the major recommendations of the September 11 commission. Recalcitrant House conservatives refused to back the bill despite the president's and vice president's personal lobbying. The bill unraveled when two influential Republican House committee chairmen, Representatives Duncan Hunter of California and F. James Sensenbrenner Jr. of Wisconsin, would not support it. Hunter, chair of the Armed Services Committee, complained that the bill would dangerously dilute the authority of the military commanders over intelligence issues and endanger troops. Sensenbrenner, chair of the Judiciary Committee, demanded a provision strongly favored by conservatives that would create federal standards for drivers' licenses to prevent states from issuing them to illegal immigrants. When House Republicans lined up behind the chairmen at a caucus meeting, Speaker Dennis Hastert pulled the plug on the bill to avoid splitting his caucus.[48] As we have seen, a compromise even-

---

[48] Philip Shenon and Carl Hulse, "House Leadership Blocks Vote on Intelligence Bill," *Washington Post,* November 21, 2004; Sheryl Gay Stolberg, "Republican Defiance on Intelligence Bill Is Surprising. Or Is It?" *New York Times,* November 22, 2004.

tually passed, but not before the president had to beg for support, even in the aftermath of his reelection.

Things looked better for the White House in the first three months of 2005, however, as the president scored important and comparatively easy victories on legislation to restrain class-action lawsuits and to revamp bankruptcy laws to make it harder for consumers to wipe out their debts. These were measures that business interests had long sought, but they represented what some observers termed "low-hanging fruit" because the newly reelected president easily picked them. The class-action bill, for example, had lingered on the verge of passage for years, and it had some important Democratic backers. The expanded Republican majority in the 2005 Senate virtually assured its enactment into law. In addition, even sympathetic observers argued that it was the K Street business lobbyists who were responsible for reforms of class action lawsuits and bankruptcy—not the president.[49] The measures received unanimous or near-unanimous support from congressional Republicans, and the minority of Democratic votes they received (beyond the handful of Senate votes needed to preclude a filibuster) were superfluous.[50]

Another bill supported by business interests, legislation to reform malpractice litigation, was a more complex and more controversial idea and proved to be more difficult for the White House. Almost everywhere President Bush traveled on the campaign trail in 2004, he lashed out at plaintiffs' lawyers for filing "junk lawsuits" that he said were sending the cost of health care spiraling upwards. Bush made clear in his State of the Union

---

[49] Novak, "Bush's Problem with Congress."
[50] There was only a single Republican vote against either bill in either chamber.

address on February 2 that he considered limiting medical malpractice lawsuits an important goal for his second term, calling
for "medical liability reform that will reduce health care costs and
make sure patients have the doctors and care they need." By the
spring, however, there was no evidence that these exhortations
had changed Congress's support for the idea as the Senate dead-
locked on the legislation and the president rarely mentioned the
topic.[51] Senate Majority Leader Bill Frist indicated that he was
willing to consider a wide range of options and urged Democrats
to "come to the table" and negotiate. Democrats, supported by
the deep-pocketed trial lawyers' lobby, did not budge. In addition,
the passage of the class-action bill, which Bush signed into law
February 18, undermined the president's efforts because many
lawmakers were loath to strike the powerful trial-lawyer lobby
more than once in a single year. Similarly, the president urged
Congress to slim the huge docket of litigation over asbestos, but
defendant companies and their insurers were unable to agree with
unions and trial lawyers on a funding level and a few other key
issues in a proposed asbestos trust fund. As a result, leaders laid
aside another Bush priority issue.

Three other significant bills passed before the summer recess.
One was a transportation bill that passed with near-unanimous
support from representatives of both parties, primarily because it
allocated billions of dollars for roads, bridges, mass transit aid,
and related projects, including virtually every congressional district in the largesse. As Democratic Senator Ben Nelson of

---

[51] Jeffrey H. Birnbaum and John F. Harris, "President's Proposed Remedy to Curb Medical Malpractice
Lawsuits Stalls: Senate Deadlocks; Democrats Plan To Use Filibuster," *Washington Post*, April 3, 2005,
p. A5.

Nebraska put it, "There's more that will unite you than will divide you, as long as you realize there are projects in Nebraska and projects in Kansas and New York and what have you." However, the same Democrats who were open to persuasion on economic issues refused to budge on issues they saw as more partisan in nature. On these issues, Nelson said, "The lines are more clearly drawn, and there's very little room to maneuver."[52]

A second bill dealt with energy and provided financial incentives for increased energy production, reduced regulation of power companies, encouraged but did not require conservation, and contained provisions to improve the electrical grid's reliability. It needed some Democratic support to pass because of Republican defectors (31 in the House, 6 in the Senate). The Republicans obtained this support with a judicious distribution of pork and the deletion of provisions opening the Alaskan National Wildlife Refuge (ANWR) to oil drilling, providing liability protection for the fuel additive MTBE, and giving cities more time to meet Clean Air Act standards. In other words, they dropped the contentious measures coveted by conservatives. No one claimed that the bill would do much to reduce U.S. oil imports or lower gasoline prices. According to Republican senator Trent Lott of Mississippi, "The only way we got the energy bill was to pick a lot of the meat out of it. This is not a particularly impressive bill."[53] Although the House Republican leadership planned to include the ANWR drilling provision in the budget reconciliation

[52] Jim VandeHei and Charles Babington, "Bills' Passage Shows the Arena Where GOP Can Flex Its Muscle," *Washington Post*, July 31, 2005.
[53] Charles Babington and Justin Blum, "On Capitol Hill, A Flurry of GOP Victories: Key Measures Advance After Long Delays," *Washington Post*, July 30, 2005, p. A1.

bill, which is not subject to a filibuster, 24 House Republicans sent a letter to the Speaker and the chair of the budget committee opposing such a move.[54] In the end, the Republicans could not pass a bill opening the ANWR to energy exploration in 2005.

One of the president's highest priorities for 2005 was passage of the Central American Free Trade Agreement (CAFTA), which would eliminate tariffs and other trade barriers on U.S. exports to Costa Rica, El Salvador, Guatemala, Honduras, Nicaragua, and the Dominican Republic and increase protections for investments and intellectual property. The bill passed the Senate in June, but House Democrats overwhelmingly opposed it, contending that it was wrong to strike a free-trade pact with poor countries lacking strong protection for worker rights (only 15 of the 202 House Democrats eventually backed the accord). To win, the White House and GOP congressional leaders had to overcome resistance from dozens of Republican members who were also loath to vote for the accord because of issues ranging from the perceived threat to the U.S. sugar and textile industries to more general worries about the impact of global trade on U.S. jobs.

The president invested a great deal of time and energy in the passage of CAFTA. He held a summit with the leaders of all six CAFTA nations, met individually with dozens of lawmakers, and gave speeches to Hispanic and other groups promoting the deal. On the day before the vote, Bush made a rare appearance on Capitol Hill, accompanied by Vice President Cheney and U.S. Trade Representative Rob Portman, at the weekly closed-door meeting of the House Republican Conference and appealed per-

---

[54] "Twenty-Four House Republicans Urge Panel to Keep ANWR Out of Reconciliation Bill," *Congressional Quarterly Weekly Report,* August 15, 2005, 2254.

sonally to fellow Republicans to close ranks behind the trade agreement with Central America. The president spoke for more than an hour and reminded Republicans that although some might oppose CAFTA for parochial interests, "we are here not only to represent our districts but to represent the nation." He stressed the national security implications of CAFTA, which are rooted in the concern that growing anti-American sentiment in Latin America would flourish if the United States refused to open its markets wider to the nations that negotiated the pact. The president also noted that Central American countries have contributed troops in the war against terrorism.[55]

In addition to the president, Vice President Cheney, National Security Assistant Stephen Hadley, U. S. Trade Representative Rob Portman, Agriculture Secretary Mike Johanns, and Commerce Secretary Carlos Gutierrez lobbied lawmakers in the Capitol and at the White House. More important than attention from high-level officials, however, were side deals offering protections for sugar and textile manufacturers.[56] On August 1 the administration also announced that it planned to seek a broad agreement with China to limit its clothing exports to the United States, keeping a promise it made to House Republicans from textile-producing states.[57] In addition, Republican leaders told their rank and file that if they wanted anything, now was the time to ask, and members took advantage of the opportunity by requesting such things as fundraising appearances by Cheney and the

---

[55] Associated Press, "Hours Before Vote, Bush Lobbies for Trade Pact," July 27, 2005.
[56] Edmund L. Andrews, "White House Makes Deals for Support of Trade Pact," *New York Times*, July 26, 2005; Paul Blustein and Mike Allen, "Trade Pact Approved By House," *Washington Post*, July 28, 2005, p. A1.
[57] Edmund L. Andrews, "Bush Administration Will Ask China to Agree to Broad Limits on Clothing Exports," *New York Times*, August 2, 2005.

restoration of money the White House had tried to cut from agriculture programs. Lawmakers also said many of the favors bestowed in exchange for votes would be tucked into the huge energy and highway bills that Congress passed shortly after CAFTA.[58] Indeed, Republican leaders delayed filing the conference report on the pork-laden highway bill until after the House voted to approve CAFTA.

There were dozens of undeclared members when the usual 15-minute voting period expired for the final vote, and the 'no' votes outnumbered the 'yes' votes by 180 to 175. House Republican leaders kept the voting open for another 47 minutes, furiously rounding up holdouts in their own party until they had secured just enough to ensure approval. In the end, CAFTA passed in a 217 to 215 vote that was announced just after midnight. Only 15 Democrats voted for the bill, but they were just enough to offset the 27 Republicans who resisted the pressure and defected.[59] On CAFTA, as well as the transportation and energy bills, the president relied heavily on his party's leaders on Capitol Hill to make the deals necessary to achieve his legislative goals.[60]

In May, after the Republicans nearly voted to end the possibility of filibustering judicial nominations, 14 senators from both parties forged a deal without White House approval that would allow some, but not all, of Bush's stalled judicial nominees to receive floor votes. The Democrats gained leverage when they focused their opposition to ending the filibuster option on the issue of fairness, arguing that the Republicans were trying to change

---

[58] Blustein and Allen, "Trade Pact Approved By House."

[59] Edmund L. Andrews, "House Approves Free Trade Pact," *New York Times,* July 28, 2005.

[60] See, for example, Mike Allen, "DeLay's Week to Reassert Command," *Washington Post,* July 30, 2005, p. A10.

rules in the middle of the game and to dismantle the checks and balances that protected the United States against one-party rule and abuse of power. They were aided in this effort by the Republicans' use of the evocative phrase, "nuclear option" to describe limiting the filibuster, which made them sound like they were ready to blow up the Senate. To the disappointment of the White House, the Republicans did not win the battle for public opinion.

The deal on judges was followed quickly by a vote to shut down a filibuster on the nomination of John Bolton to be ambassador to the UN, a vote that Bush and the Republicans lost. As soon as Congress left town for its August recess, Bush gave Bolton a recess appointment, leaving behind bitter feelings in the Senate.[61]

Troubled Times

By the fall 2005, the White House and the Republican majority in Congress faced troubled times. Chapter 4 showed that the president was slumping in the polls in response to problems in domestic and foreign policy, including rising gas prices, the furor over the government's response to Hurricane Katrina, and public discontent with the war in Iraq. Then federal investigators arrested the administration's top procurement official, who had resigned three days before, and charged him with making false statements and obstructing a federal investigation relating to the broader investigation of lobbyist Jack Abramoff. Even worse, a Texas grand jury indicted House Majority Leader Tom DeLay, forcing

---

[61] Martin Kady II, "Hard Feelings after Recess Move," *Congressional Quarterly Weekly Report,* August 8, 2005, 2186.

the congressman to step down from his leadership post. The combined loss of DeLay's leadership in the House, where he was the main enforcer of the Republican agenda, and the shift of political focus to another alleged ethics misstep, was a double blow to the president at a time when he could not easily bounce back from it. Adding to the president's troubles was the investigation of stock sales of Republican Bill Frist, an inevitable distraction for the Senate majority leader, who had already set his focus on the 2008 Republican nomination for president. In yet another blow to the White House, the special prosecutor investigating the leak that revealed the name of CIA agent Valerie Plame indicted Vice President Richard Cheney's chief of staff, I. Lewis "Scooter" Libby.

One of the most visible results of Bush's ebbing political clout was the growing number of Republicans shedding their fear of publicly challenging the White House. "I think the biggest single challenge of putting votes together for our team, frankly, was the president's numbers," declared Representative Roy Blunt, the Missouri Republican who served as acting majority leader when DeLay stepped down, referring to Bush's dip in the polls."[62] "This is partly a function of approval ratings," agreed Republican Senator John Thune of South Dakota. "People pay attention [to polls] and start saying, 'Let's take a more independent tack.' It is frankly self-interest, self-preservation."[63]

In a sharp rebuke to the White House, the Senate ignored a veto threat from Bush and voted 90-9 to ban use of "cruel, inhu-

---

[62] Quoted in Carl Hulse, "A Messy Congressional Finale," *New York Times*, December 23, 2005.
[63] Quoted in Jim VandeHei and Charles Babington, "Newly Emboldened Congress Has Dogged Bush This Year," *Washington Post*, December 23, 2005, p. A5.

man or degrading treatment or punishment" against anyone in United States government custody and require all American troops to use only interrogation techniques authorized in a new Army field manual.[64] Ultimately, the White House had to accept this language as part of the defense authorization bill.

The administration had to confront the Republican leadership in the House by opposing a bill popular among conservatives and backed by Speaker J. Dennis Hastert that would cut in half the American dues to the United Nations if it did not enact several specific budget and management reforms.[65] The House also rejected Bush by passing a measure easing his restrictions on federal funding for embryonic stem cell research, with 50 Republicans joining most Democrats despite the threat of a presidential veto.

Bush's low approval levels not only freed Republicans to vote their true views but also animated Democrats and encouraged them to attack. Following the Washington maxim of never kicking a man until he is down—and then keep kicking him—Democrats discovered they paid little or no price for defying him and attacked the president vigorously. As a result, the president faced a Democratic party more united in its opposition than perhaps at any point in his tenure. Emboldened by their defeat of the president's Social Security plan (discussed in the next two chapters), Democrats showed unusual solidarity in thwarting his agenda elsewhere. They also instituted a leadership system to discourage dissent by threatening members with the loss of committee seats if

[64] Eric Schmitt, "Senate Moves to Protect Military Prisoners Despite Veto Threat," *New York Times,* October 6, 2005.

[65] Steven R. Weisman, "White House Voices Opposition to Cutting of U.N. Dues," *New York Times,* June 15, 2005.

they work too closely with the GOP. Democratic unity in opposition forced Republicans to scramble to find votes within their own modest majorities. Not a single Democrat in the House or Senate backed the Republicans' budget cuts, for example.

Bush put up a good front. When asked at his press conference on October 4 how much political capital he had left, his upbeat response was "Plenty. Plenty."[66] Nevertheless, the president's positive posture could not heal Republican divisions. There was a wide chasm among Republicans on immigration, between the business and agri-business elements of the party that support a constant flow of lower-cost labor—as well as those who want the GOP to expand the party beyond its current base of whites and Cuban Americans—and the nativists and others who want to build a wall to curtail future illegal immigration and start wholesale deportations of those currently living in the United States without documentation. Much to the president's displeasure, Congress would not permanently renew the USA Patriot Act, extending it for a few weeks while it worked on a compromise.

Then there was the fight between those who put a premium on tax cuts above all else, and those who placed greater emphasis on balancing the federal budget. Overlaying this were differences between those representing very conservative states and districts, whose constituents wanted the smallest possible government, and those representing the Northeast and other areas, who supported more activist government. In addition, there was a general frustration among conservative Republicans who had gone along with

---

[66] The president's press conference can be found at www.whitehouse.gov/news/releases/2005/10/20051004-1.html

the administration's costly proposals such as the war in Iraq, No Child Left Behind Act, and a Medicare prescription drug benefit, only to have that same president chastise them over controlling spending. Many conservatives demanded deep spending reductions to pay for hurricane recovery, generating resistance from Republican moderates, anxious about the difficult election year approaching. They found new backbone and stood firm against drilling in the Arctic and some cuts in social programs. In the end, Republican efforts to reduce the budget reflected the party's disarray and produced few net cuts. They were also unable to pass legislation to make the tax cuts of 2001–2003 permanent.

Supreme Court Nominations

One bright spot for the White House was the confirmation of John Roberts as chief justice of the Supreme Court. Bush initially nominated him to replace Sandra Day O'Connor on the Court, but after Chief Justice William Rehnquist died, the president renominated Roberts to be chief justice. His appealing personality, distinguished legal background, and conservative credentials made it easy for Republicans to support his nomination with enthusiasm.

Democrats and their supporting coalition of interest groups faced a dilemma regarding Roberts. Although they would have preferred a less conservative nominee, Bush was certainly going to name a conservative under any circumstances. In addition, Roberts did not appear to be a fire-breathing radical. Indeed, he was not an easy target to oppose. His pleasing and professional personal demeanor and his disciplined and skilled testimony before the Senate Judicial Committee provided little basis for opposition. Moreover, the nomination came at a time when some Democrats were seeking to soft-pedal their rhetoric on abortion and appeal to more conservative voters who might be attracted to Democrats on economic issues but who felt unable to accept what they saw as the Democrats' stand on cultural issues. These Democrats did not want to fight a highly visible battle over the issue of abortion, religion, and related issues. On the other hand, traditional liberal advocacy groups and many grass-roots activists wanted to fight, and at one point they badly overreached. NARAL Pro-Choice America launched a television ad that accused Roberts of siding with violent extremists and a convicted clinic bomber while serving in the solicitor general's office, an accusation that Roberts's supporters immediately condemned as a flagrant distortion. Soon thereafter, NARAL pulled the ad. In the end, all the Senate Republicans and about half the Democrats supported Roberts.

Attention immediately turned to the president's nomination on October 2 of White House counsel Harriet Miers to replace Justice O'Connor. Because Miers was largely unknown outside the White House, it appeared that Bush and his advisors had concluded that he could ill afford a bruising ideological fight and possible filibuster over a Supreme Court nominee at a time when he and his party were besieged by problems. Bush apparently thought Miers's lack of a published record would make it easier to push her nomination through. What looked like an adroit political decision soon turned sour, however.

Many of his most passionate supporters on the right had hoped and expected that he would make an unambiguously conservative choice to fulfil their goal of clearly altering the Court's balance, even at the cost of a bitter confirmation battle. By instead settling on a loyalist with no experience as a judge and little substantive record on abortion, affirmative action, religion, and other socially divisive issues, the president shied away from a direct confrontation with liberals and in effect asked his base on the right to trust him on his nomination. Many conservatives were bitterly disappointed and highly critical of the president. They demanded a known conservative and a top-flight legal figure.

The White House was surprised at the intensity of conservatives' anger and their irritation at not being given adequate warning that Miers was the president's choice.[67] At first, it tried to pacify them by stressing Miers's conservative religious beliefs. When conservatives raised issues of her legal qualifications and liberals criticized the White House for cynically reversing its contention that John Roberts's religion was irrelevant to his confirmation, the White House tried to refocus the debate onto her legal qualifications.[68]

The nomination had additional problems. It smacked of cronyism, with the president selecting a friend and a loyalist, rather than someone of obvious merit. The comparison with Roberts only emphasized the thinness of Miers's qualifications. In the wake of the criticism of FEMA director Michael Brown over his handling of relief efforts for the victims of Hurricane Katrina and his lack of relevant qualifications for his post, Bush handed his critics additional ammunition for their argument that he was

---

[67] See, for example, Elisabeth Bumiller, "White House Tries to Quell a Rebellion on the Right," *New York Times*, October 7, 2005.
[68] Peter Baker, "White House Shifts Its Lobbying Strategy," *Washington Post*, October 15, 2005, p. A7.

prone to stocking the government with cronies rather than individuals selected solely for their qualifications.

In short order Miers withdrew from consideration, and the president nominated Samuel A. Alito Jr. a few days later. Alito was clearly a traditional conservative and had a less impressive public presence than Roberts. Response to him followed party lines, but the nominee appeared too well qualified and unthreatening in his confirmation hearings to justify a filibuster, and without one his confirmation was assured. In the background, Republicans threatened retaliation against future Democratic nominees if the Democrats filibustered the nomination, while Democrats wanted to send a warning to Bush against nominating what they viewed as extreme conservatives in the future. The Senate confirmed Alito by a vote of 58-42, and it is unlikely that Bush will hesitate to make a similar nomination if given the opportunity.

Without a mandate and with a substantial minority of the public viewing his election as illegitimate, the George W. Bush presidency commenced under difficult circumstances. In his first term, however, the president surprised many observers, who underestimated both his character and his political skills. The White House made unusually focused efforts to govern strategically and effectively exploited the context in which it was attempting to govern by focusing on priorities, moving rapidly to exploit opportunities, setting the national agenda, and displaying tactical flexibility. However, despite its sensitivity to strategy and its discipline in implementing it, the administration faced the familiar frustrations of contemporary presidents. Its core governing strategy of governing by campaigning was typically not successful, as the public was unresponsive to the president's pleas for support, and Congress was unimpressed with the president's historic 9/11-induced approval ratings. As a result, the president relied heavily on his party's congressional leadership, which effectively delivered at least the House for his legislative proposals.

Bush began his second term by substantially overestimating his political capital and overreaching with a bold and aggressive program of reform. When he could rely on his party or buy Democratic votes with pork-barrel expenditures, he met with success. When he had to persuade a skeptical public or Republicans in Congress, however, he had more difficulty. In the heady days after reelection, the president announced an ambitious agenda to avoid the traditional pitfalls of second-term presidents, including the domestic policy priorities of reforming Social Security, revising the tax code, limiting litigation, and easing immigration rules. At the end of the year, only some litigation limits had passed, and Social Security, tax, and immigration plans were dead or comatose. Lawmakers also rebuffed Bush's call to make permanent his first-term tax cuts. Chapters 6 and 7 explore his efforts to reform the nation's most expensive policy: Social Security.

As 2006 began, Republicans were openly rebelling against the White House in the area of national security, forcing the president to accept changes in the USA Patriot Act, challenging the administration's domestic wiretapping program, and moving quickly to overturn the approval of an Arab company's takeover of terminals at major American ports. Relations with Congress in the remainder of the second term were unlikely to be smooth.

CHAPTER 6

Reforming Social Security,
Part I: Going Public

The Bush White House began the president's second term as it began his first—by launching an extensive public relations effort to convince the public to support the president's reform of Social Security. Rather than wind down its campaign effort, the administration employed a permanent campaign to take its case to the public. It is a classic example of attempting to govern by going public.

Even before the inauguration, the White House announced plans to reactivate Bush's reelection campaign's network of donors and activists to build pressure on lawmakers to allow workers to invest part of their Social Security taxes in the stock market. As Treasury Secretary John W. Snow put it, the "scope and scale goes way beyond anything we have done."[1] The same architects of Bush's political victories would be masterminding the new campaign, principally political strategists Karl Rove at the White House and Ken Mehlman, who was the Bush-Cheney campaign manager, at the Republican National Committee (RNC).

Mehlman declared that he would use the campaign apparatus—from a national database of 7.5 million e-mail activists, 1.6 million volunteers, and hundreds of thousands of neighborhood precinct captains—to build congressional support for Bush's plans, starting with Social Security. "There are a lot of tools we used in the '04 campaign, from regional media to research to rapid response to having surrogates on television," he said. "That whole effort will be focused on the legislative agenda."[2] In addition to their own efforts, White House and RNC officials worked closely with the same outside groups that helped Bush win reelection in 2004, especially Progress for America.

White House allies also launched a market-research project to figure out how to sell the plan in the most comprehensible and appealing way, and Republican marketing and public relations gurus were building teams of consultants to promote it. The campaign intended to use Bush's campaign-honed techniques of mass repetition, sticking closely to the script, and using the politics of fear to build support—contending that a Social Security financial crisis was imminent. There would be campaign-style events to win support and precision targeting of districts where lawmakers

---

[1] Quoted in Jim VandeHei and Mike Allen, "Bush Rejects Delay, Prepares Escalated Social Security Push," *Washington Post*, March 3, 2005, p. A4.

[2] Mike Allen and Jim VandeHei, "Social Security Push to Tap the GOP Faithful: Campaign's Tactics Will Drive Appeal," *Washington Post*, January 14, 2005, p. A6.

could face reelection difficulties. The White House would also use hard-hitting television ads to discredit its opponents and build support for the president's plan.[3]

THE ISSUE

Both employers and employees pay Social Security taxes. Employers deduct 6.2 percent of employees' earnings (up to $90,000 in 2005) and match this amount with their own payments. Unlike other taxes, these payments do not go into the government's general revenue fund. Instead, Congress has earmarked them for a specific purpose: the Social Security Trust Fund that pays benefits to the elderly, the disabled, the widowed, and the unemployed. More than 45 million Americans receive Social Security benefits.

Social Security is less an insurance program than a kind of intergenerational contract. Essentially, the system takes money from the working members of the population and spends it on the retired members. Today, however, demographic and economic realities threaten to dilute this intergenerational relationship. Millions of baby boomers are nearing retirement, and those who retire are living longer and, therefore, drawing benefits longer. In 1940, a 3 percent tax on payrolls financed the entire Social Security system. In 1945, 50 workers paid taxes to support each Social Security beneficiary. In 2005, about three workers supported each beneficiary. By the year 2025, when people born in the late 1950s will be getting their Social Security checks, only

[3] Allen and VandeHei, "Social Security Push to Tap the GOP Faithful."

two workers will be supporting each beneficiary. Thus, under current policy, benefit costs will rise dramatically over the next few decades. Moreover, with each passing year, fewer workers will pay ever-higher benefits to an ever-larger number of retirees.

As a result, by 2018 Social Security will be paying out more than it takes in. Every year afterward will bring a new shortfall, bigger than the year before. For example, in the year 2027, the government will somehow have to come up with an extra $200 billion to keep the system afloat—and by 2033, the annual shortfall will be more than $300 billion. Social Security's trustees estimate that without corrective action, the system can pay full benefits until 2041, and after that will take in only enough through payroll taxes to cover about 73 percent of promised benefits.

In the early 1980s, Congress increased Social Security taxes so that more was coming in to the Social Security Trust Fund than was being spent. The goal was to create a surplus to help finance payments when the baby boomers retire. This money is not sitting in a vault, however. Instead, Congress spent it on other policies and issued the Social Security Trust Fund IOUs. After 2041, the Trust Fund will have to cash in some of its IOUs to pay full benefits. As President Bush put it, the only way to deal with such a demand on the federal government would be "dramatically higher taxes, massive new borrowing, or sudden and severe cuts in Social Security benefits or other government programs."

Personal Accounts

In his February 2, 2005, State of the Union message, President Bush proposed that Congress make Social Security "a better deal" for younger workers by establishing provisions for voluntary personal retirement accounts. These would work by allowing everyone younger than 55 to divert as much as 4 percent of their income subject to Social Security taxation into individual accounts. The president argued that this money would grow over time at a greater rate than anything the current system could deliver. In addition, these workers would be able to pass along the money that accumulated in their personal accounts to their children or grandchildren. The money would be theirs "and the government can never take it away."[4]

Bush promised to set careful guidelines for personal accounts, making sure that people could only invest the money in them in a conservative mix of bonds and stock funds and that hidden Wall Street fees would not eat up the earnings. There would also be provisions to protect investments from sudden market swings on the eve of retirement and to ensure that no one could empty out a personal account all at once. The government would pay out the income from these accounts over time, as an addition to traditional Social Security benefits. Finally, the president promised to make sure his plan was fiscally responsible by starting personal retirement accounts gradually and raising the yearly limits on contributions over time.

The president did not emphasize that the benefits he projected Americans to accrue from personal accounts would come in an exchange for a reduction in people's guaranteed benefits. He also did not discuss the costs of his proposal.

---

[4] The president's address is available at www.whitehouse.gov/news/releases/2005/02/20050202-11.html.

Democrats displayed no such reluctance, however. They immediately pointed out that private accounts (as they insisted on calling them) would actually make Social Security's financial problems worse in the short run, because the government would have to borrow additional trillions of dollars to compensate for funds diverted from the Social Security trust fund into these accounts. Many critics also emphasized the risks of the president's plan, questioning the reliability of net gains from personal account investments. In addition, they challenged the view that low-income persons would be able to risk not purchasing an annuity—and losing their ability to pass on their accounts in the process. More broadly, Bush's opponents expressed concern that privatizing a portion of Social Security would diminish the social insurance aspect of it in which the public collectively supported seniors' retirement income.

The Matter of Solvency

Although President Bush offered a detailed proposal for allowing workers to put part of their Social Security taxes into accounts that they could invest in the private financial markets, throughout the winter and early spring of 2005 he never said what steps he favored to put the Social Security system on a sound financial footing in order to solve the solvency problem. Instead, he maintained that it was up to Congress to offer proposals. Democrats refused to come to the bargaining table without specifics from the administration.

From the beginning, the president adamantly opposed proposals to restore Social Security's solvency by raising taxes. Although

he did not rule out an increase in the ceiling on income that is subject to payroll taxes, $90,000 in 2005, the idea was anathema to
him and most Republicans. At a press conference on March 16,
Bush admitted, "Personal accounts do not solve the issue. They
make the solution more attractive to the individual worker."[5] The
solution, of course, would have to be reduced benefits. Yet the
president still avoided dealing with the solvency issue, preferring
Congress to take the lead in proposing benefit cuts.

Even as the president struggled to sell voters on making individual investment accounts the centerpiece of any changes in the
Social Security program, some of his chief allies in Congress, such
as Republican Senator Lindsey Graham of South Carolina, were
urging him to change his focus. They argued that Bush should
emphasize the retirement program's solvency rather than private
accounts and should give lawmakers a detailed plan. "He made a
strategic mistake talking about the accounts in isolation," said
Graham, who had taken the lead on talks with Democrats on the
issue. "Ownership" is "not what people look at Social Security as
being. They look at Social Security as a safety net."[6]

On April 26, the Senate Finance Committee held its first full-
scale debate on Social Security. A standing-room-only crowd
packed the largest hearing room on Capitol Hill and heard the
committee's chair, Senator Charles Grassley of Iowa, support the
president's initiative and demand that the Democrats offer their
own proposal. The Democrats were not biting, however. Senator
John Kerry, Democrat of Massachusetts, challenged Grassley.

---

[5] The press conference can be found at www.whitehouse.gov/news/releases/2005/03/20050316-3.html.
[6] Quoted in Heidi Przybyla, "Bush Extends Social Security Tour," *Northwest Herald,* May 2, 2005.

"Where's the president's plan?" he asked. "There is no plan from the president."[7]

All the Democrats on the panel who spoke said they were resolutely opposed to the president's proposal, and some Republicans also expressed reservations, an ominous sign for the White House. Meanwhile, the partisan wars on the issue were raging outside the Capitol. In a display of party unity, scores of Democratic lawmakers, including two dozen senators, took the stage at an outdoor rally to declare their commitment to blocking private accounts. Republicans countered by saying Democrats were simply celebrating obstructionism.[8]

At the outdoor rally, Democrats characterized the Bush plan as nothing short of privatization. "Social Security is sacred ground for the American people," declared House Democratic Leader Nancy Pelosi of California. The Democratic leader of the Senate, Harry Reid of Nevada, said his party would be unrelenting in fighting Bush's plan. The rally ended with an image composed to spotlight Democratic determination: scores of lawmakers joining hands next to a giant "Declaration of Unity" placard vowing to "stop privatization."[9]

Democrats said they would try to block any Social Security bill unless Bush personally promised that investment accounts would not become part of the legislation at a later stage.[10] It was unlikely that the president would agree, however. Representative Charles B. Rangel of New York, the senior Democrat on the

---

[7] David Rosenbaum, "At Social Security Hearing, Bush's Fight Looks Largely Uphill," *New York Times,* April 27, 2005.
[8] Rosenbaum, "At Social Security Hearing, Bush's Fight Looks Largely Uphill."
[9] Rosenbaum, "At Social Security Hearing, Bush's Fight Looks Largely Uphill."
[10] Edmund L. Andrews and Eduardo Porter, "Social Security: Help for the Poor or Help for All?" *New York Times,* May 1, 2005.

House Ways and Means Committee, said he met with the president the previous week and urged him to take private accounts off the table so the two parties could work on solvency. Rangel said Bush replied, "Congressman, . . . private accounts are not coming off the table even if it's the last day I spend in the presidency."[11]

Robert C. Pozen, an investment company executive from Boston, offered a proposal that would achieve long-term solvency primarily through what he called "progressive indexing." Under this plan, low-income workers would continue to have their initial retirement benefits based on the extent to which wages nationally increased during their working years. In contrast, the government would base the retirement benefits of middle- and upper-income workers on price inflation. Over time, wages tend to rise considerably faster than prices, so the benefits of these workers would be much lower than under current law.

Bush had spoken favorably of the Pozen plan. But Pozen testified before the Senate Finance Committee that Congress should first "come to grips with the growth in benefits" and only then should they "figure out what sort of personal accounts would be complementary"[12]—implicitly criticizing the president's approach of doing just the reverse.

Progressive Indexing of Benefits

On April 27, the White House surprised nearly everyone by announcing that the president would hold a primetime press conference the next day. He could have used the occasion to cut his

---

[11] Rosenbaum, "At Social Security Hearing, Bush's Fight Looks Largely Uphill."
[12] Rosenbaum, "At Social Security Hearing, Bush's Fight Looks Largely Uphill."

losses and begin negotiating a bipartisan compromise on Social Security, perhaps without the personal accounts he had promoted for the previous several months. Instead, he continued to press for private accounts but also added a proposal that would cut Social Security spending, openly defying the longtime belief that proposing cuts in the beloved program is bad politics.

In his opening statement at the press conference, Bush proposed a version of the Pozen plan and attempted to recast the 70-year-old retirement program as one that would keep the lowest-income workers out of poverty but play a more modest role for the middle class and the affluent over the next century. Under current law, a formula based on the growth in wages throughout the economy sets initial benefits for retirees. The president proposed to leave that formula intact for low-income workers but to shift the formula to one based on prices, which tend to grow more slowly than wages, for upper-income workers. For middle-income workers, the formula would blend inflation and wage growth in setting benefits. Proponents of the president's plan said it would erase about 70 percent of Social Security's long-term deficit.

The president proposed "progressive indexation," under which a typical low-income worker who earns about $16,000 a year today would be entitled to retirement benefits equal to about 49 percent of his or her wages, the same amount that is promised today. But those earning an average income, about $36,500 in today's dollars, would see substantial changes. Instead of replacing 36 percent of that person's working pay, as promised under today's system, benefits would cover only 26 percent of pay by 2075. People who earn $90,000 a year in today's dollars would continue to pay as much as ever in taxes but would receive benefits equal to only 12 percent of pay. About 70 percent of wage earners would see a cut in benefits over time.[13]

In choosing to preserve benefits for the less well-off and not raise taxes on more affluent people, the president sought to cast himself in the Democrats' traditional role as a defender of the poor. Comments in his Saturday radio address on April 30 were typical: "By providing more generous benefits for low-income retirees, we'll make good on this commitment: If you work hard and pay into Social Security your entire life, you will not retire into poverty."[14]

The president did not back off his private accounts initiative. Indeed, he could now argue that with smaller guaranteed payments for retirees, such accounts would soften the blow from scaling back the system to keep it fiscally sound.

The president's proposal drew immediate and widespread criticism from Democrats and some Republicans. Democratic opponents of Bush's approach argued that Congress could just as easily address the issues of fairness and inequality by raising taxes on the wealthy. They proposed raising the ceiling on payroll taxes, which they claimed would maintain the system's solvency just as well, if not better, than Bush's plan while allowing it to pay out substantial retirement benefits to the 30 million more people who experts expected to be added to the rolls from the ranks of the nation's aging baby boomers. That one change would affect only 6 percent of all workers, the very highest earners, but actuarial experts estimate that it would raise almost enough money

---

[13] Andrews and Porter, "Social Security: Help for the Poor or Help for All?"
[14] The president's address is available at www.whitehouse.gov/news/releases/2005/04/20050430.html.

to eliminate the projected shortfall without needing to cut benefits at all.

Some critics charged that the slower growth in benefits would fall hardest on middle-income Americans, many of whom were highly dependent on Social Security for their retirement income. In addition, opponents feared that the president's approach would undermine a central bargain conceived during the New Deal: that Social Security is not just a welfare program for the poor but a form of social insurance that people at all income levels pay into and from which they receive benefits. If it became increasingly irrelevant for middle-income people, the critics warned, Social Security would lose public support and eventually become little more than an empty shell.

Bush's aides argued that the benefit cuts Bush proposed had to be judged against what would happen if nothing was done to shore up the system as the baby boom generation ages and life expectancy increases. The president did not focus on benefit cuts, however. On the last day of the "60 Stops in 60 Days" tour, Bush devoted only one sentence to the proposal in a 44-minute speech, and even then he said nothing about the cuts. When one of the panelists at his roundtable thanked him for trying "to reduce the rate of growth of benefits," the president ignored the remark.[15]

By May 3, however, the White House signaled that it was not wedded to a particular formula for reducing promised future benefits. Reflecting the reluctance of many members of his own party on Capitol Hill to embrace any plan that critics could portray as

---

[15] Dana Milbank, "No Light at the End of the Tour," *Washington Post*, April 30, 2005.

harming the middle class, the White House signaled that Bush would be flexible if Congress had other ideas about how to close the projected long-term gap in Social Security's finances. "He has put out his proposal on a way to protect the lowest-income workers, but that in the context of the legislative process, he'll welcome other ideas for solutions, and would welcome other ideas to perfect or to make the best system," Trent Duffy, a spokesman for Bush, told reporters.[16]

GOING PUBLIC

The day after the president presented his Social Security proposal in his State of the Union address, he embarked on a two-day campaign-style swing to North Dakota, Montana, Nebraska, Arkansas, and Florida. At each stop, he attended events to discuss Social Security with citizens and promote his plan to create private investment accounts within the retirement system and put it on sound financial footing.

The first stop on the president's trip was Fargo, North Dakota. Addressing a large crowd of students, faculty, politicians, and the general public at North Dakota State University, President Bush delivered a stump speech reminiscent of the 2004 election campaign. Then he took questions from the audience. As usual, the White House carefully staged the event (see Chapter 2). The official premise was that Bush would "converse" with "ordinary" Americans.

---

[16] Richard Stevenson, "Seeking Support, Bush Offers Assurances on Retirement Cuts," *New York Times*, May 4, 2005.

The reality was different. President Bush's campaign team had carefully screened members of the audience in his campaign rallies in 2004 to create an environment of enthusiastic support. Similarly, the audiences for the Social Security tour contained no angry protestors or political adversaries who would counter the president's remarks or ask him difficult questions. Instead, the White House's advance team handpicked the audience and those who asked questions to dramatize his points, making sure he spoke only beneath giant campaign-style banners in front of crowds of cheering supporters.

Not only did the president's staff recruit the panelists for these conversations from administration supporters, but sometimes they also rehearsed them the night before, with a White House official playing the president. One participant told the *Washington Post*, "We ran through it five times before the president got there." At the last minute staffers dismissed potential panelists who varied just slightly from the administration's pitch.[17]

The following dialogue (from the White House website), in which a female veteran addresses the president during the question period in the president's Fargo appearance, was not unusual.[18]

The President: All right, Tricia Traynor, welcome.

Mrs. Traynor: Welcome.

The President: Thank you. You are married? For how long?

Mrs. Traynor: Three months—almost three months. My husband, Dan—

---

[17] Frank Rich, "Enron: Patron Saint of Bush's Fake News," *New York Times,* March 20, 2005.
[18] www.whitehouse.gov/news/releases/2005/02/20050203-6.html, "President Participates in Social Security Conversation in North Dakota," February 2, 2005.

The President: Where is he?

Mrs. Traynor: He is over to the right, waving his hand.

The President: There he is. Fine-looking man. That a boy, Dan. (Applause.) The interesting thing about Tricia is she is a—

Mrs. Traynor: Major in the Air Force Reserve.

The President: There you go. (Applause.) Have you been overseas yet?

Mrs. Traynor: Yes. I was in the Middle East for six months in 2003, for Operation Iraqi Freedom.

The President: Good. Thanks for serving. (Applause.) Your nation is grateful . . . . (Applause.) So tell me what's on your mind about Social Security. You're young.

Mrs. Traynor: We're in our 30s.

The President: Yes, you fall in the category of those who should be worried about whether or not Congress—and the President—has got the will to act.

Mrs. Traynor: We'd like to make sure that the money we are investing in Social Security now will be there 30 years from now, 40 years from now.

The President: Right. . . . let me ask you something. So you've heard about personal retirement accounts. Give me—just tell the folks here what you thought when you heard it. I mean, people need to kind of get a sense for how souls such as yourself, an educated person, obviously interested in the future, worried about your and Dan's life, think about a new concept for Social Security.

Mrs. Traynor: Mr. President, it gives us hope that somebody is willing to address the issue. It's too easy to just push it down the road and it's better to prevent the crisis before the crisis takes place.

The President: That's the first threshold issue. Thank you. (Applause.) . . . You probably think I hired her, or something. (Laughter.) Did you talk to my mother this morning? (Laughter.) Thanks.

Look, here's the thing. The threshold question is whether there's a problem that needs to be solved. And if there is, then who can come up with solutions that work.

And so thank you for saying that. I—it's in my nature to confront problems. And I really enjoyed giving the speech last night and trying to do the very best I could to kind of educate people, is to explain as rationally as possible why we have a problem. And the Major is typical of many 30-year-old citizens around. In the course of two campaigns, I campaigned on this issue. Some were saying, oh, don't talk about the issue, it's the third rail of American politics. If you touch it, you know, you become politically electrocuted. (Laughter.)

. . . I believe that the whole issue has shifted over time. Once older citizens are sure they're going to get their check—and I assure you you're going to get your check—that younger workers begin to—will have a voice in deciding how this issue turns out. Once people say, well, there is a problem, what are you going to do about it? That's what the Major just said. And so, Major, personal accounts, any feel for that at all?

Mrs. Traynor: The thrift savings plans were opened up to the military just a couple years ago.

The President: You're in one?

Mrs. Traynor: I am in one. I participate. What it is, is it's a safe investment, and it allows me to take a portion of the income I'm earning and put it away to save it for the future. And I'm happy with that, and I like the idea of sharing that with the American public, and not just limiting it to federal employees.

The President: Federal employees. See, she's in a thrift savings plan very similar—in other words, we're not inventing something new. What's new is that it would be associated with a retirement through Social Security. It's not new. It's already being used. It's a plan that is—that federal employees are able to take advantage of. The way we proposed the plan is that you could put $1,000—up to 4 percent of your income, whichever is less—in your account. And over time, the $1,000 grows. Is that right—up to $1,000, 4 percent, which ever is less. Yes, I think that's right. It better be right. (Laughter.)

So in other words, if you're making $90,000 you'll eventually be able to put $3,600 a year away in a personal account. But it starts at $1,000 and phases in over time, in order to make sure that the—is fiscally responsible. So I don't want to know your income, but you could start with $1,000, and over time it grows. And as interest compounds, Tricia and her husband would have a nice nest egg to complement that which would be coming out of Social Security.

Is that the way you see it?

Mrs. Traynor: Yes.

The President: That's the way it's going to be. If only we can get Congress to vote it in. (Applause.)

The administration also employed other techniques to influence the public. Republican National Committee Chairman Ken Mehlman started a contest on the Web—"National March Madness: Preserve Social Security Champion," complete with a spinning basketball—to encourage college students to collect signatures for the party's Social Security petition.[19] The president even enlisted his mother, Barbara Bush, in his campaign to overhaul Social Security. In March and July 2005, the former first lady—who turned 80 in June—played a cameo role as a participant in "conversations" on the issue, appearing with him on stage to express her concern about the program's solvency. "I'm here because I'm worried about our 17 grandchildren, and so is my husband," Mrs. Bush declared. "They will get no Social Security."[20]

On April 6, the Treasury Department held "Social Security Radio Day" at its headquarters from 8 A.M. to 8 P.M. At Treasury Secretary John Snow's invitation, more than 25 radio hosts from around the country broadcast interviews on Social Security from the Treasury Department. The hosts transmitted hundreds of interviews with administration surrogates, including Snow, senior White House advisor Karl Rove, Secretary of Commerce Carlos M. Gutierrez, White House Budget Director Joshua B. Bolton, and four of Snow's lieutenants at the Treasury Department.[21]

The Republican National Committee reported that in the week of February 21, when Congress was in recess, COMPASS (Coalition for the Modernization and Protection of America's Social Security)—a coalition of business lobbies including the Business Roundtable, the U.S. Chamber of Commerce, the National Association of Manufacturers, the National Retail

---

[19] Mike Allen and Peter Baker, "Hill Takes a Back Seat on Social Security: Administration, Republican National Committee Lead Drive to Add Private Accounts," *Washington Post,* April 6, 2005, p. A4.

[20] See, for example, Elizabeth Bumiller, "Stumping on Social Security, Bush Gets Motherly Help," *New York Times,* March 19, 2005; Jim VandeHei, "Mother and Son Bush Talk Medicare to Seniors," *Washington Post,* July 23, 2005, p. A2; David E. Rosenbaum, "Bush Urges Retirees to Get Behind His 'Senior Security Package,'" *New York Times,* July 23, 2005.

[21] Edmund L. Andrews, "Treasury Takes Social Security to Airwaves," *New York Times,* April 7, 2005, p. A16; Allen and Baker, "Hill Takes a Back Seat on Social Security."

Association, the National Restaurant Association, the Associated General Contractors, and the Alliance of Automobile Manufacturers—made 267,694 phone calls to build support for Bush's proposal. It also mobilized 3,100 advocates to attend town hall meetings, call talk show programs, and reach out to the national media; linked 247 Web logs to a pro-Bush online petition; placed 38 Progress for America spokesmen on 38 radio shows; and placed 28 letters to the editor.[22]

At the end of President Bush's "60 Stops in 60 Days" campaign to promote his Social Security proposals, the Treasury Department reported on its website that 31 administration officials had made 166 stops outside the beltway, visiting 40 states and 127 cities, and given more than 500 radio interviews in 50 states. Administration officials also placed opinion columns in newspapers with circulation totaling 7.94 million during this period, and they participated in 61 town hall meetings with 30 members of Congress in their constituencies.[23]

As we will see later, all this effort did not succeed in convincing the public to support the president or his Social Security proposal. So the president kept on stumping in an effort to reverse the dwindling public support for his plan. The continuation of the campaign-style trips underscored the challenge Bush faced. It appeared that it was unlikely that he could obtain congressional backing for his proposal until he won more public support. "Social Security reform is stuck in the mud on Capitol Hill," said Stuart Rothenberg, editor of the nonpartisan *Rothenberg Political*

---

[22] "By the Numbers: A Snapshot of One Week in the GOP Effort to Change Social Security," *Congressional Quarterly Weekly Report*, March 7, 2005, 547.
[23] www.strengtheningsocialsecurity.gov/60stops/accomplishments_042705.pdf

Report. "The only way to move this issue forward is to create a groundswell at the grassroots."[24]

WORKING WITH AFFILIATED GROUPS

In addition to their own efforts, the White House and the Republican National Committee worked closely with the same outside groups that helped Bush win reelection in 2004. Many of these interest groups also backed the Bush administration's tax cuts, the 2003 Medicare prescription drug legislation, and proposed energy initiatives. As President Bush began his second term, the alliance had become an institutional fixture, providing both money and manpower to further the Bush agenda and strengthen the Republican party apparatus. Thus, corporations, the financial services industry, conservative think tanks, much of the Washington trade association community, and GOP lobbyists and consultants prepared to spend $200 million or more on lobbying, television advertising, grass-roots campaigning, letter-writing, and phone calls to help the president obtain passage of his priority domestic policy proposals, the most important of which was personal accounts under Social Security.[25]

To coincide with Bush's new drive, Progress for America, a Republican political advocacy group, ran ads on Fox News and CNN that compared Bush to Franklin Roosevelt, the father of

---

[24] Quoted in Przybyla, "Bush Extends Social Security Tour."
[25] Thomas B. Edsall, "Conservatives Join Forces for Bush Plans; Social Security, Tort Limits Spur Alliance," *Washington Post*, February 13, 2005, p. A4.

Social Security. The group also phoned or e-mailed Republicans to enlist their help in selling the Bush plan, either by donating money or talking up the plan to neighbors. As a spokesman for the group said, it was applying the lessons it learned electing a president to selling a public policy.[26] In March, the organization began a $2 million campaign of television commercials, rolling out a minute-long advertisement supporting President Bush's Social Security plan.[27]

By early April, Progress for America had spent about $9 million on the campaign, including sponsoring traffic reports in 25 cities so that commuters would continually hear the message, "There's a crisis in Social Security—and it's coming sooner than you think."[28] One of the group's television ads likened Social Security's impending financial problems to the Titanic's approaching the iceberg that would send the ship to the ocean floor.[29] The group even signed up a 9-year-old from Texas, who agreed to travel supporting the president's proposal as a volunteer spokesman while on spring break from elementary school.[30]

Business groups also immediately arrayed to assist the president. The Alliance for Worker Retirement Security, housed at the National Association of Manufacturers, organized to pressure Congress directly. COMPASS announced a costly nationwide television and grass-roots pressure campaign. These efforts were in

---

[26] Allen and VandeHei, "Social Security Push to Tap the GOP Faithful."
[27] Glen Justice, "Group Opens $2 Million Drive for Bush Social Security Plan," *New York Times,* March 8, 2005.
[28] Allen and Baker, "Hill Takes a Back Seat on Social Security."
[29] Associated Press, "Democrats Hit Road in Social Security War," April 3, 2005.
[30] Glenn Justice, "At 9, He's Out Stumping for President's Social Security Plan," *New York Times,* February 26, 2005.

addition to those of pro-Bush groups such as Progress for America, Freedom Works, and USA Next, which announced plans to raise and spend substantial amounts to help the president's Social Security initiative.[31]

When Bush visited Indiana and New Jersey on March 4, for example, his supporting coalition went into action. In Indiana, the Business Roundtable recruited dozens of Bush supporters carrying "Fix Social Security Now!" signs and buttons. Former Republican representative J.C. Watts, now a lobbyist, gave an interview on Indiana Network talk radio. In New Jersey, the same group turned out 60 supporters at the president's speech and placed an opinion piece favoring private accounts in the *Newark Star-Ledger* by Sam Beard, a Democrat on the organization's board. Progress for America arranged for radio stations in the two states to interview experts and politicians who favored Bush's initiative.[32]

On Fridays, the Republican National Committee held a meeting on Social Security that Barry Jackson, White House senior advisor Karl Rove's deputy, who handled much of the day-to-day oversight of the Social Security campaign, often attended. Also in attendance were representatives of Progress for America and COMPASS. Although the groups operated independently of the White House, they had close ties to the administration and to Rove. Terry Nelson, who was one of Rove's top aides as political director of Bush's reelection campaign, ran COMPASS's cam-

---

[31] Jeffrey H. Birnbaum, "Group to Coordinate Attack on Bush Plan Social Security Proposal Is Targeted," *Washington Post*, February 25, 2005, p. A19.
[32] Peter Baker and Jeffrey Birnbaum, "For Bush and Foes, Dueling Social Security Efforts," *Washington Post*, March 5, 2005, p. A2.

paign. Charles Blahous, the White House's Social Security expert, once ran the Alliance for Worker Retirement Security.[33]

Despite the organizations supporting the president, he faced formidable organized opposition to his proposal for personal accounts. Most important was the nation's largest lobby, the Association for the Advancement of Retired Persons (AARP), with 35 million members. The AARP's $800 million budget is five times that of the U.S. Chamber of Commerce, the country's biggest business association, and it delivers its *Magazine* and *Bulletin* to 22 million households. It also has offices in all 50 states, a national radio show, a heavily visited website, and a 650,000-circulation Spanish-language magazine, *Segunda Juventud* (Second Youth). With 1,800 employees, it mobilizes senior citizens better than any other group, and seniors are a powerful voting bloc. In addition, the AARP has taught 1.5 million members how to contact their elected representatives. These activists receive their own publication, as well as periodic "alerts" that launch them into action from every congressional district. Half way through the president's "60 Stops in 60 Days" tour, the organization reported that members of Congress had received more than 460,000 phone calls complaining about Bush's private-account plan.[34]

The AARP worked hard to defeat the president's Social Security plan and spent millions of dollars on ads attacking it. In addition, it held AARP forums in states with swing-vote senators,

---

[33] Richard Stevenson, "With Bush Safely Re-elected, Rove Turns Intensity to Policy," *New York Times,* March 28, 2005.
[34] Jeffrey H. Birnbaum, "Bush's Plan Faces Formidable Foe: AARP Leads With Wallet In Fight Over Social Security," *Washington Post,* March 30, 2005, p. A1.

generally drawing 300 people per meeting, and it dispatched volunteers to protest the president's plan for individual accounts at town meetings held by members of Congress. When President Bush arrived in Iowa on March 30 to talk up his private-accounts proposal, the senior citizens group countered him with two news conferences, the release of a national poll, full-page newspaper advertisements, and commercials on radio and television.[35]

In Indiana and New Jersey, the AARP greeted Bush's visits with full-page newspaper ads warning that his plan would turn the program into "Social Insecurity." Other Bush opponents staged news conferences, placed newspaper ads and commentaries, and aired radio commercials targeting the two House Republicans who hosted the president on his visits. Outside the Joyce Center at the University of Notre Dame, about 100 protesters greeted Bush's motorcade with signs such as "Social Security, Another Big Fat Lie." As was often the case in the battle over Social Security reform, there was the spectacle of competing public demonstrations, for and against the president, sometimes just a few hundred yards apart.[36]

The president's supporters were not idle in the face of this opposition. One focus was to discredit the AARP on Social Security. USA Next hired some of the same consultants who worked for Swift Vets and P.O.W.s for Truth, which made headlines in 2004 for its attacks on Senator John Kerry's record in the Vietnam War. In February, USA Next ran an Internet advertisement linking the AARP to support for same-sex marriage. The advertisement,

---

[35] Birnbaum, "Bush's Plan Faces Formidable Foe."
[36] Baker and Birnbaum, "For Bush and Foes, Dueling Social Security Efforts."

which ran briefly on *The American Spectator* website, had two pictures, one of an American soldier in camouflage crossed out by a red X and the other showing two men in tuxedos kissing each other accompanied by a green check mark. The advertisement carried the caption, "The real AARP agenda." "We are going to be revealing areas where the AARP is out of touch with a large number of their members, including the issue of marriage," declared Charlie Jarvis, the group's chief executive. The fact that the AARP had never taken a position on same-sex marriage did not stop USA Next.[37]

The inflammatory nature of this ad caused a riff among Bush's supporters. The Cato Institute, the libertarian research organization that had long been a leader in promoting private Social Security accounts, lashed out at USA Next. "This is not very bright politics," Michael Tanner, the director of health and welfare studies at Cato, said. "Introducing homophobia and other things that are not relevant to Social Security reform is not helpful." "You need to build a coalition to win this fight. You're not going to get Social Security reform passed just through the right wing of the Republican Party. Groups like gays are disadvantaged by the current system, and I'd think we would want to bring them into the campaign, not insult them."[38] Nevertheless, Charlie Jarvis, the president of USA Next, said his group would not back down. "We are going to make sure their members know their position on that and every

---

[37] Glen Justice and David D. Kirkpatrick, "Group Makes Pre-emptive Strike Against AARP on Benefits Plan," *New York Times*, February 23, 2005.
[38] Sheryl Gay Stolberg and Richard W. Stevenson, "Flare-Ups in Battle Over Bush's Social Security Plan," *New York Times*, February 24, 2005.

other issue," he said of AARP, adding, "They can run, but they cannot hide."[39]

Labor Unions were also in the forefront of the opposition to the president. In February, the American Federation of State, County, and Municipal Employees (AFSCME) played a leading role in forming Americans United to Protect Social Security (discussed below) to serve as an umbrella for groups opposed to Bush's proposal. The union also helped organize protests in cities Bush had visited to publicize his proposal, and it organized "town hall" meetings in the districts of Republican members who had not stated a clear public position on the issue.[40]

Unions also staged demonstrations in dozens of cities, packed congresspersons' town meetings with union members, and collected tens of thousands of signatures to denounce Bush's call for personal Social Security investment accounts.[41] In addition, organized labor made firms that aligned with the administration targets of public protests. The AFL-CIO and its local affiliates took aim at members of the Alliance for Worker Retirement Security, a business group that backed the White House proposal and suggested that its pension managers would look elsewhere to invest their billions as long as the firms were members of the alliance.[42]

The AFL-CIO spotlighted four large companies that had joined the Alliance for Worker Retirement Security. Not wishing to risk losing the opportunity to manage the more than $400 billion

---

[39] Stolberg and Stevenson, "Flare-Ups in Battle over Bush's Social Security Plan."
[40] "Unions Hit the Field in Overhaul Battle," *Congressional Quarterly Weekly Report*, March 28, 2005, 768–769.
[41] Steve Greenhouse, "Unions Protest Against Bush's Social Security Proposal," *New York Times*, April 1, 2005.
[42] "Unions Hit the Field in Overhaul Battle."

in pension funds that unions have invested nationwide, Edward Jones and Waddell & Reed dropped out of the lobbying group, and the other two, Charles Schwab and the Wachovia Corporation, stayed in the alliance but insisted they had no official position on Bush's ideas. In addition, the Financial Services Forum, a financial services industry association, dropped out of COMPASS.[43]

On May 3, the Department of Labor sent a letter to the AFL-CIO, saying it was "very concerned" that pension plans might be spending workers' money to "advocate a particular result in the current Social Security debate." The Labor Department also warned the federation that pension plans could be violating their fiduciary responsibilities by suggesting that they might take their investment business away from Wall Street firms that support the president's plans.

At the urging of Democratic leaders in Congress, some political campaign veterans worked with organized labor to form Americans United to Protect Social Security. The organization served as an umbrella group to coordinate the attacks of about 200 organizations on President Bush's drive to create personal investment accounts. It also launched "60 Faces over 60 Days: The Real Faces of Social Security"—a program featuring personal stories of 60 people to highlight what it perceived as the dangers of Bush's plan. Other major players in the coalition included USAction, a grass-roots issues network, and the Campaign for America's Future, an activist group that pushes issues from the perspective of the political left. The group worked closely with the

---

[43] Glen Justice, "Group Opens $2 Million Drive for Bush Social Security Plan," *New York Times,* March 8, 2005; Edmund Andrews, "U.S. Warns AFL-CIO on Protests About Social Security," *New York Times,* May 5, 2005.

Democratic leaders in the House and Senate to fight Bush's Social Security proposal.[44]

Another advocacy group, Campaign for America's Future, accused Representative Jim McCrery of Louisiana (chair of the House Ways and Means Committee's subcommittee on Social Security) of conflict of interest, saying he had accepted nearly $200,000 in contributions over four years from securities firms and commercial banks that could benefit from Bush's plan to let workers invest in retirement accounts. The group also ran newspaper advertisements against McCrery under the headline, "Who Does This Man Work For?" in his hometown of Shreveport, Louisiana. In addition, it used the Internet to raise money for television advertisements. McCrery responded by accusing the group, which is backed by labor unions and liberal philanthropists (including George Soros), of "extreme liberal bias" and conducting "a meritless campaign" attacking his integrity.[45]

REACHING THE PUBLIC

Although the president traveled across the country on behalf of his Social Security proposals, devoting speech after speech and even a rare primetime news conference to his top legislative priority, he faced a number of obstacles to focusing the public's attention. Perhaps the greatest distraction was that international affairs kept forcing itself onto his agenda. The elections in Iraq and

---

[44] Jeffrey H. Birnbaum, "Group to Coordinate Attack on Bush Plan Social Security Proposal Is Targeted," *Washington Post*, February 25, 2005, p. A19; Peter Baker and Jeffrey Birnbaum, "For Bush and Foes, Dueling Social Security Efforts," *Washington Post*, March 5, 2005, p. A2.
[45] Stolberg and Stevenson, "Flare-Ups in Battle over Bush's Social Security Plan."

Bush's soaring rhetoric in his inaugural address calling for an end to tyranny and promising to promote democracy in the Middle East and elsewhere generated substantial coverage by the media, as did the death of Yasser Arafat and the withdrawal of Syrian troops from Lebanon after decades of occupation. These stories were good news for the president, but they forced him to speak and act on issues that diverted the public's attention from his persuasive efforts focused on Social Security.

Other circumstances forced Bush to confront several growing threats that distracted from his domestic goals. Violence continued in Iraq at a frightening pace, and American military officers reported that there was no end in sight to the insurgency. They also argued that U.S. forces were spread too thinly to undertake major new responsibilities. U.S. opposition to nuclear arsenals in North Korea and Iran were certain headline grabbers. "Right now, one of the defining aspects of this period is lowered barriers to the acquisition of very destructive technologies," said one former national security official. The threats of North Korea and Iran, "two countries perched to be breakthrough" nuclear powers, he added, would dominate any president's time. "You can't wish that away."[46]

Even unexpected complications in his trip to Europe in May to celebrate the anniversary of the end of World War II intruded on his efforts to move the public on his domestic policy initiative. His statements about Soviet domination of the Baltic states irritated the Russians and provided a natural story line of conflict between major powers.

---

[46] Jim VandeHei and Peter Baker, "Events Pull Attention From U.S.," *Washington Post*, May 7, 2005.

Other matters forced the president to rearrange his schedule to deal with issues other than Social Security. He made a special trip from his ranch to Washington to sign legislation affecting Terri Schiavo. The president's support of federal intervention in determining the fate of the comatose woman boosted the already extraordinary media attention devoted to her case—and irritated the public in the process. Then Bush had to fly to Rome for the high-profile funeral of Pope John Paul II. All the while, gas prices remained high at the pump, forcing the administration to ask oil producing countries to increase their output of oil.

To refocus attention on his flagging Social Security reform proposal, the White House announced on Wednesday, April 27, 2005, that the president would hold a primetime press conference the next day at 8:30 P.M. (EDT). Although it might seem reasonable to assume that holding such a press conference would be a straightforward activity in which the president could obtain a hearing from the American people, such an assumption would be incorrect. Examining the press conference illustrates additional frustrations the president experienced in attempting to lead the public.

This was the president's first primetime press conference in more than a year. However, in scheduling it the president's aides had not considered one very important factor. The evening press conference was to occur on the first night of the May sweeps period, one of three main times in the year in which companies like Nielsen closely track network ratings, with important implications for setting advertising rates for the next year.[47]

---

[47] Jacques Steinberg, "How the President's News Conference Ended Up Live on Four Networks," *New York Times*, April 29, 2005.

Had it decided to carry the news conference at 8:30, NBC would have had to bump, or at least delay, *Will and Grace* and delay the start of *The Apprentice,* among its most popular shows. Like a game of dominoes, a delay in starting *The Apprentice* would have delayed the start of *E.R.,* also among its most popular shows, and that could have then jeopardized the starts of local newscasts, at least on the East Coast. In the end, NBC decided that it could afford to pre-empt *Will and Grace,* but not *The Apprentice,* so it complained to the White House.

Neither CBS nor Fox thought that it could afford to pre-empt the popular one-hour shows that they broadcast beginning at 8 P.M, *Survivor* and *The O.C.,* respectively. Both networks announced early on Thursday that they did not intend to broadcast the president's remarks live on their main networks. ABC, lacking a popular show on Thursday evening, announced early in the day that it intended to carry the president live.

Faced with three of the four largest broadcast networks snubbing Bush's news conference for regular primetime programming, the White House released a one-sentence statement at 5 P.M., Thursday: "Due to the complications of network programming, the White House is moving the time of tonight's news conference to 8:00 P.M."

The White House's decision to move up the time of the press conference, and NBC's decision to carry it, put sufficient pressure on CBS and Fox to prompt them to announce that they, too, would carry the news conference live on their main networks, according the president considerably wider television exposure than he would have otherwise received for his primetime news conference. Bush obtained an audience of 37 million viewers (plus those watching on PBS), more than for his State of the Union message but fewer than the 41 million of his previous primetime press conference in April 2004. It is entirely possible that the president got a bigger audience than he might otherwise have attracted because viewers were tuning in for the usual highly rated Thursday night programs on the networks. Because the White House did not schedule the press conference until Wednesday, a sizable share of viewers probably tuned in thinking they were about to watch their favorite Thursday shows, such as CBS's *Survivor.*

As if obtaining airtime was not difficult enough for the president, he had to endure one final indignity. After sacrificing one hour of primetime, CBS, NBC, and FOX cut off the president in mid-sentence at 9 P.M. (EST). The president was left standing on the stage as NBC rushed to Donald Trump on *The Apprentice,* FOX to Paris Hilton on *The Simple Life,* and CBS to *Survivor.* Sensing he was running into trouble, Bush joked, "We better finish this up, there are TV programs to show. And I want to help the economy." But it was too late. They had already pulled away.

Bush faced problems with more routine coverage as well. On May 19, 18 days after the president's 60-day road show was to have ended, the president traveled to Milwaukee to host his thirty-second Social Security event. The president delivered the same spiel that he had given dozens of times before while Washington—and the media—focused on violence in Iraq, the Senate's consideration of the nomination of John Bolton to be ambassador to the United Nations, and the Senate's debate over limiting the use of filibusters for judicial nominations. As a result, the press charter plane that travels with the president was only half filled. None of the networks sent its regular White House correspondents and *USA Today,* the *Washington Times,* and other papers that usually cover presidential trips saw no reason to cover this one. Even some White House aides had grown weary of the barnstorming and privately rolled their eyes and groaned at the notion of yet another Social Security trip.[48]

FRAMING THE ISSUE

Central to the White House's strategy in the fight for reforming Social Security was the language employed in the battle. At the core of the struggle was the question of whether President Bush was proposing to create "personal" or "private" accounts in the program.

At the end of January 2005, congressional Republicans emerged from an annual retreat to launch their campaign to try to convince constituents that rewriting the Social Security law would be cheaper and less risky than leaving it alone. They carried with them a 104-page playbook titled *Saving Social Security,* a deliberate echo of the language President Bill Clinton used to argue that the government should build up the retirement system's trust fund in anticipation of the baby boomers' retirement. Republican leaders developed this plan with the advice of pollsters, marketing experts, and communication consultants and urged the lawmakers to promote the "personalization" of Social Security, suggesting ownership and control, rather than "privatization," which "connotes the total corporate takeover of Social Security."[49]

---

[48] Peter Baker, "Bush Continues Social Security Campaign: Polls Show President's Roadshow Failing to Drive Up Support for His Plan," *Washington Post,* May 20, 2005, p. A4.
[49] Mike Allen, "Congressional Republicans Agree to Launch Social Security Campaign," *Washington Post,* January 31, 2005.

Polls and focus groups for both sides showed that voters—especially older ones, for whom Social Security policy is most salient and who vote in disproportionately large numbers—distrusted any change that has the word "private" attached to it. Pollsters found that privatization conveyed to people a fundamental change in Social Security, one that put their retirement at the mercy of private-sector forces over which they had little or no control.

Frank Luntz, a Republican consultant with extensive experience with focus groups on language, added that "'Private' is exclusive. 'Private' is limiting. 'Private' is something that's not available to all." However, "'Personal' is encompassing. It's individual. It's ownership. In the end, you need the combination of 'personal' and 'security'."[50]

As a result, Bush and his supporters employed the terms "personal accounts" instead of "private accounts" to refer to his plan to let younger workers invest part of their payroll taxes in stocks and bonds. The president protested that "'privatization' was a trick word," intended to "scare people." Republican officials called journalists to complain about references to "private accounts."[51]

Democrats returned the favor, insisting that the president was really proposing the "privatization" of Social Security. They pointed out that the very people advocating the individual investment accounts the president was proposing had described them as a form of "privatization" for many years. The Cato Institute, which had long promoted the accounts, originally called its effort the Project on Social Security Privatization.

---

[50] Robin Toner, "It's 'Private' vs. 'Personal' in Social Security Debate," *New York Times*, March 22, 2005.
[51] Toner, "It's 'Private' vs. 'Personal' in Social Security Debate" ; Mike Allen, "Semantics Shape Social Security Debate," *Washington Post*, January 23, 2005.

Conflict over framing issues erupted during the House Ways and Means Committee's first major hearing on overhauling Social Security on May 12. Representative Jim McCrery, the chair of the subcommittee on Social Security, complained about the Democrats' repeated use of the term "privatization" to describe the president's plan. "Democrats on the panel use it ad nauseam," said a visibly angry McCrery. "Nobody is talking about privatizing Social Security. Get over it." He also objected to the Democrats' characterization of "progressive indexation." "It's not means-testing," he proclaimed. "It's further income-relating the benefit." When Democrats on the panel began to laugh, McCrery retorted: "There is two different things. I mean, you either know it or you don't." Moments later, Representative Sander M. Levin, a Democrat from Michigan, responded: "You don't like the term. I'm sorry. It's privatization."[52]

Taking a different tact, White House officials and Republican strategists also focused on persuading African Americans and Hispanics that Social Security was a bad deal for them. They argued that the current Social Security system shortchanged blacks because they tend to die earlier than do whites and to collect retirement benefits for fewer years. In a parallel effort aimed at Hispanics, Republicans focused on the wealth that people could build through the individual investment accounts that the Bush administration had proposed.[53] African American and Hispanic leaders wasted no time in attacking the White House for making what they saw as misleading arguments.

---

[52] Robin Toner, "House Social Security Hearing Opens With Sharp Partisan Debate," *New York Times,* May 13, 2005.
[53] Edmund L. Andrews, "G.O.P. Courts Blacks and Hispanics on Social Security," *New York Times,* March 20, 2005.

Democrats had their own framing problem: They did not want the public to see the Social Security system in "crisis"—as the president often described it. Instead, they preferred to discuss future Social Security shortfalls as a "challenge" and argued that Bush was attempting to manufacture a crisis to justify making changes that the Democrats opposed as unnecessary.[54]

As the president encountered opposition to his proposals, the White House's efforts to frame the debate changed in an attempt to counter it. When critics complained that personal accounts would force the government to add to the national debt by borrowing trillions of dollars, the administration argued that the plan's "transition costs" were really just "prepayment" of national debt that would be incurred later if Congress did not change Social Security.

Even the slogan at the president's public events changed. For example, by the third week of March 2005, it was clear that seniors strongly opposed the president's proposal and were concerned that they would lose some of their benefits. Thus, the White House changed the banners that once declared the president's interest in "Strengthening Social Security" to a more targeted message: "Keeping Our Promise to Seniors." Bush had to spend more time reassuring older voters that their Social Security payments were not in jeopardy, reducing his ability to focus on demanding the bold restructuring of the program.[55]

By May, the president's meticulously stage-managed presentations on Social Security shifted into yet another phase, one in

---

[54] Allen, "Semantics Shape Social Security Debate."
[55] Anne E. Kornblut, "Bush Opens Door to Changes in His Plan," *New York Times*, March 23, 2005.

which White House aides found young people to share the stage with the president and assert that Social Security would not be there at all when they retired. Rather than correcting them on their misconception—official estimates concluded that after 2041, Social Security would still be able to pay at least three-quarters of currently promised benefits without any changes—Bush congratulated them on their perceptiveness. The president then appealed to Congress to protect benefits for younger citizens.[56] Some viewed this effort as a scare campaign.

After he outlined the two biggest components of his approach to Social Security, cutting benefits from promised levels for most workers and establishing investment accounts, President Bush began trying to turn the focus to another aspect of the debate: the response of the Democrats. The White House and its allies increasingly prodded Democrats to make a counter proposal for dealing with the retirement system's projected long-term problems. For example, an e-mail release from the Republican National Committee in early May was headlined, "Democrat Forecast on Social Security: Severe Obstruction, No Ideas." The president badly needed Democratic support for benefit cuts, tax increases, or other painful changes in Social Security to provide his party with political cover for making unpopular decisions. Throughout the spring, however, Democrats refused to play along, reasoning that Bush's approach was sinking of its own accord and there was no reason to jump in the quicksand with him.[57]

---

[56] Dan Froomkin, "Exploiting a Misconception," *Washington Post*, May 20, 2005.
[57] Richard W. Stevenson, "On Social Security, a Search for Rivals," *New York Times*, May 9, 2005.

There was another good reason for Democrats to keep the focus on Bush's approach. To the degree that they acknowledged there was a problem that the government needed to address, they would have little choice but to back some benefit reductions of their own, plus an array of tax increases that would not be popular with voters. Democrats had not forgotten that Republicans regained control of Congress in 1994 in part by running aggressively against the tax increases, primarily on upper-income people, that Democrats adopted in 1993 to help reduce the budget deficit.

President Bush began his second term by launching perhaps the most extensive public relations campaign in the history of the presidency on behalf of reforming Social Security. It was a classic example of the permanent campaign, employing the same public relations techniques, party apparatus, and allied groups that were responsible for his reelection. So the White House continued to attempt to govern by going public. Chapter 7 explores the president's success in moving the public and, ultimately, Congress to support his proposals.

CHAPTER 7

Reforming Social Security, Part II: Persuading the Public and Congress

The Bush administration launched a campaign-style effort to persuade the public and thus the Congress to support the president's proposals for reforming Social Security. This was a high-stakes gamble in which the president had the possibility of demonstrating mastery over the political system but also the prospect of taking his case to the people and being dramatically rebuffed. Success in his endeavor would pave the way for future victories while failure could undermine his efforts to enact the rest of his agenda.

This chapter examines the president's success in obtaining public support and, ultimately, congressional passage of his proposals. We start with the question of the implications of the 2004 election for Social Security reform.

A MANDATE FOR REFORM?

In the 2004 presidential campaign, President Bush did not detail his plans for Social Security reform. Although the basic idea of personal accounts had been around for several years, it was not until *after* the election, on February 2, 2005, that the White House released its official document entitled *Strengthening Social Security for the 21st Century*. The document is only a few pages long and devotes only four pages to personal accounts. Nowhere does the document make clear that there is a tradeoff between personal accounts and current guaranteed benefits. The document also does not offer a plan for financing the transition to personal accounts, only making the argument that the costs would be manageable.

The lack of attention to Social Security compromised Bush's ability to govern after the election, because his claims of a mandate for his reform proposals lacked credibility. The president began his second term with an exaggerated sense of his mandate and the extent of his political capital. In reality, as noted in Chapters 4 and 5, he had received no mandate for his Social Security proposals, and the public held mixed views about his stewardship as president. The situation on the ground provided a weak basis for major reform of a major program.

By May 19, Bush recognized this. After his visit to Milwaukee, a reporter asked him whether he thought his election victory in November was an expression of support by voters for his Social Security plans. (In an interview with the *Milwaukee Journal Sentinel*, Vice President Dick Cheney had declared that the election was a mandate for personal accounts.) Bush answered with a more nuanced and reasonable response.

It's hard to break down a specific issue, and an issue in a race in which there was a lot of issues. We had Iraq, we had foreign policy . . . we had values. Social Security was clearly an issue, however. . . . I think they voted for me in large part because they knew I would not be afraid to take on a tough issue.[1]

There were also limits on what a mandate could do for a president in the context of polarized politics. Leon E. Panetta, who served as White House chief of staff under President Bill Clinton, remarked about Bush, "You can't slam-dunk issues in Washington. You can't just say, 'This is what I want done' and by mandate get it done. It's a lesson everybody has to learn, and sometimes you learn it the hard way."[2]

PUBLIC OPINION

As 2005 began, Americans were in principle open to the idea of introducing private accounts into the Social Security system. In January, a clear majority of Americans—55 percent—supported the president's proposal to allow younger workers to put some of their Social Security savings into stocks or bonds.[3] In practice, however, the public believed it was more important to retain a guaranteed monthly Social Security benefit than it was to let younger workers invest in private accounts whose value would rise or fall depending on how their investments performed. The preference for a guaranteed Social Security benefit had grown

---

[1] Quoted in Craig Gilbert, "Bush Not Dissuaded by Shaky Support for Social Security," *Milwaukee Journal Sentinel*, May 19, 2005.
[2] Peter Baker and Jim VandeHei, "Bush's Political Capital Spent, Voices in Both Parties Suggest Poll," *Washington Post*, May 31, 2005, p. A2.
[3] *Washington Post*/ABC News poll, January 12–16, 2005.

since the end of the 1990s stock market boom. In early 2005, 65 percent of the public preferred retaining a guaranteed monthly benefit, compared with 54 percent in October 2000.[4]

As noted in Chapter 6, by February the president had admitted that personal accounts would do little to fix the long-term solvency issues facing Social Security, but he had not specified the mix of tax increases, benefit cuts, and deficit spending he would support to make the system solvent for generations to come. Instead, Bush said he would leave those details to Congress, which had shown little interest in raising taxes or cutting benefits. It appears that the more people found out about personal accounts, the more they understood that personal accounts would make the solvency problem worse, threatening guaranteed benefits.

Table 7.1 provides the results of Gallup polls employing questions with different wordings inquiring about support for personal accounts under the Social Security system. Support for private accounts is always lower when the question mentions reducing guaranteed benefits, but the trends are the same. Once the president launched his public drive for personal accounts in January 2005, support for his proposal dropped. Indeed, a majority of the public opposed his plan (despite an anomalous increase in support in the end of April poll). In early May, the Gallup Poll reported, "There has been no statistically significant change in support for private investment accounts since Gallup first tested this in December."[5]

---

[4] Pew Research Center for the People and the Press poll, January 5–9, 2005.
[5] Lydia Saad, "Bush Fails to Ignite Public Support for Reform," *Gallup News Service*, May 4, 2005.

TABLE 7.1
Support for Personal Social Security Accounts

POLL DATE	FAVOR	OPPOSE	NO OPINION
17–19 December 2004*	48%	48%	4%
18–20 March 2005*	45	47	8
1–2 April 2005*	39	56	5
20 April–1 May 2005	44	52	4
24–26 June 2005	44	53	3

SOURCE: Gallup Poll question: "As you may know, a proposal has been made that would allow workers to invest part of their Social Security taxes in the stock market or in bonds, while the rest of those taxes would remain in the Social Security system. Do you favor or oppose this proposal?"
*Asked of half a sample.

POLL DATE	GOOD IDEA	BAD IDEA	NO OPINION
7–9 January 2005	40%	55%	5%
4–6 February 2005	40	55	5
7–10 February 2005	36	60	4
18–20 March 2005	33	59	8
1–2 April 2005	33	61	6
29 April–1 May 2005	44	52	4

SOURCE: Gallup Poll question asked of half a sample (except April 29–May 1, 2005): "As you may know, one idea to address concerns with the Social Security system would allow people who retire in future decades to invest some of their Social Security taxes in the stock market and bonds, but would reduce the guaranteed benefits they get when they retire. Do you think this is a good idea or a bad idea?"

In a survey of results from a number of polling organizations, Jacobson found that when people were asked if they backed personal accounts if they were accompanied by a reduction in guaranteed future benefits, average support dropped to 39 percent. In surveys that specified that the cut in guaranteed benefits could be up to one-third, matching the proportion of Social Security taxes diverted into private accounts, support dropped to an average of 22 percent. If personal accounts added $2 trillion to the national debt over the next ten years, on average only 27 percent of respondents favored it.[6] Of course, both of these last two specifications were actually part of the president's plan.

One problem the president faced was that the people most receptive to his proposal were the least engaged in the debate, and those most engaged were also the most opposed. Members of Congress encountered angry public responses at town hall meetings in their constituencies (and many urged the administration to back off or provide them with some kind of political cover). The fact that the stock market dropped during the winter and spring certainly did not help Bush's cause.

Equally significant, the Pew Research Center found that awareness fueled opposition, as people who were paying more attention to the issue were also less supportive than those paying less attention were. Results from its March 18–21, 2005, poll showed that only 41 percent of those who reported that they had heard or read a lot about the proposal supported it while 52 percent opposed it. On the other hand, 47 percent of those who knew less about the issue supported it and 30 percent opposed it. Similarly, the more the president pressed his proposal, the larger the majority of the public that disapproved of his handling of Social Security (see Table 7.2). By June, nearly two-thirds of the public disapproved of the president's handling of the issue.

---

[6] Gary C. Jacobson, *A Divider, Not a Uniter* (New York: Longman, 2006), chap. 8.

TABLE 7.2
Bush's Handling of Social Security

POLL DATE	APPROVE	DISAPPROVE	NO OPINION
9–11 March 2001	49%	31%	20%
10–11 July 2001	49	35	16
22–24 March 2002	47	40	13
7–9 January 2005	41	52	7
4–6 February 2005	43	48	9
25–27 February 2005	35	56	9
1–2 April 2005	35	57	8
29 April–1 May 2005	35	58	7
20–22 May 2005	33	59	8
24–26 June 2005	31	64	5

SOURCE: Gallup Poll question: "Do you approve or disapprove of the way George W. Bush is handling Social Security?"

It is especially interesting that this pattern of awareness breeding opposition was significant even for those under 30, who were supposed to be the primary beneficiaries of the president's proposal. People under age 30 who had heard a lot about the proposal were more than twice as likely as their less engaged peers to oppose the idea (45 percent vs. 19 percent). During the heart of his effort to obtain the public's support, the president lost 17 percentage points among those under 30, with their support declining from 66 percent to 49 percent in the Pew polls from February 16–21 to March 18–21, 2005.

Younger and higher income Americans were the most supportive of personal accounts, but they did not expect benefits or did not depend on them for retirement income. Even those who never expected to see any Social Security benefits still opposed the president's plan. The more someone cared about Social Security and depended on its continued existence, the less he or she supported private accounts.[7]

In the face of clear public opposition to his proposals for reforming Social Security, the president and other administration officials repeatedly declared that the first stage of their effort was persuading the public that there was a crisis in Social Security that required immediate action. They also often proclaimed success in this endeavor. Nevertheless, by early May a Gallup Poll showed it was clear that a majority of Americans did not believe the need for action was urgent. Although 81 percent agreed that major changes in Social Security would be needed in the foreseeable future, only 45 percent thought that such changes were needed in the next year or two. Thirty-six percent said changes should be made within the next ten years, and 16 percent thought major changes were unnecessary. In January, 49 percent favored quick action.[8]

What concerned many Republicans the most was the intense level of opposition to restructuring Social Security even before policymakers discussed in detail the most politically unappealing aspects of the plan, including a reduction in guaranteed benefits.[9] As noted in Chapter 6, on April 28 the president made a bid to restore momentum to his flagging proposal to restructure Social Security—and to his presidency—by proposing progressive index-

---

[7] William Schneider, "Political Pulse: Crisis of Confidence?" *National Journal,* February 12, 2005, 492.
[8] Gallup poll, April 29–May 1, 2005.
[9] Jim VandeHei, "Social Security Plan Meets Doubt in Iowa," *Washington Post,* March 30, 2005.

ing of Social Security benefits. Democrats immediately branded Bush's proposal a massive cut in Social Security benefits.

How did the public respond to the president's proposal? In the April 29–May 1, 2005, Gallup poll taken just after the press conference, the president's overall approval rating and approval of his handling of Social Security was unchanged. Americans were also resistant to the idea of indexing Social Security benefits for future retirees. Only 38 percent favored the president's proposal, while 54 percent opposed it. Indeed, the public was so opposed to this means-testing proposal that, when given a choice, the majority, 53 percent, said they would rather see taxes raised than have benefits cut (38 percent).[10]

In its May 11–15 poll, the Pew Research Center for the People and the Press found that negative opinions of Bush's handling of Social Security outnumbered positive ones by about a two-to-one margin (59 percent to 29 percent). Even worse for the president was the fact that his association with a plan to limit the growth of Social Security benefits appeared to undermine support for the concept. Pew split its large sample and, as Table 7.3 shows, by a 53 percent to 36 percent margin most Americans said they would support limiting the growth of benefits for wealthy and middle-income retirees, while keeping the current system intact for lower-income people. This was a considerably higher figure than the 38 percent level of support Gallup found about two weeks earlier. However, the public's support was significantly lower when Pew explicitly associated the proposal with Bush. When the phrase

---

[10] Gallup poll, April 29–May 1, 2005.

TABLE 7.3

Effect of Bush Association with Social Security Indexing

	ALL	REPUBLICANS	DEMOCRATS	INDEPENDENTS
DESCRIBED WITHOUT BUSH'S NAME[1]				
Favor	53%	47%	54%	55%
Oppose	36	41	37	36
Don't Know	11	12	9	9
DESCRIBED AS BUSH'S PROPOSAL[2]				
Favor	45	62	34	43
Oppose	43	27	57	47
Don't Knoiw	12	11	9	10
CHANGE IN SUPPORT				
	−8	+15	−20	−12

Source: Pew Research Center for the People and the Press poll, May 11–15, 2005.

[1] "One proposal for dealing with Social Security's financial situation is to keep the system as it is now for lower income retirees, but limit the growth of future benefits for wealthy and middle income retirees. Would you favor or oppose this proposal?"

[2] "George W. Bush has proposed dealing with Social Security's financial situation by keeping the system as it is now for lower income retirees, but limiting the growth of future benefits for wealthy and middle income retirees. Would you favor or oppose this proposal?"

"George W. Bush has proposed . . ." preceded the idea, the public was divided (45 percent in favor, 43 percent opposed).

Equally striking were the responses of different partisan groups. Without any mention of Bush, the proposal was slightly more popular among Democrats than among Republicans (54 percent to 47 percent). When pollsters attributed the proposal to Bush, however, Republican support increased 15 percentage points to 62 percent while Democratic support dropped 20 points to 34 percent. Support among Independents for limiting future benefit growth for wealthy and middle-income retirees dropped

12 percentage points, from 55 percent to 43 percent, when the poll question attributed the proposal to the president.[11]

Pew also found that public support for adding private accounts to Social Security appeared to have stabilized, with a plurality (47 percent) in favor of the idea of allowing younger workers to invest a portion of their Social Security taxes in private retirement accounts, though 40 percent were opposed (Bush's endorsement of this proposal was not mentioned in this survey question). Unfortunately, Pew did not mention the inevitable trade-off with guaranteed benefits in its question.

On May 19, the president suffered another blow to his private accounts proposal, however. As Bush visited Milwaukee to promote his Social Security plan, Robert C. Pozen, the business executive who developed the theory behind the president's plan to index Social Security benefits, urged Bush to drop his proposal for personal accounts. Pozen declared that the president's approach to investment accounts would destroy the chances for a Social Security bill in Congress and would make it more difficult to resolve the long-term financial problems facing the system. He argued the president's plan to let workers divert some of their payroll taxes to private accounts would reduce tax revenues and lower guaranteed retirement benefits too much. He also suggested the president consider a surcharge on payroll taxes for people who earn more than $90,000 a year (the current limit to the income on which wage earners paid Social Security taxes) and the possibility of using some of that added revenue for private investment accounts.[12]

---

[11] For another example of divergent partisan responses to the president, see ABC/*Washington Post* poll, March 10–13, 2005.

[12] David E. Rosenbaum and Edmund L. Andrews, "Adviser Splits With Bush on Social Security Accounts," *New York Times*, May 19, 2005.

The lack of public support for the president and his proposals discouraged potential allies. By the middle of May, COMPASS, the coalition of business lobbies, had only 300 members, compared with well over a 1,000 business groups that united to support the president's energy plans and tax cuts. Companies appeared to be wary of getting behind an initiative that was unpopular with their workers and appeared to be floundering.[13]

By June, 66 percent of the public reported that they were uneasy about Bush's ability to make sound decisions on Social Security, while only 25 percent said they approved of the way he was handling Social Security. Moreover, 45 percent said the more they heard about the Bush plan, the less they liked it. Most said they did not think Bush's plan for private accounts would do anything for the system's long-term solvency, and only 25 percent thought that personal accounts would make Social Security more financially secure. Although the public favored the prospects of earning more for their retirements and leaving their accounts to their children, they did not like the increased risk or reduction in guaranteed benefits these potential benefits would entail, nor did they favor the increased borrowing that paying for the personal accounts would require.[14]

CONGRESS

The president thought he had a mandate for his Social Security proposals. He also anticipated unified Republican support in Congress. The House, under the tight control of his party's major-

---

[13] "COMPASS Alliance Needs Some Pointers," *National Journal*, May 21, 2005.
[14] CBS News/*New York Times* poll, June 10–15.

ity, had given him most everything for which he asked during his first term. The principal challenge, he thought, would be the Senate, where he would need some Democratic support to overcome a filibuster.

Pressuring Democrats

When Bush began barnstorming on behalf of his Social Security plan, his goal at many stops was to convince congressional Democrats that backing his call for individual investment accounts would be good politics. Journalists reported that at the outset, White House officials simply assumed that a presidential appearance in a state that Bush carried in 2004 and where a Democrat was up for reelection in 2006 would frighten that Democrat into backing the proposal.[15]

As noted in Chapter 6, the day after the president presented his Social Security proposal in his State of the Union address, he embarked on a two-day campaign-style swing to North Dakota, Montana, Nebraska, Arkansas, and Florida. Bush carried each of these states in his reelection campaign the previous year, and each state had at least one Democratic senator (and a total of seven), some of whom had been helpful to him in the past. The senators included Bill Nelson of Florida, Ben Nelson of Nebraska, and Kent Conrad of North Dakota, who were up for reelection in 2006; Max Baucus of Montana, the top Democrat on the Finance Committee, who supported the president's 2001 tax cut, along with Ben Nelson; and Blanche Lincoln and Mark Pryor of Arkansas

---

[15] See, for example, Richard W. Stevenson, "Bush Finds Some Republicans Need Wooing," *New York Times,* March 11, 2005.

potential swing votes. Lincoln supported Bush's first tax cut. The president's itinerary suggested that he was especially intent on pressuring this handful of Democratic senators to back his approach by demonstrating local support for him and his proposal.

From February 8–16, 2005, Bush visited five additional states, three of which he did not win in his reelection bid the previous fall. Criticism of the president's plan was heating up, however, and on March 3, the White House launched a "60 Stops in 60 Days" tour of administration officials to convince the public to support the president's Social Security reform. During this period the president visited 15 states (including Florida again) in 17 stops. However, he only visited one state (New Jersey) that he did not carry in 2004. Once again, rather than attempting to convince the large number of Americans who were skeptical of his proposals, it appears that the president was seeking friendly audiences where he already enjoyed support to create favorable images and stories for the media.

Democrats were unimpressed, however. The White House not only overestimated the president's political capital but it also underestimated the resistance of Senate Democrats to the president's proposal.

Perhaps Bush's earlier successes were catching up with him. His tax cuts helped foster huge deficits that now made financing his plan a harder sell to fiscal conservatives. His take-no-prisoners approach to politics had alienated Democrats who had helped him in the past. In 2002, he campaigned against Sen. Mary Landrieu of Louisiana after she broke with her party to support him on tax cuts. In 2003, Senate Democrats who backed a compromise on a drug benefit later found themselves all but shut out of final negotiations. Now, Bush's campaign-style appearances in Democratic senators' states suggested that he hoped to pressure them rather than seduce them.[16]

Conditions during the winter and spring of 2005 also emboldened Democrats, who united against Bush. Gas prices rose to near-record highs, the stock market lost much of its gains over the past year, trade deficits ballooned, and casualties in Iraq occurred at an alarming pace. The public was not happy with the president's handling of the Terri Schiavo case. With the president at modest levels in the polls, Democrats not only resisted his proposals, they went on the offensive to oppose him aggressively.

Many Democrats highlighted their position on Social Security in their constituencies during Congress's Presidents' Day recess and the two-week Easter vacation. Others traveled throughout the country to campaign against President Bush and his Social Security proposals, including a "Fix It, Don't Nix It" swing. Some Democratic members of Congress even made their case in the districts of Republican colleagues who were wary about embracing Bush's idea of private accounts. Representative Sandy Levin of Michigan held a town meeting in Battle Creek, Michigan, the district of Republican Representative Joe Schwarz. Democratic Representative Betty McCollum of Minnesota held a town hall meeting in the district of her Republican colleague from that state, Representative Mark Kennedy. Democrat Earl Pomeroy of North Dakota met with voters in the district of Minnesota Republican Gil Gutknecht.[17]

---

[16] Richard Stevenson, "Seeking Support, Bush Offers Assurances on Retirement Cuts," *New York Times,* May 4, 2005.
[17] Associated Press, "Democrats Hit Road in Social Security War," April 3, 2005.

Bush had also boxed himself in on working with the Democrats. Although he repeatedly declared that he was willing to look at all ideas, he insisted that personal accounts be part of the package. Moreover, his characterization of Social Security as in a "crisis" and thus requiring sweeping changes made it difficult to reach small compromises with opponents. He had in effect positioned himself so he could not consider "fix it" options.

Containing Republicans

The president's strategy in going public seemed to be to talk only about the benefits of Social Security reform and not the costs. He did not focus on the reduction of guaranteed benefits that would accompany personal accounts or the risks inherent in investments. He also avoided discussing paying for the transition to personal accounts and, until the end of April, reductions in benefits for most retirees, independent of personal accounts. He left it to Congress to do the heavy lifting when it came to the costs of reform. He also frequently invoked ideas from Democrats as suggestions that had been made in the past—but he steered clear of offering his own proposals for as long as he could. Although this strategy denied his opponents fodder for their criticisms, it also did not provide his supporters with political cover for the difficult choices he wanted them to make.

The White House did try to support Republicans in other ways. Early on, Republicans received a playbook, with a golden nest egg on the cover, offering advice on how to support the president such as "talk in simple language," "keep the numbers small," and "avoid percentages; your audience will try to calculate them in their head."[18] The president's top political strategist, Karl Rove, played an important role in deciding where the president, Vice President Cheney, and other administration officials went as they crisscrossed the country trying to win public support. He oversaw an intelligence-gathering effort that closely tracked the positions of every Republican in Congress and made sure they received phone calls, invitations to the White House, rides on Air Force One, or other expressions of support if they came under pressure from Bush's opponents.[19]

Nevertheless, the White House faced dissension on Capitol Hill. First, there were deep splits among supporters of personal accounts over issues like how big the accounts should be, whether to include deep benefit cuts in any overhaul of the retirement system, and whether the president needed to put forth more details for reform.[20]

More importantly, Republicans were receiving negative feedback from the public. Stung by a spate of rowdy, critic-packed town hall meetings about Social Security over the Presidents' Day break in February, Republicans shied away from such open forums during the two-week Easter recess. Instead, they stuck mainly to workshops in which administration officials did most of the talking and the lawmakers stepped up to answer a few questions after lengthy presentations from Bush appointees.[21]

---

[18] Mike Allen, "Congressional Republicans Agree to Launch Social Security Campaign," *Washington Post,* January 31, 2005.
[19] Richard Stevenson, "With Bush Safely Re-elected, Rove Turns Intensity to Policy," *New York Times,* March 28, 2005.
[20] Sheryl Gay Stolberg and Richard W. Stevenson, "Flare-Ups in Battle over Bush's Social Security Plan," *New York Times,* February 24, 2005.
[21] Mike Allen and Peter Baker, "Hill Takes a Back Seat on Social Security: Administration, Republican National Committee Lead Drive to Add Private Accounts," *Washington Post,* April 6, 2005, p. A4.

Republicans sometimes publicly voiced their nervousness over the public's response to the president's proposals, but the White House wasted no time in suppressing dissent within Republican ranks. Representative Jim McCrery raised questions about President Bush's plan to overhaul Social Security, pointing out that the proposal would give Democrats and the AARP an opening to attack Republicans for undermining the Social Security trust fund. The White House responded quickly to put the squeeze on him. Four of the president's men descended on Capitol Hill to pay McCrery a visit, surrounding him with charts and figures in a fevered effort to get him to endorse the company line. After this session, McCrery still said the plan would be a tough sell on Capitol Hill, but he mollified the other end of Pennsylvania Avenue by adding that Congress should give it a chance.[22]

On March 1, the administration once again had to steady its drive for Social Security legislation. That day, the Senate's top Republican, Majority Leader Bill Frist of Tennessee, declared that Bush's bid to restructure Social Security might have to wait until 2006 and might not involve individual accounts. The press widely understood his remark as a sign that Social Security reform was in serious trouble. Hoping for action before Congress headed into the midterm election year, the Bush administration did not welcome the senator's comments and went to work on Frist. Two

---

[22] Sheryl Gay Stolberg, "In Eye of Social Security Storm, Quiet Power Broker Is Courted," *New York Times*, February 22, 2005; Stolberg and Stevenson, "Flare-Ups in Battle over Bush's Social Security Plan."

days later, Frist's tune was different. He took the floor of the Senate to declare that he was committed to bringing Social Security legislation to the floor in 2005: "We need to do it this year. This year. Not next year."[23]

On February 28, Senator Charles E. Grassley of Iowa, the chairman of the Finance Committee—which handles Social Security—argued that if public opinion did not soon begin to swing in favor of the president's Social Security plan, it would be an indication that the plan was in trouble. After a meeting with the other Republicans on his committee, Grassley repeated to reporters what he had been saying for weeks: The success or failure of the plan depended on whether the president could persuade voters at the grassroots that the Social Security system was in jeopardy and that his approach was the right way to fix the problem.[24]

Three days later, Senator Grassley sparked a wave of speculation when he told Iowa reporters that people had focused too much attention on personal accounts. "Since personal accounts don't have a lot to do with solvency," he said, "maybe we ought to focus on solvency and just bring people to the table on what you do about solvency over the next 75 years." He added that personal accounts had given Democrats a target and a way of avoiding "the responsibility we all have about the solvency of it."

---

[23] Mike Allen and Charles Babington, "Social Security Vote May Be Delayed: Critics Could Force Proposal to Change," *Washington Post,* March 2, 2005, p. A1; Robin Toner, "Bush Denies That Private Accounts Are in Serious Trouble," *New York Times,* March 4, 2005.
[24] David E. Rosenbaum, "Public Views on Social Security Need to Swing Soon, Senator Says," *New York Times,* March 1, 2005.

Representative Charles B. Rangel of New York, the ranking Democrat on the House Ways and Means Committee, praised Grassley for putting Social Security's fiscal health first, "over the ideology of privatization" that has "nothing to do with improving Social Security's solvency." Later, on March 3, however, Grassley issued a statement suggesting he was not breaking ranks with the administration, declaring, "Personal accounts are still on the table along with all the other ideas to strengthen Social Security."[25]

Despite the administration's efforts to maintain Republicans' support, they continued to express reservations about the president's proposals. In early May, for example, both of Mississippi's conservative Republican senators attended a Bush rally in their state. Afterwards, each indicated that he was not yet prepared to embrace the details of the president's approach. Senator Trent Lott said he was "not overjoyed" by the way the administration's approach would work. Senator Thad Cochran was more evasive, replying that he wanted to see Congress and the administration come together to work out a plan.[26]

In a sign of the trouble he was facing on Social Security reform, Bush increasingly used his travels to buck up—or even win over—members of his own party. In his initial set of events, from February 3–10, the president visited the districts of six Democrats and just two Republicans. Both Republicans attended the events in their districts but none of the Democrats did. From

---

[25] Toner, "Bush Denies That Private Accounts Are in Serious Trouble."
[26] Richard Stevenson, "Seeking Support, Bush Offers Assurances on Retirement Cuts," *New York Times*, May 4, 2005.

February 16 through the end of March, however, 11 of the president's 13 events took place in the districts of Republican members of the House. Eight of the 11 Republicans attended with the president, as did one of the two Democrats.

In April through July, Bush held events or delivered speeches on Social Security another 17 times. In this period, he visited the districts of five Republicans and seven Democrats (four of the events were in the District of Columbia and two took place in the same congressional district), but only three of these members of Congress attended the events. When the White House staged an event in Milwaukee on May 19, only one of Wisconsin's four Republican representatives, Paul Ryan, accompanied him. Ryan's fellow Republicans had been noncommittal about Bush's proposals[27] and the local representative was a Democrat. Thomas Reynolds, a Republican from upstate New York, attended the president's event held outside Rochester. He had been under pressure from labor and other local groups that opposed the president's plans. Although he introduced Bush, he did not specifically support his proposals.

From February 16 through the end of March, Bush visited 12 states, all of which but New Jersey had at least one Republican senator and five of which had two. In April through July, Bush visited 11 additional states and also returned to Pennsylvania. Two Republican senators represented seven of these states. The president apparently had shifted his itinerary from the states of

---

[27] Craig Gilbert, "Bush Not Dissuaded by Shaky Support for Social Security," *Milwaukee Journal Sentinel,* May 19, 2005.

"persuadable" Democrats to those of Republicans under fire[28] or skeptical of his plan. In only four of the states did the senators attend the events with the president.

The reluctance of congressional Republicans to take center stage was emblematic of the low-key role that they had adopted in the debate over Social Security. For the first third of 2005, they had served largely as bystanders in the president's campaign to restructure Social Security and had taken a back seat to the effort being driven by the White House, the Treasury Department, the Republican National Committee, and the administration's business allies.[29]

The White House and House leaders had wanted the Senate Finance Committee to craft a narrow bill based largely on the president's proposal first. They figured that the Finance panel would have more luck attracting bipartisan support while House leaders did not want to force their rank and file to vote on a measure that had no chance of Senate passage.[30] Given the public's opposition to the president, some House Republicans were reluctant to cast politically difficult votes for a Social Security bill unless they knew that a bill would also pass the Senate. As one representative put it, "People are prepared to bleed, but they're not prepared to bleed for no reason." Democrats said they were convinced that they could hold their ranks against any legislation that created private investment accounts in Social Security financed by payroll tax revenue. If that were the case, the Democ-

---

[28] Allen and Baker, "Hill Takes a Back Seat on Social Security."

[29] Allen and Baker, "Hill Takes a Back Seat on Social Security."

[30] Jonathan Weisman and Jeffrey H. Birnbaum, "Bush Ally in House Alters Social Security Debate Strategy," *Washington Post,* May 5, 2005, p. A5.

rats could use the filibuster, if necessary, to prevent action in the Senate. The House would then have to pass legislation on a strict party-line vote to keep the president's proposals alive[31]—an unappealing prospect.

Nevertheless, sensing that the president's top domestic priority was fading fast and that the fallout from the public's opposition might harm them, some congressional Republicans began to act. In a major shift in legislative strategy that caught the House leadership by surprise,[32] Representative Bill Thomas of California, Republican chair of the House Ways and Means Committee, announced that he would try to rejuvenate the president's initiative by holding hearings beginning on May 12 and adding provisions on retirement savings, long-term care, and private pensions. His goal was to build a broader constituency for a plan that sorely needed one.[33]

Thomas believed that it made no sense to consider changes in Social Security without addressing the entire array of government policies affecting retirement. Thus, Congress should address broader issues confronting an aging society. He also felt that only a bill adorned with long-sought sweeteners could attract enough support to reach the president's desk. For example, life insurers were determined to prevent Social Security reform legislation from being so generous with its savings incentives that it reduced the market for life-insurance products. Others, especially airlines and automakers, wanted pension-law changes that would make it

---

[31] Robin Toner and David E. Rosenbaum, "Lawmaker May Hold Key to Bush Social Security Plan," *New York Times,* May 12, 2005.
[32] Weisman and Birnbaum, "Bush Ally in House Alters Social Security Debate Strategy."
[33] Toner and Rosenbaum, "Lawmaker May Hold Key to Bush Social Security Plan."

easier for them and other troubled industries to deal with the huge retirement obligations they owed their former employees. They wanted measures designed to bolster traditional corporate pensions without imposing tough new funding requirements. Labor unions and their Democratic allies also saw such provisions as vital. Retailers were anxious that Congress did not add a sales or value-added tax to pay for Social Security benefits. With so much on the table, Thomas's actions ignited a lobbying frenzy.[34]

On May 19, Thomas chaired a hearing in which he turned his committee's attention away from Social Security (and thus the president's proposals) and toward retirement savings. He disregarded the methods favored by the president to encourage workers to save for retirement—mostly tax incentives for the affluent—and offered completely different proposals of his own, including encouraging new forms of annuities that would be attractive investments for low-income workers and requiring employers who offered their workers 401(k) plans to enroll the workers automatically unless the workers specifically opted out, instead of leaving it to workers to take the initiative to sign up.[35]

By June, the Senate Finance Committee was at an impasse on Social Security. Democrats were united in their opposition to the president's call for personal accounts, and at least three committee Republicans were also skeptical. But the committee also did not have the votes to pass a plan that would preserve Social Security's solvency without the personal accounts because too many Republicans wanted them. In addition, at least some Republicans had concluded that Democrats would not pay a political price for killing the president's plan without offering their own. Thus, Senate leaders told the White House that it was time to look for an exit strategy.[36] "Nobody really talks too much about Social Security," Grassley complained of his fellow Republican senators. "They all want it to go away."[37]

White House officials recognized the problem but were afraid that pulling back from private accounts would undermine Bush's congressional allies with no guarantee that a compromise could be reached without the accounts. Instead, the president responded to the impasse by dispensing his cautious calls for bipartisanship in favor of far tougher rhetoric that blamed the Democrats for the stalemate. "On issue after issue, they stand for nothing except obstruction," Bush declared at a Republican fundraiser on June 14. This shift in strategy set the stage for blaming the Democrats—instead of the president's proposal—if his plan failed.[38]

In an attempt to pressure Democrats to negotiate, House Republican leaders and some Republican senators presented their own versions of personal accounts in late-June. The proposals would create a temporary system of personal accounts, taking money from the surplus that the Social Security trust fund is running and parcel it out to individual accounts that would later be used to pay for workers' retirement benefits and could be inherited by their heirs. Both the House and Senate plans had

---

[36] Alex Wayne, "Pressing Against a Security 'Balloon'," *Congressional Quarterly Weekly Report*, June 13, 2005, 1570; Jonathan Weisman and Jim VandeHei, "Exit Strategy on Social Security Is Sought," *Washington Post*, June 16, 2005, p. A9.
[37] Quoted in "House Leaders Pledge Vote on Social Security Accounts," *USA Today*, June 29, 2005.
[38] Weisman and VandeHei, "Exit Strategy on Social Security Is Sought."

complicated financing schemes and did nothing to address the solvency issue. In the end they would cause the government to borrow even more money. In addition, the House plan would drop efforts to close the gap between promised future benefits and anticipated tax revenue by cutting benefits or raising taxes. When the House Republicans announced their plan, they offered only a single sheet consisting of a dozen sentences and no dollar figures.[39]

Not everyone was impressed with the Republicans' effort. As political analyst Charlie Cook put it, "Anyone who thinks that you can sell members of a typical Rotary or Kiwanis Club, or American Legion or VFW Post, or just about any other reasonably intelligent adult that there is enough of a Social Security surplus to buy a vente skim latte at Starbucks has been in Washington way too long. It boggles the mind to think that anyone believes that Republicans could sell this country the idea that there is a Social Security surplus."[40]

Nevertheless, House Republican leaders, needing to provide their rank and file some political cover, promised to vote on their scaled-down version of personal retirement accounts by the end of the year. They planned to incorporate the measure into Thomas's broader bill making changes in pensions and other areas relating to retirement. Mindful of the political sensitivity of the issue, Republicans began closed-door meetings at which they advised members how to describe the program to their constituents over the July 4 break.[41]

[39] Mike Allen and Jonathan Weisman, "GOP Sounded the Alarm But Didn't Respond to It," *Washington Post*, June 24, 2005, p. A8.
[40] Charlie Cook, "Surplus? What Surplus?" *Off to the Races*, June 28, 2005.
[41] Quoted in "House Leaders Pledge Vote on Social Security Accounts."

It did not help. One House Republican declared that the plan was "more symbol than substance" while another called it "a smoke-and-mirrors thing." Republican Jim Kolbe of Arizona concluded that the House Republican leadership had "decided nothing's going to happen on Social Security. They don't see a way out of the box, so they're looking for something that gets them politically off the hook but doesn't cause them too much political grief."[42]

The White House was also uncooperative. In mid-July, Ben S. Bernanke, the new chairman of Bush's Council of Economic Advisors, told reporters the president would insist that any Social Security legislation include a fix to the program's long-term financing problems, undercutting House leaders' efforts to craft a compromise that ignored the solvency question.[43]

Social Security assumed a lower profile in the weeks that followed as the White House turned more attention to Iraq and the economy. With no consensus in sight, even among Republicans, the chairmen of the Senate and House committees with jurisdiction over Social Security decided to postpone further consideration of the issue at least until the fall.[44] At that point the president was hitting new lows in the polls in the wake of continued violence in Iraq, surging gasoline prices, and Hurricane Katrina. Proponents on both ends of Pennsylvania Avenue quietly shelved Social Security reform and turned their attention to other issues.

---

[42] Jonathan Weisman, "Happy 70th Birthday, Social Security," *Washington Post,* August 14, 2005, p. A5.
[43] Jonathan Weisman, "Aide Says Bush Wants Solvent Social Security," *Washington Post,* July 19, 2005, p. A4.
[44] David E. Rosenbaum, "Lawmakers Postponing Bush Priority on Benefits," *New York Times,* July 15, 2005.

Chapter 6 shows that George W. Bush began his second term by launching an intensive campaign to reform Social Security. This chapter shows how Bush's attempts to govern by campaigning failed. His failure to detail his Social Security proposals in the 2004 election undermined his claim to a mandate on the issue. When he took his case to the people, they did not respond. At least they did not support his policies. Instead, the more the president advocated change, the less the public backed his proposals, and majorities opposed him. Congress was no more enthusiastic. In the face of firm Democratic opposition and mixed support among Republicans, his efforts at reform were going nowhere. After the president fell further in the polls in late summer, Congress turned its attention to other pressing matters and quietly dropped consideration of Social Security reform. One of the most explicit efforts to govern by campaigning in U.S. history had failed, apparently surprising the White House but not those who closely study the president's ability to move public opinion.[45]

---

[45] See George C. Edwards III, *On Deaf Ears: The Limits of the Bully Pulpit* (New Haven: Yale University Press, 2003).

CHAPTER 8

Governing by Campaigning

George W. Bush has endeavored to revolutionize public policy. Despite his detractors' claims that he is not up to the job, his has been a presidency of ideas. We need not agree on the wisdom of his proposals to concur that he has tackled big issues and sought significant departures from the policy status quo. Not unexpectedly, his efforts to transform policy have met spirited opposition and contributed to the historic levels of partisan polarization the U.S. experiences today.

To accomplish his goals and overcome the adamant resistance of his opponents, Bush has adopted the permanent campaign as his core governing strategy. Without a mandate for change, with close party divisions in Congress, and substantial hostility to his efforts to transform policy and create a lasting Republican majority, the president has taken his case to the public in an unprecedented fashion. For a period in his first term, the public's enthusiastic response to his leadership in the war on terrorism kept him high in the polls and was a critical factor in his reelection and the Republicans' success in congressional elections.

Despite the Bush administration's skill and discipline in public relations and its extraordinary investment of time and energy in seeking popular support, the public has been largely unresponsive to the White House. Rather than moving Congress by first obtaining the public's support, the president has relied heavily on his party's strong congressional leadership, which effectively delivered at least the House for his legislative proposals.

In both his policies and his politics, Bush has been a divider, not a uniter.[1] Such an approach was reasonably successful when the country was tolerant of his policy experimentation. Democrats as well as Republicans supported the general goals of improving education and adding prescription drug coverage to Medicare. There was no effective organized opposition to the war in Iraq. In addition, the budget surplus (and then projected surpluses) provided at least the perception of resources available for tax cuts and new expenditures. When his party was united, the president could obtain much of what he sought from Congress.

None of these conditions characterize the beginning of Bush's sixth year in office. The president is well below 50 percent approval in the polls, there is widespread dissatisfaction with the direction of the country, the war in Iraq, the state of the economy, and other areas of policy, and the budget deficit shows no sign of disappearing. Republican unity is fraying over social issues, the government's performance on issues ranging from Iraq to Hurri-

---

[1] See Gary C. Jacobson, *A Divider, Not a Uniter* (New York: Longman, 2006).

cane Katrina, and the general growth of both the government and the budget. At least some of Bush's fellow partisans are less willing to accord him the benefit of the doubt. Equally important, the president has lost the public's trust.

From at least one perspective, he has no one to blame but himself. His policies made a significant contribution to polarizing the country and spending its treasury. The president's fall from the public's grace may also be a reaction to years of governing by campaigning. Bush has pushed arguments for his policies to the limit (his critics allege he made exaggerated claims, manipulated information, and misled the public, most notably regarding the war in Iraq), and challenged his critics' patriotism. At least partially as a result, large segments of the public no longer trust him, and the discourse of politics is often harsh. In addition, it is quite natural that members of both Congress and the public are reacting to his stewardship as head of the executive branch and his decisions and decision-making style regarding the occupation of Iraq, Supreme Court nominations, and other critical matters.

In addition, the president also seemed to lose his strategic sense and began his second term by grossly overestimating his political capital and launching the most extensive public relations campaign in the history of the presidency on behalf of reforming Social Security. It was a classic example of the permanent campaign, employing the same public relations techniques, party apparatus, and allied groups that were responsible for his reelection. The president's most vigorous effort to alter public opinion was a significant failure. Not only was the public unresponsive to his appeals for support, but the more the president talked, the less the public supported his ideas. As a result, Congress quietly dropped consideration of the president's proposals. The administration's experience once again raises serious questions about the efficacy of the permanent campaign.

Bush's emphasis on governing by campaigning does not represent a sharp break with the past, of course. For most modern presidents, both politics and policy revolve around their attempts to garner public support for themselves and for their policies. Ronald Reagan took office oriented to using his communications skills to persuade the public and thus the Congress to do his bidding, and the Clinton White House accelerated the trend. The Bush administration is merely the latest stage in an evolution that we can trace back to Theodore Roosevelt and Woodrow Wilson. The irony is that, like George W. Bush, presidents typically fail to increase public support for their policies.

In addition, a governing strategy based on the mistaken belief that the White House can reliably move the public has other disadvantages. It may encourage presidents to underestimate their opponents and eschew necessary compromises. In the process, the president may suffer significant opportunity costs as he overlooks less dramatic, but more realistic, chances for success.

Overreaching may lead to even greater problems than the failure to achieve immediate policy goals. It may also result in political disasters. Not long after Bill Clinton failed to obtain even a vote in either house of Congress on his health care reform proposal, which was to have been his centerpiece legislation, the Democrats lost majorities in both the House and the Senate for the first time in four decades. The administration's health care proposal was the prime example of the Republicans' charge that the Democrats were ideological extremists who had lost touch with the wishes of Americans. Summing up the health care reform debacle, Jacobs and Shapiro conclude that the "fundamental political mistake committed by Bill Clinton and his aides was in grossly overestimating the capacity of a president to 'win' public opinion and to use public support as leverage to overcome known political obstacles—from an ideologically divided Congress to hostile interest groups."[2]

There are broader problems with governing by campaigning. When political leaders take their cases directly to the public, they have to accommodate the limited attention spans of the public and the availability of space on television. As a result, the president and his opponents often reduce choices to stark black-and-white terms. When leaders frame issues in such terms, they typically frustrate rather than facilitate building coalitions. Such positions are difficult to compromise, which hardens negotiating positions as both sides posture as much to mobilize an intense minority of supporters as to persuade the other side. *The permanent campaign is antithetical to governing.*

Given the nature of White House efforts at public persuasion, it is not the case that even a failed effort at going public will be useful for educating the public and thus pave the way for eventual passage of proposals. Major initiatives have few second chances in contemporary America. In addition, there is little evidence that presidents' public relations campaigns actually do much educating. In governing by campaigning political leaders do not look for ways to insulate controversial or difficult policy decisions from

---

[2] Lawrence R. Jacobs and Robert Y. Shapiro, *Politicians Don't Pander* (Chicago: University of Chicago Press, 2000), p. 115.

their vulnerability to demagoguery and oversimplification.[3] Often the White House is as likely to mislead as it is to educate.

Indeed, as political scientist Hugh Heclo argues, campaigning to govern is anti-deliberative. Campaigning focuses on persuasion, competition, conflict, and short-term victory. Campaigns are waged in either/or terms. Conversely, governing involves deliberation, cooperation, negotiation, and compromise over an extended period. Campaigns prosecute a cause among adversaries rather than deliberate courses of action among collaborators. The goal of campaign communications is to win rather than to educate or learn. Thus, the incentives for leaders are to stay on message rather than to engage with opponents and to frame issues rather than inform their audience about anything in detail. Similarly, campaigning requires projecting self-assurance rather than admitting ignorance or uncertainty about complex issues and counterattacking and switching the subject rather than struggling with tough questions. It is better to have a campaign issue for the next election than deal with an issue by governing. Thus, the more campaigning infiltrates into governing, the more we should expect the values of a campaign perspective to dominate over values of deliberation.[4]

Traditionally, presidents attempted to build coalitions in Congress through bargaining. The core strategy was to providing benefits for both sides, allowing many to share in a coalition's success and to declare victory. Going public is fundamentally different.

---

[3] Norman J. Ornstein and Thomas E. Mann, "Conclusion: The Permanent Campaign and the Future of American Democracy," in *The Permanent Campaign and Its Future,* ed. Norman Ornstein and Thomas Mann (Washington, DC: American Enterprise Institute and Brookings Institution, 2000), p. 225.
[4] Hugh Heclo, "Campaigning and Governing: A Conspectus," in *The Permanent Campaign and Its Future,* ed. Norman Ornstein and Thomas Mann (Washington, D.C.: American Enterprise Institute and Brookings Institution, 2000), pp. 11–15, 34.

The core strategy is to *defeat the opposition,* creating winners and losers in a zero-sum game. In going public, the president tries to intimidate opponents by increasing the political costs of opposition rather than attracting them with benefits. As we have seen, such an approach is unlikely to win the president the benefit of the doubt from skeptical legislators. Governing by campaigning too often revolves around destroying enemies rather than producing legislative products broadly acceptable to the electorate. The tendencies are for civility to lose out to conflict, compromise to deadlock, deliberation to sound bites, and legislative product to campaign issues.[5]

The increasing ideological distinctiveness of the two major parties exacerbates these narrowing and anti-deliberative propensities of the permanent campaign. Partisan polarization encourages presidents and members of Congress to view those on the other side of the aisle as enemies to defeat rather than opponents with whom to compromise. Moreover, the media is biased toward viewing politics as a game and more likely to cover communications that are critical and conflictual. This orientation provides additional incentives to publicity hungry officials to attempt to govern by campaigning and attack their opponents.

Finally, the enormous amount of money required to run a permanent campaign also discourages building broad coalitions. To raise such sums, presidents need to tailor their messages to attract those most predisposed to support them, those with "special interests," instead of focusing on building support within broad

---

[5] David Brady and Morris Fiorina, "Congress in the Era of the Permanent Campaign," in *The Permanent Campaign and Its Future,* ed. Norman Ornstein and Thomas Mann (Washington, D.C.: American Enterprise Institute and Brookings Institution, 2000), p. 156.

coalitions. In addition, it is often the case that frightening people about the evils of the opposition is the most effective means of raising money. Such scare tactics encourage harsh attacks on opponents while discouraging the comity necessary for building coalitions. Interest groups, which provide substantial funds for the permanent campaign, enforce ideological rigidity by closely monitoring policy makers and rapidly attacking deviations from the group's line.[6] As fund-raising structures are institutionalized and produce ever-increasing amounts of money for the permanent campaign, we should not be surprised that policy making is more ideologically charged and personally hostile and resembles sustained political warfare more than democratic consideration of policy alternatives.

What would we expect if governing by campaigning is not a successful strategy and actually makes coalition building more difficult? We would expect partisan polarization, legislative gridlock, and public cynicism. It is not coincidental that these are central characteristics of contemporary American politics.

---

[6] For more on groups in the permanent campaign, see Burdett Loomis, "The Never Ending Story: Campaigns without Elections," in *The Permanent Campaign and Its Future,* ed. Norman Ornstein and Thomas Mann (Washington, D.C.: American Enterprise Institute and Brookings Institution, 2000), pp. 162–184.

Index

9/11 attacks, 1, 8, 11, 31, 45, 61, 64, 80–81, 87, 90, 95, 99–101, 105, 164–165, 170
  policy, impact on, 132, 165
  public blame for, 129, 132
  rally from, 47, 80, 128–132, 181
  See also Iraq war; Terrorism, war on

A

Abortion, 23, 50, 125–126, 171, 173, 210–211
Abramoff, Jack, 205
Abramowitz, Alan I., 182
Abu Ghraib. *See* Prisoner abuse
Addresses, televised 49, 63–64, 73–74, 78–90, 135, 146, 164
  audiences for, 81–90
  public approval, and, 78–90
  television coverage of, 87–88

Afghanistan war, 1, 59, 105, 132, 135, 165
Agenda, Bush, 3–13, 27, 164–168, 188, 242–244, 246, 279
Agenda, public, 132, 134, 164–168, 242–244, 246
Agenda, Congress. *See* Congress
AFL-CIO, 240–241
Agriculture policy, 169, 171, 203
Airport security, 170
Alito, Samuel A., Jr., 212
Alliance for Worker Retirement Security, 235, 237, 240–241
Alliance of Automobile Manufacturers, 233
Al Qaeda, 33, 45, 61, 64, 68, 100
American Federation of State, County, and Municipal Employees (AFSCME), 240